Colonial America

**Recent Titles in
Historical Facts and Fictions**

The Victorian World: Facts and Fictions
Ginger S. Frost

The Vikings: Facts and Fictions
Kirsten Wolf and Tristan Mueller-Vollmer

American Civil War: Facts and Fictions
James R. Hedtke

The Middle Ages: Facts and Fictions
Winston Black

The History of Christianity: Facts and Fictions
Dyron B. Daughrity

The History of Buddhism: Facts and Fictions
Geoffrey C. Goble

Ancient Egypt: Facts and Fictions
Stephen E. Thompson

Ancient Rome: Facts and Fictions
Monica M. Bontty

William Shakespeare: Facts and Fictions
Douglas J. King

Colonial America

Facts and Fictions

K. David Goss and A. A. Grishin

Historical Facts and Fictions

BLOOMSBURY ACADEMIC
NEW YORK • LONDON • OXFORD • NEW DELHI • SYDNEY

BLOOMSBURY ACADEMIC
Bloomsbury Publishing Inc
1385 Broadway, New York, NY 10018, USA
50 Bedford Square, London, WC1B 3DP, UK
29 Earlsfort Terrace, Dublin 2, Ireland

BLOOMSBURY, BLOOMSBURY ACADEMIC and the Diana logo
are trademarks of Bloomsbury Publishing Plc

First published in the United States of America by ABC-CLIO 2021
Paperback edition published by Bloomsbury Academic 2025

Copyright © Bloomsbury Publishing Inc, 2025

Cover Photo: The First Thanksgiving 1621, by J.L.G. Ferris. (Library of Congress)

All rights reserved. No part of this publication may be reproduced or
transmitted in any form or by any means, electronic or mechanical,
including photocopying, recording, or any information storage or retrieval
system, without prior permission in writing from the publishers.

Bloomsbury Publishing Inc does not have any control over, or responsibility for,
any third-party websites referred to or in this book. All internet addresses given
in this book were correct at the time of going to press. The author and publisher
regret any inconvenience caused if addresses have changed or sites have
ceased to exist, but can accept no responsibility for any such changes.

Library of Congress Cataloging-in-Publication Data
Names: Goss, K. David, 1952- author. | Grishin, A. A., 1971- author.
Title: Colonial America : facts and fictions / K. David Goss and A. A. Grishin.
Description: Santa Barbara, California : ABC-CLIO, [2021] | Series:
Historical facts and fictions | Includes bibliographical references and index.
Identifiers: LCCN 2020016834 (print) | LCCN 2020016835 (ebook) |
ISBN 9781440864261 (hardback) | ISBN 9781440864278 (ebook)
Subjects: LCSH: United States—History—Colonial period, ca. 1600–1775.
Classification: LCC E188 .G65 2020 (print) |
LCC E188 (ebook) | DDC 973.2—dc23
LC record available at https://lccn.loc.gov/2020016834
LC ebook record available at https://lccn.loc.gov/2020016835

ISBN: HB: 978-1-4408-6426-1
PB: 979-8-2163-6609-6
ePDF: 978-1-44086-427-8
eBook: 979-8-2160-6295-0

Series: Historical Facts and Fictions

To find out more about our authors and books visit www.bloomsbury.com
and sign up for our newsletters.

To
Rebecca J. Goss
and
Cheri L. Grishin
with appreciation, admiration and affection

Contents

Preface	ix
Introduction	xi
1. Columbus Was the First European to Discover the Western Hemisphere	1
2. Captain John Smith and Pocahontas Had a Romantic Relationship	27
3. Puritans and Pilgrims Are the Same People	51
4. The First Thanksgiving Was a Shared Harvest Celebration	71
5. Manhattan Island Was Purchased for $24	95
6. Witches Were Burned in Salem	117
7. The Boston Tea Party Participants Threw Chests of Tea into the Sea to Hurt the British	129
8. The American Revolution Was Fought by United Patriots against an Evil Oppressor	149
9. Paul Revere Completed His Famous Ride Alone	173
10. George Washington Had Wooden Teeth	193
Bibliography	213
Index	223

Preface

The colonial period in the history of the United States is often defined in a narrow sense, starting in the early sixteenth century and only including the events that transpired during the active stage of European colonization of North America. In choosing the topics for this book, we operated on the assumption that our readers' interest would extend to the earliest recorded attempts of Europeans to settle in the New World. This necessitated a discussion of Columbian voyages, still perceived by many as the earliest contact between the "Old World" and the "New World." Despite being a monumental milestone, these voyages were preceded by the discovery of North America by the Norse Vikings. The plethora of written and archaeological evidence for these early contacts allowed us to place the bottom boundary for the period discussed in this book in the tenth century CE. The Revolutionary War understandably acts as the second boundary for the book's time line.

The text is not a continuous narrative of historic events that occurred between these two boundaries. Instead, individual events that have the baggage of false notions and bizarre misconceptions have been chosen as highlights. This results in what may seem as gaps in coverage, but a better way to look at the chapters' selection is through realizing that there are distinct clusters of narratives that naturally attract people's attention: the early beginnings of British colonization in the seventh century and the American War of Independence, along with events leading into it.

Arranged in a historic order (as much as possible), the chapters of the book cover (1) the supposed discovery of America by Columbus, (2) the myth of the romantic union between Captain Smith and Pocahontas,

(3) the persistent failure of the public to differentiate between the Pilgrims and the Puritans, (4) the late date interpretation of certain events as the First Thanksgiving, (5) the myth of the purchase of Manhattan for $24 worth of trinkets, (6) erroneous beliefs about the fate of the Salem witch hysteria victims in 1692, (7) misconceptions surrounding the destruction of the tea in Boston, (8) false notions about the national and ethnic composition of the active combatants during the Revolutionary War, (9) the myths about Paul Revere's midnight ride, and (10) George Washington's supposed wooden teeth.

The use of primary sources in this book, outside of the strictly utilitarian purpose of dismantling outdated and embarrassing myths, was also dictated by our desire to demonstrate how comprehensive and sophisticated historic records can be, even as we look at points in time so distant and different from the world in which we now live. The nature of these documents varies considerably; this book includes references to periodicals, broadsides, private letters, scholarly treatises, commercial advertisements, poems, theatrical productions, and accounting books, among others. In certain cases, the choice was made to include short excerpts from sources in the main body of the text; in other situations, the sources are presented separately, in full or in part, at the end of the chapters.

The authors extend their gratitude to our editors, whose support and consideration has been invaluable. We would also like to encourage the readers of this book to direct their attention to other volumes available in this series, which we hope will cultivate an appreciation of history in this era of widely available primary resources.

Introduction

In this country's history, designating the span of events preceding the establishment of the United States as the *colonial period* is more than just a matter of convenient nomenclature. The term *colonial* bears many connotations essential for understanding this time period. The origin of the word lies in the common practices present in ancient civilizations, most notably in the Greco-Roman world, where the prevalent model for territorial and cultural expansion was the founding of *coloniae*, purposefully planned settlements that were populated by a particular group of individuals and often transplanted from the same area of the home country (e.g., the same Greek *polis*). Such settlements enjoyed a great degree of independence, especially during earlier times, but also maintained strong filial links with their historic homelands. Colonies addressed a variety of needs in ancient societies, including the need for resources, a remedy for overpopulation, and locations for defense against potential threats on the outskirts of civilization as understood by the Greeks and the Romans.

The fragmentation of cultural and political life as well as the economic decline that followed during the centuries after the fall of the Western Roman Empire caused a decline in this effective practice. However, the model was alive and well even among the Norse Vikings, whose explorations often resulted in the establishment of far-flung colonies interconnected through shared culture and carefully preserved kinship. Some of their settlements were eventually abandoned, but we owe the first attempts at the colonization of North America to these efforts.

INTRODUCTION

The Age of Discovery opened up vast opportunities for Europeans to make full use of colonialism to the point of reinventing it as a mode of existence for countries with imperial aspirations: Spain, Portugal, England, France, and others. However, internal and external circumstances dictated different approaches toward allowing large groups of citizens to settle overseas. For instance, while Spain and Portugal resorted to direct exploitation of the colonies, the goals of the English crown were originally determined by the political situation within the country.

Often lacking the resources needed for exploration, England relegated colony founding to special interest ventures, such as chartered joint-stock companies and religiously motivated groups. By necessity, such settlements received a fair amount of independence and remained self-governed, even in those situations when a charter was revoked and the status changed to that of a *crown colony*. Generations of British subjects who resided in these colonies developed a sense of relative autonomy while continuously deferring to the rule of overseas monarchs as the guarantors of safety, stability, and legitimacy. Even as we consider the history of the Salem witch trials (the event seemingly steeped solely in religious sensitivities of the time), it becomes evident that the situation in Massachusetts during that period was a result of the colony's charter having been revoked several years prior. The new charter was brought to the colony amid the witch hysteria by the newly appointed governor William Phips, whose handling of the crisis ended up being incompetent. It was the new Massachusetts charter that enabled the infamous Court of Oyer and Terminer to be created, giving legitimacy to the verdicts and capital punishments that would soon follow.

It is therefore crucial to understand that historic events of the colonial era were an integral part of British history when they occurred. The men and women of the English-speaking colonies in North America usually represented their home country in their dealings with the native occupants of the land, and they often followed known European practices in almost all spheres of life. The significance of many events that transpired on American soil was sometimes perceived as negligible by the people actively involved in them (as appears to be the case with the events that have since been reinterpreted as the First Thanksgiving). Perhaps in the grand scheme of British history, this was a justified view of things. However, the creation of an independent nation combining the North American colonies of the United Kingdom shifted the perspective on many events.

On the one hand, this change was justifiable and proper; on the other hand, the situation created ample opportunities for mythmaking. Often (if not always) done with the best of intentions, this reinvention of colonial history was cemented by poets, storytellers, and educators alike, who shaped the perception of America as we know it. According to this self-image, colonial America was populated by pious and industrious people who acted fairly toward the native population, encouraging peace, prosperity, and inclusion. Above all, the newly arrived colonists cherished freedom and learned to live in harmony with each other despite a few easily reconcilable differences.

The episode that seems to be the darkest hour in this saga of humble but mighty beginnings (the Salem witch trials) came to be discounted as a clear remnant of medieval superstition, complete with the inquisitors' method of execution by fire that modern Americans cannot relate to in any meaningful way beyond the textbook knowledge of horrific practices from the Middle Ages. When these freedom-loving men and women bravely faced the British Empire's increasing attempts to oppress them, they responded in unison with utmost resolve, using only fair and well-considered measures to fight off the monarch and ministry determined to violate their rights as Englishmen. Heroes that were brought to the forefront by this surge of patriotism showed stamina and determination (e.g., Paul Revere), yet they remained human in their suffering and almost vulnerable in their everyday appearance (e.g., George Washington). This book does not simply question the validity of these perceptions; it provides original sources that reveal the truth that sometimes augments what is commonly believed and occasionally paints an entirely different picture.

What is to be gained by questioning a self-image that is essentially positive and should only create positive results, motivating people to act in ways that reflect all the worthy values shared and promoted by colonial Americans? In other words, can historic truth be more detrimental to a nation than historic misinformation?

It is entirely likely that no harm will ever come to someone who is convinced that George Washington had wooden teeth. Even if the people of this nation were convinced that the accused witches in Salem were burned at the stake instead of being hanged, there may be little effect on the country's well-being and prospects for the future. Ignorance about major historical facts is not always a problem, but it is nearly always a symptom, a cautionary warning that something has gone awry in one's personal upbringing or public education, allowing for a dismissive approach to historic reality. Such an approach is not harmless. It represents a pattern of inattention to the truth that can be replicated in the way people view and interpret current events and shape the future that is to come. And it only gets worse from here. Most of the myths addressed in this book have already been debunked over many decades in various publications directed at diverse audiences. Nevertheless, these misconceptions manage to persist and prosper.

For example, people may be well aware of the fact that the story of the First Thanksgiving, as told by their elementary schoolteachers, has little to do with the real events of the early seventeenth century. Yet, the choice is often made to repeat this myth simply because it is convenient, easy to remember, entertaining, and flattering in many respects. Unfortunately, this is when the perpetuation of myth does become a serious issue. It can, and sometimes does, lead to public hostility and, ultimately, social conflict.

The problem is that historical events are frequently what they are because they are the result of conflicts: societal, economic, geopolitical, and the like. Any interpretive account of history that superficially glosses over unresolved conflicts perpetuates them and will lead to more hostility. If one is convinced that the love affair between Captain Smith and Pocahontas represents the happy marriage between Native Americans and European newcomers that has lasted four hundred years, this misconception is both unfair and troubling—besides being patently wrong. More importantly, past conflicts that have shaped our history cannot be neatly erased or compartmentalized in their given time periods. They represent patterns that repeat themselves with frightening regularity. It is simply unwise to ignore the historic truth as long as it saves us from being complacent and negligent about the present. Even the smallest details of past records bind us to the realities of today's world and increase our understanding of it.

Therefore, it is not the debunking of outlived myths that represents a problem for the development of a nation's self-image. Ignorance about the past stalls the progress, and outright lying about history resulting from purposeful intention to the historic truth is indeed dangerous. Nothing is more subversive to the present than lies about the past. The nation's perception of its own history can only benefit from being purged of myths and misconceptions. History can become more real as it becomes more complex, and it is no less illustrious as accents are shifted and glaring inaccuracies are removed. One's appreciation of the Boston Tea Party will not diminish after understanding that the time period was defined by internal strife over what it meant to be loyal. Paul Revere's famous midnight ride to Concord does not lose its strange appeal when we realize that his heroic effort required the help of others. One can find renewed admiration for the Pilgrims and the Puritans as it becomes evident that they were distinctly different from each other, although both groups contributed to form the earliest Colonial society. Some facts may be harder to digest than others, of course, but in the end, investing in the historic truth is a worthy endeavor.

It is the good fortune of any student of American history that there are great and numerous sources available for virtually every decade of it. This nation's colonial history is no exception. The nation's history has many voices that deserve to be heard.

1

Columbus Was the First European to Discover the Western Hemisphere

What People Think Happened

Inside the great cathedral of Seville in southern Spain stands an imposing monument to Christopher Columbus (1451–1506). Four crowned figures (representing the four Spanish kingdoms of Castile, Aragon, Leon, and Navarre) solemnly carry the casket bearing the earthly remains of the great explorer. Along the base of the pall runs an inscription—long recognized as Columbus's official epitaph:

A Castilla y Leon // Nuevo mundo dio Colon
(To Castile and Leon, Columbus gave a New World)

This brief motto essentially summarizes the claim made by all subsequent generations of cartographers and historians since the early sixteenth century that this "most famous native son of Genoa" is credited with discovering an entirely new world and essentially giving it to the foremost European nation of his time.

While the centuries following Columbus's death have greatly added to our understanding of geography and world history, his role as the essential discoverer of the New World remains virtually unchallenged. Recent scholarship has found it much easier to question Columbus's status as a hero or his ethics as an administrator than to deprive him of his notable achievements as an explorer *extraordinaire*. But was he indeed the "discoverer of the New World"?

Certainly, no doubt can be placed upon the clear anthropological evidence of several Ice Age migrations of Asian tribes moving into North America across the land bridge that once joined eastern Siberia to present-day Alaska. More recent research has even speculated that the Western Hemisphere was visited by prehistoric European people who crossed from Northern Europe along the perimeter of an ice bridge that once connected Northern Europe to North America during the last Ice Age, over ten thousand years ago. And early modern historians have had no difficulty believing that the Atlantic Ocean might well have been traversed by ships blown off course from ancient times to the Middle Ages. More recent authors have furnished research of varying value suggesting that the New World was discovered and explored prior to Columbus by Chinese navigators and even the Knights Templar fleeing persecution in Europe.

And yet, when one is asked who should properly be called the discoverer of America, the name Christopher Columbus will almost always come up—if not right away then after some deliberation. He is generally considered the first European to claim areas of the Western Hemisphere for a European nation and to have first established a marginal foothold in the New World that would eventually grow to become a massive colonial empire in the name of the Spanish crown. In recent years, Columbus's reputation as an enslaver of human beings and an exploiter of native peoples has cast a dark shadow on his name, but despite these moral failings, his title as the "Discoverer of the New World" has not, as yet, been stripped away. And this is because every history text that includes the period known as the Age of Exploration and Discovery provides at least a summary of Columbus's struggles and achievements, usually concluding with the point that although he was persuaded he had reached islands off the coast of Asia, he had in fact discovered the Western Hemisphere. Some authors go so far as to suggest that Columbus was responsible for demonstrating conclusively for the first time that Earth is indeed round.

And lest we believe that such a myth could not possibly persist into the mid-twentieth century, one need only examine the chapter entitled "Columbus's First Voyage" in Harvard historian Samuel Eliot Morison's classic text *The Oxford History of the American People*, published in 1965, in which we read, "America was discovered accidentally by a great seaman who was looking for something else; when it was not wanted; and most of the exploration for the next fifty years was done in the hope of getting through or around it" (Morison 1994, 23).

This then is what people, both the educated and uneducated, thought happened. This is the misconception taught from textbooks and in classrooms since before the founding of the United States. As a consequence, Columbus has been honored for his alleged "achievement" in a variety of ways, occupying a prestigious—almost mythical—position in Western culture. To anthropologists and historians, the entire way of life of native peoples in the Western Hemisphere is divided between the pre- and post-Columbian eras. The transference of ideas, technology, diseases, and agricultural innovations has come to be called the "Columbian Exchange."

And naturally, although Columbus's personal reputation may have lately been damaged, his name is still proudly borne by the charitable and benevolent Roman Catholic fraternal organization known as the Knights of Columbus. In addition, the South American country of Colombia is his namesake, and in the United States, eighteen cities bear his name as well as the District of Columbia.

All of the preceding honors are directly attributable to the popular misconception that Christopher Columbus was (1) the first European explorer to sail across the Atlantic, (2) the first European to set foot in the New World, (3) the first European to establish an American colonial settlement, (4) the first European to interact and trade with the native peoples, and (5) the first European to introduce the Christian faith to the Western Hemisphere. All these ideas were popularly held for centuries, and, interestingly, all of these ideas are essentially incorrect.

How It Became Popular

When did this general idea of Columbus as the "Discoverer of the New World" originate? Although the monument in the Seville Cathedral only dates to the very end of the nineteenth century, the famous epitaph emblazoned across it is much older. According to legend, the two-line motto identifying Columbus as the giver of the New World to the Spanish royal house was the gift of his patrons turned beneficiaries, King Ferdinand and Queen Isabella. It is this motto that serves as the earliest known evidence for the creation of the Columbus myth.

That said, there is absolutely no primary source dating from Columbus's lifetime (he died in 1506) that identifies the Spanish royal couple as the source of the motto. Instead, the motto made its first appearance in 1535, when it was printed by Gonzalo Fernandez de Oviedo in his publication *A General History of the Indies* (or *La Historia General de las Indias*). Here the wording is slightly different and perhaps even more fitting: "Por Castilla e por Leon // Nuevo Mundo hallo Colon" ("For Castile and for Leon // Columbus found a New World"). This marks the official beginning of the myth purporting that it was Columbus who was responsible for finding "a new world," when in fact the world he "discovered" had already been reached, colonized, and explored by Europeans almost five hundred years previous.

As to how the myth initially became popular, some of the credit must go to Columbus's descendants, in particular his son Ferdinand Columbus, who sought to capitalize on his father's fame by adopting the aforementioned motto as his own in 1537. Throughout the 1500s and 1600s, historians and cartographers believed that an epitaph praising Columbus for giving the New World to Spain was inscribed on the first monument raised to him in 1506 over the admiral's tomb in the Cathedral of Valladolid—then the capital city of the Kingdom of Spain under Ferdinand and Isabella.

What is interesting is that the great explorer seems to have traveled nearly as much after his death as before it. Each relocation was accompanied by a ceremonial cortege that increased the great man's visibility. Columbus's remains were initially relocated from his first tomb at Valladolid to the monastery of La Cartuja in Seville. Later, his son Diego Columbus arranged for his father's body to be transported across the Atlantic to the city of Santo Domingo, the capital of the Island of Hispaniola, where Diego served as the royal governor. Here it remained until 1795, when the French seized the island, forcing the Spanish authorities to remove their greatest national hero to a fourth tomb in Havana, Cuba. One hundred years later, when Havana, Cuba, fell to the forces of the United States during the Spanish American War, colonial authorities decided to return Columbus to Seville, Spain, and created for him the aforementioned monument in the city's cathedral bearing the now famous motto declaring Columbus to be the discoverer of the New World.

This extended postmortem expedition is significant because it clearly demonstrates that Columbus, for over four hundred years, remained a Spanish national symbol of American colonization. As that great empire dwindled and eventually lost its foothold in the Americas, the only place where Columbus could finally rest in peace was in his adopted homeland. To add further intrigue to the story, following the removal of Columbus's alleged body to Spain, construction workers in Santo Domingo uncovered a lead-lined metal box inscribed "Don Christopher Columbus" that contained human remains. Not wanting to neglect the possible vestiges of a legendary national hero, the contents of the metal box were interred in yet another tomb in the Dominican Republic. This alternative Columbian tomb only adds to the striking duality of this historic figure, who is symbolically, if not literally, buried on both sides of the Atlantic. Two cities now claim the honor of being Columbus's final resting place—an honor derived from the belief that he and his navigational accomplishments are unique in the annals of history.

It should be noted that DNA testing of the body contained in the Seville tomb when compared to that of other members of the family has confirmed the positive identity of the person buried there. No testing has yet been conducted upon the alleged Columbian remains in the Dominican Republic. Each nation still lays claim to their share of Columbus's legend.

Thus, the myth of Columbus, despite his Genoese origins, began and still remains within the context of the Spanish-speaking world—both Spain and the Western Hemisphere. Over the centuries, it grew and flourished among those who took national pride in his accomplishments. And those accomplishments are not only the result of popular speculation but also based in part on the claims made by Columbus himself.

In a famous letter to Juana de la Torre, a lady-in-waiting at the Spanish royal court, Columbus expresses his personal reasons for his greatness:

> I ought to be judged as a captain sent from Spain to the Indies, to conquer a nation numerous and warlike, with customs and religion altogether different to ours; a people who dwelt in the mountains, without regular habitations for themselves or for us, and where, by Divine will, I have subdued another world to the dominion of the King and Queen, our sovereigns; in consequence of which, Spain that used to be called poor, is now the most wealthy of kingdoms. (Columbus et al. 1870, 170)

Interestingly, in his narrative, Columbus avoids claiming to have discovered a new world but rather only purports to have been sent to the Indies—the East Indies—and been responsible for conquering a people in the name of Spain, thus making Spain rich. Columbus never actually believed that he had discovered the Western Hemisphere. Indeed, to his dying day, he believed he had merely reached islands off the coast of Asia. Thus, Columbus would never lay claim to the title of "Discoverer of the New World," but it would be applied to him shortly after his death by those who more fully understood the impact of what his exploratory voyages had accomplished.

It is important to stress that for the purposes of this chapter we are not primarily focusing on Columbus's status as a heroic explorer, enslaver, and brutalizer of Native American peoples or even as an overzealous champion of the Christian faith. Rather, our goal is simply to reconsider and disprove wholesale assumptions concerning his mythical status as the first European to discover and colonize the New World.

Was Columbus's mythical status ever challenged? The closest contemporary attempt to unseat Columbus as the discoverer of the Western Hemisphere occurred when the renowned German cartographer Martin Waldseemuller published his famous 1507 map naming the continents of North and South America after the Florentine explorer Amerigo Vespucci (1454–1512)—whose exploratory journals he had used to determine that the newly discovered land masses were in fact the Western Hemisphere of the globe and not in any respect a part of Asia.

Despite the naming of the continents after Vespucci, in popular literature, the Florentine explorer remained a relatively obscure figure, while the Genoese "Admiral of the Ocean Sea" emerged at the end of the sixteenth century as an even greater figure when another cartographer, Theodor De Bry, published his extremely accurate map of the known world in 1594 and credited Columbus with the discovery of America, virtually ignoring the role of Vespucci. With the publishing of De Bry's definitive world map, Columbus's reputation—which was already established—grew and expanded exponentially from where it was at the time of his death in 1506.

Legends are often created through popular artistic images and poetry, and the legend of Columbus is no exception. Within one hundred years of De Bry's published map, writers describing the Western Hemisphere began looking for a Western geographical counterpart to the visual image of the goddess Europa. Europa came to be associated with the European continent as far back as the eighth century CE, when ecclesiastical cartographers used the Greek name *Europa* when referring to that portion of the continent under the rule of Emperor Charlemagne. Europa—a Greek female divinity—thus came to symbolically personify the continent of Europe. After Columbus's explorations, cartographers needed a similar historical connection to the renowned "discoverer of the Western Hemisphere," and so they developed the Latin female name for "Columbus," "Columbia," a mythical character whose name and visual image was soon adopted by mapmakers and artists to symbolize the continents of the Western Hemisphere.

The resulting image of Columbia, the divine American counterpart to Europa, thus came into existence. During the seventeenth century, she represented both North and South America, but by the mid-eighteenth century, the Greek female image primarily came to represent North America alone. Her appearance frequently incorporated clothing and items associated with the untamed West: a feathered native headdress, a loincloth, and moccasins holding a bountiful cornucopia.

Because the Columbian goddess represented a geographical place, the newly created patron goddess Columbia soon rivaled Amerigo Vespucci's namesake, making "Columbia" a popular alternative to the name "America" and thus further enhancing the Columbus legend. After the 1730s, and up to the time of the American Revolution, the term "Columbia" became a popular symbolic reference to the thirteen colonies as a whole—especially in the English public press. In this respect, Columbia formed a direct trans-Atlantic counterpart to England's symbolic patron deity, Britannia. Indeed, the name "Columbia" as a toponym for America first appeared in 1738 in the weekly publication of the debates of the British Parliament in Edward Cave's *The Gentleman's Magazine*. By the post-Revolutionary period, the visual image of Columbia changed from that of a Native American "Indian princess" to that of a more classical Greco-Roman demigoddess draped in a flowing white gown. This modification established for Columbia a clear, visual connection to the democratic traditions of ancient Greece and the Roman Republic. It was this classical symbolic image of Columbia that, by the early 1800s, commonly appeared in public print and was portrayed leading the American people as they began to undertake movement westward—fulfilling their Manifest Destiny of discovery and conquest in the best tradition of Admiral Columbus himself.

It was during the early national period that the names of Columbus and his female namesake, Columbia, were to become commonly recognized as the nation grew and expanded. As a result, the reputation and legend of Columbus became commonplace among the American people. By 1784, King's College in New York was renamed Columbia College, and two years later, South Carolina established its new capital city at Columbia. By 1801, the national capital was designated the City of Washington, District of Columbia, and "The President's March" by Philip Phile, which was used during the early presidential inaugurations, was renamed "Hail Columbia"; it is still in use today as the vice presidential entrance march.

In many ways, in the popular press and in works of popular art throughout the nineteenth century, the symbolic role of Uncle Sam was often visually usurped by the more popular and attractive patron goddess of the United States named in honor of the "Discoverer of America"—ultimately coming to be called "Lady Columbia"! Foremost of her proponents among nineteenth-century American artists was the legendary political cartoonist Thomas Nast, who depicted Lady Columbia in countless newspapers across the country in the 1860s and 1870s.

The Columbian legend reached its high point in 1893 when the nation held the World's Columbian Exposition in Chicago. This was a world fair specifically designed to celebrate the four hundredth anniversary of Christopher Columbus's arrival in the New World in 1492. The national impact of this event cannot be overestimated in advancing the myth of Columbus as the "Discoverer of the New World." The area of the exposition occupied over 690 acres of Chicago real estate, the centerpiece of which was a huge central pool representing the long voyage Columbus took to the New World. Most impressive was the total attendance figure for the event: over 27,300,000 people at a time when the entire U.S. population was 62,979,766. The event's attendance represented approximately one out of every three Americans in the country.

Most importantly, the exposition famously included life-size reproductions of Christopher Columbus's three ships, the *Niña* (or *Santa Clara*), the *Pinta*, and the *Santa María*, which were sailed from Spain and across the Great Lakes to the exposition site. This small fleet was the result of cooperative partnership between the United States and Spain and was one of the most popular exhibits at the exposition. A supremely ironic Columbian Exposition exhibit was the contribution from Norway: a full-scale replica of the recently excavated ninth-century Gokstad ship known as *The Viking*, which, like the reproduction Columbus fleet, had been sailed across the Atlantic to the exposition site.

With "Columbus fever" in the air following the World's Columbian Exposition, it is perhaps not surprising that a nationally known poet would compose a popular poem that would become one of the most widely known American poems, recited by legions of schoolchildren. That classic poem is Joaquin Miller's "Columbus." Perhaps more than any historical account in any history book, this single poem did more to entrench the Columbus myth in the hearts and minds of the American people. The poem speaks for itself:

"Columbus"
by Joaquin Miller

Behind him lay the gray Azores,
Behind the Gates of Hercules,

COLUMBUS WAS THE FIRST

Before him not the ghost of shores,
Before him only shoreless seas,
The good mate said: "Now must we pray,
For lo! The very stars are gone.
Brave Admiral speak, what shall I say?"
"Why say, 'Sail on! sail on! and on!'"

"My men grow mutinous day by day;
My men grow ghastly wan and weak."
The stout mate thought of home; a spray
Of salt wave washed his swarthy cheek.
"What shall I say, brave Admiral, say
If we sight not but seas at dawn?"
"Why you shall say at break of day,
'Sail on! sail on! sail on! and on!'"

They sailed and sailed, as winds might blow,
Until at last the blanched mate said;
"Why, now not even God would know
Should I and all my men fall dead.
These very winds forget their way,
For God from these dread seas is gone.
Now speak, brave Admiral, speak and say"—
He said: "Sail on! sail on! and on!"

They sail, they sailed. Then spake the mate:
"This mad sea shows his teeth tonight.
He curls his lip, he lies in wait,
With lifted teeth as if to bite!
Brave Admiral say but one good word:
What shall we do when hope is gone?"
The words leapt like a leaping sword:
"Sail on! sail on! sail on! and on!"

Then, pale and worn, he kept his deck,
And peered through darkness. Ah, that night
Of all dark nights! And then a speck—
A light! A light! A light! A light!
It grew, a starlit flag unfurled!
It grew to be Time's burst of dawn.

> He gained a world; he gave that world
> Its grandest lesson; "On! sail on!"
> (Stedman 1900, 426)

The Columbus myth was best supported by the creation of a national holiday on October 12 honoring Christopher Columbus as the "Discoverer of the New World." Such a celebratory event would not be officially recognized in the United States until 1934; yet, there were many earlier steps that finally led to the creation of that observance. Starting with the administration of President George Washington, the first acknowledgment of Columbus and his discovery took place in New York City in 1792, when New York was the first capital of the United States.

The organization responsible for the first Columbus Day event was the Tammany Society, which had only been established six years earlier, in 1786, as a society for pure Americans who resented the "aristocratic" Federalists of New York and wished to oppose them, taking on the character of anti-federalists. To these politically motivated New Yorkers, the idea of annually celebrating the actions of Columbus seemed appropriate because he was credited with having made a literal break with the aristocracy of Europe and establishing a New World outside Europe, where immigrants—untainted by the poison of traditional nobility—could rise in society on the basis on their own natural skills and intelligence. This Columbus Day tradition continued until the Tammany Society's demise in 1967.

At the same time, for entirely historical reasons, the Massachusetts Historical Society celebrated the three hundredth anniversary of the arrival of Columbus in 1792. The practice was followed by others who felt that, historically and culturally, the discovery of America needed to be recognized and the discoverer honored. Not surprisingly, in 1866, a large contingent of recently arrived immigrants from Italy also held their first Columbus Day celebration in New York City, which at the time held the largest concentration of Italian Americans in the United States. But nothing previously observed could compare to the national outpouring of Columbus Day festivities resulting from the presidential injunction of President Benjamin Harrison, who in 1892 strongly urged all patriotic Americans to recognize and honor the discovery of America by Christopher Columbus. As a direct result of Harrison's influence, the "myth of Columbus" was finally established on a national scale and firmly entrenched in every household, village, town, city, church, library, and school, both primary and secondary. All that remained was an act of

Congress to officially acknowledge the debt owed to Columbus for the discovery of the New World, the discovery of North America, and the founding of the United States. None of which, in reality, he was responsible for doing.

Nonetheless, in April 1934—largely as a result of a national lobbying campaign on the part of Italian Americans and, in particular, the Italian community in New York City aided by support from the Knights of Columbus—President Franklin Delano Roosevelt signed a proclamation making October 12 a federal holiday under the name of Columbus Day. After this activity, the population of the United States was firmly and legally convinced of the myth that Columbus was indeed the first European to sail across the Atlantic, the first European to set foot in the New World, the first European to establish a colonial settlement, the first European to trade with Native Americans, and the first to introduce the Christian faith.

What Really Happened

Beyond all the speculative theories of pre-Columbian visits to North and South America by the Chinese, Polynesians, Egyptians, Phoenicians, Welsh, Irish monks, and refugee members of the Knights Templar, there is one group that unquestionably (1) crossed the Atlantic Ocean, (2) visited a variety of locations in the Western Hemisphere, (3) established at least one year-round colonial settlement, (4) traded with the Native Americans, and (5) introduced the Christian faith by bringing it with them. What makes these dramatic events even more interesting is that they were all accomplished by Scandinavian seafarers five hundred years before Columbus set sail from Spain.

The primary difference between the Norse and the Spanish exploratory voyages was their motivation. The Norse explorers responsible for discovering and settling in the Western Hemisphere were not, like Columbus, searching for a lucrative Western trade route to the riches of the Far East. Rather, they were exploring an unsettled maritime region in an attempt to support and sustain a westward colonizing effort that began in Norway in the late ninth century, moving gradually westward past the Shetland Islands, the Orkney Islands, the Faroes, the Outer Hebrides, Iceland, and Greenland before finally reaching the northeast coastal region of North America by the year 1000 CE. This was in reality a migration, not a business venture, in that it was conducted primarily in cargo-bearing knars, not warlike long ships.

Those that finally arrived and settled in North America also brought women, produced children, transported livestock, and built year-round dwellings for themselves and their families with the intention of settling down in an early medieval Scandinavian community along the northeast coast of North America. According to the primary source narratives, known as *sagas*, and more recent archeological discoveries, this is what really happened. And it significantly undermines the list of unique claims and first-time achievements traditionally attributed to Christopher Columbus—making him actually a relative latecomer among those medieval Europeans who previously reached the New World.

The literary evidence for much of this remarkable story rests in medieval manuscripts written in Old Norse and archived in repositories in Iceland and Denmark. The primary sources that are the most reliable are *The Greenlanders' Saga* (Anonymous, thirteenth century), *Erik the Red's Saga* (Anonymous, thirteenth century, ca. 1265 CE)—note that *Erik the Red's Saga* is preserved in two versions, *The Hauksbok* (fourteenth century) and *The Skalholtsbok* (fifteenth century)—and Adam of Bremen's *Descriptio Insularum Aquilonis* (*A Description of the Northern Isles*, written ca. 1075 CE). Together, *The Greenlanders' Saga* and *Erik the Red's Saga* are known as the "Vinland sagas" and were both written approximately two hundred years after the Norse discovery of the New World.

In *The Greenlanders' Saga*, the reader is introduced to the important Norse explorer who discovered and colonized Greenland, Erik the Red. Erik is a non-Christian, or a traditional Viking who originated in Norway, and the son of a Viking leader named Thorvald. Both father and son are accused of committing manslaughter in Norway and banished. They decide to travel to the newly settled island of Iceland and acquire an estate called Drangar. Shortly after settling in Iceland, Thorvald dies, leaving his son in possession of the new estate. Erik soon marries Thjodhild, the daughter of Jorund, a prominent Icelandic leader. If Erik the Red could have avoided further bloodshed, he may have remained in Iceland, but in his own saga, *Erik the Red's Saga*, we read of more killings committed by him in a blood feud that finally results in yet another banishment:

> Then did Eirik's thralls cause a landslip on the estate of Valthjof, at Valthjofsstadr. Eyjolf the Foul, his kinsman, slew the thralls beside Skeidsbrekkur (slopes of the race-course), above Vatzhorn. In return Eirik slew Eyjolf the Foul; he slew also Hrafn the Dueller, at Leikskalar (play booths). Grerstein, and Odd of Jorfi, kinsman of Eyjolf, were found willing to follow up his death by a legal prosecution; and then was Eirik banished from

Haukadalr. He occupied then Brokey and Eyxney, and dwelt at Tradir, in Sudrey, the first winter. At this time did he lend to Thorgest pillars for seatstocks. Afterwards Eirik removed into Eyxney, and dwelt at Eiriksstadr. (*Erik the Red's Saga* in Sephton 1880, 7)

In relocating to a place distant from his earlier home of *Eiriksstadr*, Erik removed the sacred wooden pillars that constituted his family "seat," and because he needed time to construct a new dwelling at *Tradir*, he entrusted the keeping of these sacred pillars (probably brought from his original family home in Norway) to his friend and former neighbor Thorgest. When his new dwelling—also named *Eiriksstadr* (Erik's dwelling place)—was completed, he returned to Thorgest to take back his family's pillars, but Thorgest refused to surrender them to Erik the Red because he had given them to his friends residing at *Breidabolstadr*. When Erik discovered where his family's sacred pillars were, he went to take them back by force, and Thorgest went after him with his sons and a company of armed men to stop Erik from further violence. Erik the Red and his supporters confronted Thorgest and fought him:

> And Thorgest went after him. They fought at a short distance from the hay-yard at Drangar, and there fell two sons of Thorgest, and some other men. After that they both kept a large body of men together. Styr gave assistance to Eirik, as also did Eyjolf, of Sviney, Thorbjorn Vifilsson, and the sons of Thorbrand, of Alptafjordr (Swanfirth). But the sons of Thord Gellir, as also Thorgeir, of Hitardalr (Hotdale), Aslak, of Langadalr (Longdale), and Illugi, his son, gave assistance to Thorgest. Eirik and his people were outlawed at Thorsnes Thing. (*Erik the Red's Saga* in Sephton 1880, 7)

(*Note:* The custom of a gathering of free Icelanders voting on laws in the absence of a monarch makes Iceland the oldest continuously operating democratic republic in the world.)

The Discovery of Greenland

With Erik the Red again outlawed and banished for manslaughter (not murder) at a public meeting (*Thorsnes Thing*), he could not long remain in Iceland—as the court granted the relatives of the victim the right to hunt him down and kill him—he therefore decided to explore the waters to the west. Erik's next voyage was prompted by stories he had heard from an old Viking (Gunnbjorn Ulfsson) who claimed to have seen islands to the west of Iceland after he had been blown several days off course by a storm. He named them the *Gunnbjorn Skerries*, which are generally thought today to be the small cluster of coastal islands situated off *Tasiilaq*, located off the shore of northeastern Greenland.

> Eirik said to his people that he purposed to seek for the land which Gunnbjorn, the son of Ulf the Crow, saw when he was driven westwards over the ocean, and discovered Grunnbjarnarsker (Gunnbjorn's rock or skerry). He promised that he would return to visit his friends if he found the land. Thorbjorn, and Eyjolf, and Styr accompanied Eirik beyond the islands. They separated in the friendliest manner, Eirik saying that he would be of the like assistance to them, if he should be able so to be, and they should happen to need him. Then he sailed oceanwards under Snoefellsjokull (snow mountain glacier), and arrived at the glacier called Blaserkr (Blueshirt); thence he journeyed south to see if there were any inhabitants of the country. He passed the first winter at Eiriksey, near the middle of the Vestribygd western settlement). (*Erik the Red's Saga* in Sephton 1880, 8)

For the next three years, Erik explored the coastline of what he would later name "Greenland" and then returned to Iceland—after the end of his period of banishment—with stories of its attractive qualities as a place of settlement:

> Now, afterwards, during the summer, he proceeded to Iceland, and came to Breidafjordr (Broadfirth). This winter he was with Tngolf, at Holmlatr (Island-litter). During the spring, Thorgest and he fought, and Eirik met with defeat. After that they were reconciled. In the summer Eirik went to live in the land which he had discovered, and which he called Greenland, "Because," said he, "men will desire much the more to go there if the land has a good name." (*Erik the Red's Saga* in Sephton 1880, 8)

As a result of Erik's expedition and leadership, a number of Viking families were convinced to leave Iceland and establish farms and settlements in Greenland. As to why Erik was so successful and so many colonists were persuaded to relocate to the Greenland environment, it appears that the average temperature was significantly warmer in the 900s and the growing season longer, or as Robert Ferguson explains, "This was about midway through the 'Medieval Warm Period,' and the relatively mild temperatures in the region and ice-free approaches from the sea will have made the name Greenland seem less fanciful than we might now be inclined to suppose" (Ferguson 2014, 281). As to exactly how many colonists followed Erik the Red, *The Book of the Settlements* identifies ten Viking lords who, together with their families, thralls, and livestock, chose to move to Greenland, ultimately establishing two large coastal communities—an eastern settlement at the southernmost tip of Greenland and a "smaller Western Settlement 400 miles further up the west coast, in the Nuuk area around Godthaab (Good Hope) and *Lysufjord*, where Erik's younger son, Thorstein, owned a half-share in a farm" (Ferguson 2014, 282).

Erik the Red's Saga continues the story of his migration, saying that he chose to establish his home, a farm called "*Brattahlid*," at the head of a long inlet on Greenland's western shore, which he named "Eiriksfjord." It was here that he and his wife, Thjodhild, raised their sons, or as the saga relates,

> Eirik had a wife who was named Thjodhild, and two sons; the one was named Thorstein, and the other Leif. These sons of Eirik were both promising men. Thorstein as then at home with his father; and there was at that time no man in Greenland who was thought so highly of as he. Leif had sailed to Norway, and was there with King Olaf Tryggvason. Now, when Leif sailed from Greenland during the summer, he and his men were driven out of their course to the Sudreyjar. They were slow in getting a favourable wind from this place, and they stayed there a long time during the summer reaching Norway about harvest-tide. (*Erik the Red's Saga* in Sephton 1880, 8)

Leif Erikson, as he was then known, had decided to leave his family in Greenland and seek his fortune in Northern Europe in the service of the king of Norway as a supporter of the royal household. Had his career continued in this direction, continental North America might never have been discovered until the time of Columbus. But the narrative of *Erik the Red's Saga* provides a fascinating turn of events involving the impact of recent Roman Catholic missionary efforts to convert the Norse population of Scandinavia from their belief in Nordic paganism to Christianity. Apparently, Leif was himself, since his arrival in Norway, a recent convert to the new faith:

> He joined the body-guard of King Olaf Tryggvason, and the king formed an excellent opinion of him, and it appeared to him that Leif was a well-bred man. Once upon a time the king entered into conversation with Leif, and asked him, "Dost thou purpose sailing to Greenland in summer?" Leif answered, "I should wish so to do, if it is your will." The king replied, "I think it may well be so; thou shalt go my errand, and preach Christianity in Greenland." Leif said that he was willing to undertake it, but that, for himself, he considered that message a difficult one to proclaim in

Greenland. But the king said that he knew no man who was better fitted for the work than he. "And thou shalt carry," said he, "good luck with thee in it." "That can only be," said Leif, "if I carry yours with me." (*Erik the Red's Saga* in Sephton 1880, 9)

This discussion clearly implies two things. First, the King Olaf Tryggvason was a deeply devoted Christian ruler of Norway. This fact is borne out in his warlike rise to power, which included the slaughter of all his pagan enemies, royal and otherwise, or as described by Robert Ferguson,

> According to the accepted chronology, Olaf (Tryggvason) was twenty-seven years old when he was hailed as the new king in *Trondelag* (capital of Norway). At once he set about the task . . . of converting the country to Christianity. Not for him the subtle and disappointed compromise between cross and hammer; at an early stage in the campaign he herded eighty priests of the old faith, men and women now regarded as sorcerers, into a temple and burned them along with the images of the gods. Report of the sheer terror inspired by his methods preceded him as he travelled the country. The *Trondelag*, a bastion of Norwegian Heathendom, was cowed into acceptance of the new faith. (Ferguson 2014, 278)

The second point was simply that as daunting a task as converting the population of Greenland to Christianity might be, Leif Erikson felt it was preferable to declining King Olaf's request to do so. Clearly, King Olaf believed that the Kingdom of Norway was well within its rights to exert its authority over Greenland as an overseas territory or colony.

In terms of size and property value, was this struggling island colony worth the effort for Norway's king to claim and establish the right of rule and conversion? According to the Danish colonial records, the number of farms located around the Eastern Settlement of Greenland was approximately 190, and the number of farms around the Western Settlement was recorded at 90. Ferguson further observes that a substantial colonial population existed that might have varied between a minimum of two thousand and a maximum of four thousand colonists ruled locally by an assembly of residents, or "*althing*" as was employed in Iceland (Ferguson 2014, 283).

Returning to *Erik the Red's Saga*, the narrative traces one version of Leif Erikson's fateful journey westward:

> Leif set sail as soon as he was ready. He was tossed about a long time out at sea, and lighted upon lauds of which before he had no expectation. There

were fields of wild wheat, and the vine-tree in full growth. There were also the trees which were called maples; and they gathered of all this certain tokens; some trunks so large that they were used in house-building. Leif came upon men who had been shipwrecked, and took them home with him, and gave them sustenance during the winter. Thus, did he show his great munificence and his graciousness when he brought Christianity to the land, and saved the shipwrecked crew. He was called Leif the Lucky. (*Erik the Red's Saga* in Sephton 1880, 9)

The Greenlanders' Saga also has a passage describing the first sighting of land beyond Greenland. In this narrative, however, the credit for the first sighting of the New World was given to a lost Norse mariner named Bjarne Herjulfson, who while en route to Greenland from Iceland in about 986 CE accidentally found himself sailing off the coast of unknown lands. He does not attempt to land or explore the new territory but simply observes them from the safety of his vessel and finally returns to Greenland with reports of lands to the west. Once again, Leif Erikson enters the narrative:

There was now much talk about voyages of discovery. Leif, the son of Erik the Red, of Brattahlid, went to Bjarne Herjulfson, and bought the ship of him, and engaged men for it, so that there were thirty-five men in all. Leif asked his father Erik to be the leader on the voyage, but Erik excused himself, saying that he was now pretty well stricken in years, and could not now, as formerly, hold out all the hardships of the sea. Leif said that still he was the one of the family whom good fortune would soonest attend; and Erik gave in to Leif's request, and rode from home soon as they were ready; and it was but a short way to the ship. The horse stumbled that Erik rode, and he fell off and bruised his foot. Then said Erik, "It is not ordained that I should discover more countries than that which we now inhabit, and we should make no further attempt in company." Erik went home to Brattahlid, but Leif repaired to the ship, and his comrades with him, thirty-five men. (*The Greenlanders' Saga* in Sephton 1880, 10)

The Greenlanders' Saga provides a far more detailed account of Leif Erikson's voyage to the New World, with topographical descriptions of the landscape corresponding to some identifiable locations today:

There was a southern man on the voyage, who was named Tyrker. Now prepared they their ship, and sailed out into the sea when they were ready, and then found first that land which Bjarne had found last. There sailed they to the land, and cast anchor, and put off boats, and went ashore, and saw there no grass. Great icebergs were over all up the country, but like a plain of flat stones was all from the sea to the mountains, and it appeared to them that this land had no good qualities. Then said Leif, "We have not done like Bjarne concerning this land, in that we have been upon it. Now will I give the land a name, and call it Helluland." (*The Greenlanders' Saga* in Sephton 1880, 10)

Scholars generally translate the place-name of *Helluland* as "land of rocky slabs," the northernmost of Leif's discoveries. It is treeless, with little or no vegetation, and covered in a surface of broken fragments of stone corresponding to the present-day appearance of Baffin Island, which borders the west shore of the Davis Strait, which separates it from the western coastline of Greenland at a distance of approximately three hundred nautical miles. Thus, the Leif Erikson expedition begins at a place relatively close to home and gradually works its way southward. The narrative continues:

They then went on board and after that, sailed to sea and found another land; they sailed again to the land, and cast anchor, then put off boats and went again on shore. This land was flat and covered with wood, and white sands were far around where they went, and the shore was low. Then said Leif, "This land shall be named after its qualities, and called Markland (wood-or-forestland)." They then immediately returned to the ship. Now sailed they thence into the open sea, with a northeast wind and were two days at sea before they saw land, and they sailed thither and came to an island which lay to the eastward of the land, and went up there, and looked around them in good weather, and observed that there was dew upon the grass; and it so happened that they touched the dew with their hands, and raised the fingers to the mouth, and they thought that they had never before tasted anything so sweet. (*The Greenlanders' Saga* in Sephton 1880, 11)

After that they went to the ship, and sailed into a, which lay between the island and a ness which ran out to the eastward of the land; and then steered westward past the ness. It was very shallow at ebbtide, and their ship stood up, so that it was far to see from the ship to the water. But so much did they desire to land, that they did not give themselves time to wait until the water again rose under their ship, but ran at once onto the shore, at a place where a river flows out of a lake; but so, as soon as the waters rose up under the ship, they took their boats, and rowed to the ship, and floated it up to the river, and then into the lake, and there cast anchor, and brought up from the ship their skin cots, and made their booths. (*The Greenlanders' Saga* in Sephton 1880, 12)

After this took they counsel, and formed the resolution of remaining there for the winter, and build there large houses. There was no want of salmon either in the river or in the lake, and larger salmon than they had before seen. The nature of the country was, as they thought, so good that cattle would not require house-feeding in winter, for there came no frost in winter, and little did the grass wither there. Day and night were more equal than in Greenland or Iceland, for on the shortest day was the sun above the horizon from half past seven in the forenoon, till half past four in the afternoon. (*The Greenlanders' Saga* in Sephton 1880, 12)

But when they had done with the house building, Leif said to his comrades: 'Now I will divide our men into two parts, and have the land explored, and half of the men shall remain at home at the house, while the other half explore the land; but however, not go further than they can come home in the evening, and they should not separate.' Now they did so for a time, and Leif changed about, so that the one day he went with them, and on the other remained at home in the house. Leif was a great and strong man, grave and well-favored, therewith sensible and moderate in all things. (*The Greenlanders' Saga* in Sephton 1880, 12)

Interestingly, unlike several other accounts of visits to Markland and Vinland, *The Greenlanders' Saga* makes no mention of an encounter with native people, usually referred to as "Skraelings," who occasionally traded with Norse explorers and sometimes fought with them, effectively using the bow and arrow as a range weapon.

It happened one evening that a man of the party was missing, and this was Tyrker, the German. This took Leif much to heart, for Tyrker had long been with his father and him, and loved Leif much in his childhood. Leif now took his people severely to task, and prepared to seek for Tyrker, and took twelve men with him. But when they had gotten a short way from the house, then came Tyrker towards them, and was joyfully received. Leif soon saw that his foster-father was not in his right senses. Tyrker had a high forehead, and unsteady eyes, was freckled in the face, small and mean in stature, but excellent in all kinds of artifice. (*The Greenlanders' Saga* in Sephton 1880, 13)

Then said Leif to him: "Why wert thou so late, my fosterer, and separated from the party?" He now spoke—first for a long-time in German, and rolled his eyes about to and from different sides—and twisted his mouth—but they did not understand what he said. So after a time, he spoke Norse. "I have not been much further off, but still I have something new to tell of; I found vines and grapes." "But is that true, my fosterer?" quoth Leif. "Surely it is true," replied he, "For I was bred up in a land where there is no want of either vines or grapes." They slept now for the night, but in the morning, Leif said to his sailors: "We will now set about two things, in that in one day we gather grapes, and the other day cut vines and fell trees, so from thence will be a loading for my ship," and that was the counsel taken, and it is said that their longboat was filled with grapes. Now was a cargo cut down for the ship, and when the spring came, they got ready and sailed away, and Leif gave the land a name after its qualities, and called it Vinland, or Wineland. (*The Greenlanders' Saga* in Sephton 1880, 13)

They sailed now into the open sea, and had a fair wind until they saw Greenland, and the mountains below the joklers. Then a man put in his word and said to Leif: "Why do you steer so close to the wind?" Leif answered, "I attend to my steering, and something more, and can you not see anything?" They answered that they could not see anything extraordinary. "I know not," said Leif, "whether I see a ship or a rock." Now they looked and said it was a rock. But he saw so much sharper than they, that he perceived there were men upon the rock. "Now let us," said Leif, "hold our wind so that we come up to them, if they should want our assistance, and the necessity demands that we should help them; and if they should not be kindly disposed, the power is in our hands, not theirs." Now sailed they under the rock, and lowered their sail, and cast anchor, and put out another little boat, which they had with them. Then asked Tyrker who their leader was? He called himself, Thorer, and said he was a Northman; "but was is your name?" said he, and Leif told him his name. "Art you a son of Erik the Red of Brattahlid?" quoth he. Leif answered that so it was. "Now will I," said Leif, "take you all on board my ship, and as much of your goods as my ship can hold." They accepted this offer and said thereupon to Eriksfjord with the cargo, and thence to Brattahlid, where they unloaded the ship. (*The Greenlanders' Saga* in Sephton 1880, 13)

This important part of the story—the saving of Thorer's shipwrecked crew—is confirmed in *Erik the Red's Saga* as an essential precursor to the explanation in both cases for how Leif earned his nickname, "Leif the Lucky." This is borne out in the following segment of the narrative:

After that, Leif invited Thorer and his wife, Gudrid, and three other men to stop with him, and got berths for the other seamen elsewhere, as well as that of Thorer himself. Leif took fifteen men from the rock; he was, after that, called Leif the Lucky. Leif had earned by now both riches and respect. The same winter came a heavy sickness among Thorer's people, and carried off, Thorer himself, as well as many of his men. That winter died also Erik the Red. Now was there much talk about Leif's voyage to Vinland, and Thorwald, his brother, thought that the land had been much too little explored. Then Leif said to Thorvald, "You can go with my ship, brother, if thou wilt, to Vinland, but I wish first that the ship will go and fetch the timber, which Thorer had upon the rock . . .," and so was done. (*The Greenlanders' Saga* in Sephton 1880, 14)

This passage concludes the narrative describing Leif Erikson's exploratory voyage to Vinland, which based on the vegetation described and the approximate time of sunrise on the winter solstice of that time is estimated by many contemporary scholars to be situated approximately near the Gulf of Saint Lawrence and the present-day Canadian province of New Brunswick. Similarly, it is generally accepted that "Helluland" was, in all probability, a portion of Baffin Island, and the forested "Markland" might well be the southern part of the present-day province of Newfoundland-Labrador.

Allowing for the fact that both the *Erik the Red's Saga* and *The Greenlanders' Saga* were transmitted separately by oral tradition until finally recorded about 250 years after the events they describe, they are surprisingly consistent in a number of key points, particularly the following: (1) the return cargo of house-framing timbers cut from the forests of Vinland, (2) the presence of grapevines, (3) the much milder climate and longer growing season of Vinland, (4) the identical geographic descriptions of topography, and, finally, (5) the homeward-bound rescue of a shipwrecked captain and his crew.

The later portion of *The Greenlanders' Saga* provides the reader with a detailed account of Leif's brother Thorvarld's expedition to Vinland, which contemporary scholars estimate as having taken place in 1002 CE, and begins with Thorvald and his crew of thirty seamen arriving in Vinland to occupy the houses built by Leif Erikson's crew and situated near the coast. As a result of their exploration, Thorvald's men discover a corn-shed but little evidence of native people until they "saw there were three skin boats (canoes) and three men under each." Unfortunately, this resulted in the slaughter of eight Skraelings (native people), with only one escaping to raise an alarm. In short order, the Norse explorers were soon confronted with "an innumerable crowd of skin boats" and native warriors, prompting Thorvald to order his men to "put out the battle-screen (shield wall), and defend ourselves as well as we can, but fight little against them" (*The Greenlanders' Saga* in Sephton 1880, 14).

So did they, and the Skraelings shot at them for a time, but afterwards ran away . . . . Then asked Thorvald his men if they had gotten any wounds; they answered that no one was wounded. "I have gotten a wound under the arm," said he, "for an arrow fled between the edge of the ship and my shield, in under my arm, and here is the arrow, and it will prove a mortal wound to me. Now counsel I you, that you get ready to instantly depart, but you first shall bear me to that cape, where I thought it best to dwell; it may be that a true word fell from my mouth that I should dwell there for a time; there shall you bury me, and set up crosses at my head and feet; and call the place, Krossaness forever in all time to come." Now Thorvald died, but they did all things according to his directions, and then went away, and returned to their companions, and told to each other the tidings which they knew, and dwelt there for a winter and gathered grapes and vines to load the ship. But in the spring they made ready to sail back to Greenland, and came with their ship in Eriksfjord, and could now tell great tidings to Leif. (*The Greenlanders' Saga* in Sephton 1880, 14–15)

These Norse sagas and other primary sources remained fairly obscure during the Middle Ages, having been relegated to minor monastic archival repositories and generally not known by the academic communities, with the exception of Adam of Bremen, who around the year 1075 CE wrote in his *Descriptio Insularum Aquilonis* that during a visit at the court of the Danish king Svend Estridsen, he heard about islands discovered by Norse sailors far out in the Atlantic, of which Vinland was the most remote. Or, as Adam of Bremen wrote, "He (King Svende) told me that in this part of the Ocean many have discovered an island, which is now called Vinland because there are grapevines growing wild, which produce the best of wines. From trustworthy Danes rather from fantastic tales, I have also heard that there is an abundance of cereal which is self-sown" (Adam of Bremen 1978, 62).

But evidence of the Norse discovery and settlement of North America prior to Columbus, as described by the aforementioned sagas, is not limited to medieval manuscripts alone. Tangible proof of Nordic colonization was conclusively uncovered by the archaeologists Helge and Stine Ingstad in 1960 at L'Anse aux Meadows, near the Strait of Belle Isle, leading into the Gulf of Saint Lawrence. Here, at the northernmost tip of Newfoundland, once existed a small medieval town of Scandinavian people consisting of a population of between seventy to ninety colonists living in three "residential halls" among a total of seven structures, including a blacksmith's forge. As to dating the small medieval colony, "about a third of the 150 radio-carbon dates for the L'Anse aux Meadows are connected to the period of Norse settlement there, dating it between 980 and 1020 A.D." (Ferguson 2014, 294).

More excavations of the colony have taken place since the initial discovery—most importantly those of Brigitta Wallace, who in comparing the descriptions provided in the sagas against the archaeological and topographical evidence has concluded that the L'Anse aux Meadows site was described in the *Erik the Red's Saga* as "the Fjord of Currents," known in Old Norse as "Straumfjord," a year-round settlement that sent out expeditions to gather resources and supplies from areas farther to the south. Evidence of this was the discovery at L'Anse aux Meadows of white walnut (or butternut) shells among the wood-shavings refuse. As walnut trees—and wild grapes—grow no farther north than present-day New Brunswick, it appears that desirable foodstuffs were brought to feed the settlers of the Newfoundland colony from North American sources farther down the Atlantic coastline. As to what the primary export item from L'Anse aux Meadows might have been, the answer is timber—by far the most valuable, needed, and most difficult to acquire commodity back home in Greenland.

The fate of the settlement seems to have been a voluntary withdrawal or relocation of the Norse community. As indicated in the sagas themselves, relations with the "Skraelings," or native people, did not go well. Mutual suspicion and cultural misunderstandings were a problem that resulted in open hostility and warfare. The archaeological evidence, however, does not appear to reflect the colony's destruction by violence; yet, a peaceable retreat after years of residence to another place seems to have happened at L'Anse aux Meadows, leaving fragments of nails, foundations of buildings, and Norse artifacts as silent testimony to the Nordic discovery of the New World during the European Middle Ages.

Today, the Canadian government has created a national park at L'Anse aux Meadows that is open to tourists and scholars researching North American Viking culture. What remains is for the world in general, and the United States in particular, to recognize that Columbus was far from the first European to discover and explore the Western Hemisphere.

Further Reading

Adam of Bremen. 1978. *Beskrivelse af øerne i Nordern* [*Description of the Islands in the North*]. Copenhagen: Wormianum.

Brittain, Alfred. 1903. *The History of North America*. Philadelphia: Barrie.

Castiglioni, Luigi, Antonio Pace, Joseph Ewan, and Luigi Castiglioni. 1983. *Luigi Castiglioni's Viaggio*. Syracuse, NY: Syracuse University Press.

Columbus, Christopher, Diego Alvarez Chanca, Giuliano Dati, Richard Henry Major, Diego Méndez de Segura, and Luis de Santángel. 1870. *Select Letters of Christopher Columbus*. London: Printed for the Hakluyt Society.

Desai, Christina M. 2014. "The Columbus Myth: Power and Ideology in Picture Books about Christopher Columbus." *Children's Literature in Education* 45 (3): 179–196.

Ferguson, Robert. 2014. *The Vikings*. New York: Penguin Books.

Fitzhugh, William W., Elisabeth I. Ward, and National Museum of Natural History (U.S.), eds. 2000. *Vikings: The North Atlantic Saga*. Washington, DC: Smithsonian Institution Press in association with the National Museum of Natural History.

Gleach, Frederic W. 1997. *Powhatan's World and Colonial Virginia: A Conflict of Cultures*. Studies in the Anthropology of North American Indians. Lincoln: University of Nebraska Press.

Ingstad, Anne Stine. 1977. *The Discovery of a Norse Settlement in America*. Oslo: Universitetsforlaget.

Jones, Gwyn. 1986. *The Norse Atlantic Saga: Being the Norse Voyages of Discovery and Settlement to Iceland, Greenland, and North America*. Oxford, and New York: Oxford University Press.

Koning, Hans. 1991. *Columbus: His Enterprise: Exploding the Myth*. New York: Monthly Review Press.

Kunz, Keneva, ed. 2008. *The Vinland Sagas: The Icelandic Sagas about the First Documented Voyages across the North Atlantic; The Saga of the Greenlanders and Eirik the Red's Saga*. New ed. Penguin Classics. London: Penguin Books.

Love, Ronald S. 2006. *Maritime Exploration in the Age of Discovery, 1415–1800*. Westport, CT: Greenwood Press.

Morison, Samuel Eliot. 1994. *The Oxford History of the American People*. New York: New American Library.

Ogilby, John. 1671. *America Being the Latest and Most Accurate Description of the New World*. London: Printed by the author.

Reeves, Arthur Middleton, and William Dudley Foulke. 1895. *The Finding of Wineland the Good*. London: Frowde.

Rowe, Elizabeth Ashman. 2005. *The Development of Flateyjarbók*. Odense: University Press of Southern Denmark.

Sephton, John. 1880. *The Greenlanders' Saga and Erik the Red's Saga: A Translation*. Liverpool: D. Marples & Co.

Stedman, Edmund Clarence. 1900. *An American Anthology, 1787–1900*. Boston, MA: Houghton-Mifflin and Co.

Symonds, William. 1612. *The Proceedings of the English Colonie in Virginia.* Oxford: Joseph Barnes.

Vespucci, Amerigo, Luciano Formisano, and David Jacobson. 1992. *Letters from a New World: Amerigo Vespucci's Discovery of America.* Marsilio Classics. New York: Marsilio.

Winroth, Anders. 2014. *The Age of the Vikings.* Princeton, NJ: Princeton University Press.

2

Captain John Smith and Pocahontas Had a Romantic Relationship

What People Think Happened

The story of Pocahontas (also known as Matoaka and Rebecca Rolfe ca. 1596–1617) and Captain John Smith (1580–1631) looms large in the annals of the early settlement of Jamestown, Virginia Colony, and, indeed, colonial America. Americans have heard the story of how the young Indian "princess," the favorite daughter of Chief Powhatan (or Wahunsenacawh, ca. 1547–1618), risked her life to save the handsome English explorer from execution at the hands of her father—a story told in great detail by Captain Smith himself in his popular 1624 book, *The Generall Historie of Virginia*.

It is from this primary source that a mythical assumption has been made. Many people—from film producers and historians to schoolchildren—have assumed that Pocahontas and Captain John Smith were somehow romantically involved. Indeed, such an assumption was most recently reaffirmed to the general public by the writers and producers of Walt Disney's 1995 animated film *Pocahontas*.

Although the questionable idea of a romantic involvement between these two significant historical figures is certainly the dominant myth, there are several other associated misconceptions deserving of attention that also require further clarification. These misunderstandings include

(1) whether Captain John Smith's 1624 published narrative—when compared to his earlier 1608 version—was a factually reliable account or greatly exaggerated and (2) whether it is possible that the famous incident of Smith's life, being saved by Pocahontas, might be an entirely fictional narrative fabricated by the famous explorer to enhance his reputation.

Over the past four hundred years, these myths and misconceptions about Captain John Smith and Pocahontas have shaped and distorted the public's conception of what actually happened in early Virginia that ultimately led to what historians have called the "Peace of Pocahontas" and the end of the "First Anglo-Powhatan War." It is this peace, established by Pocahontas, that gave rise to a brief but important period of stability and commercial prosperity for the Jamestown Colony. Unfortunately, there is a great deal of conflicting and erroneous information concerning the relations between native and English people living in Virginia at this time.

It is possible that much of what we think we "know" about Pocahontas and Captain Smith is a creative combination of truth and a fictional narrative made up to retrospectively mask and rationalize the exploitation and destruction of an indigenous people by the newly arrived English settlers.

How It Became Popular

The myth of John Smith and Pocahontas has its point of origin in the prolific writings of Captain John Smith himself, who emphasized that among the many ladies who came to his aid during his many travel adventures—in the Ottoman and Russian Empires and the Anglo-American colonies—Pocahontas was certainly one of the most important. In his first published account, *A True Relation* (1608), he describes his initial meeting with Chief Powhatan's daughter, introducing a very young Pocahontas as her father's diplomatic representative to negotiate the release of a small group of native prisoners then being held in Smith's custody. During this initial encounter, the twenty-eight-year-old professional soldier developed a very favorable impression of her physical appearance, intelligence, and personal enthusiasm. He further asserts that she was among the highest-quality (nonpareil) native people he had yet to encounter in Virginia. What is somewhat surprising is his estimate of her as being merely a child of ten years old, which seems quite young to be engaged in a serious negotiation. Later in the narrative, Smith mentions that he only decided to free the captive natives into the hands of Pocahontas on the basis of her handling of the situation:

In the afternoon, they (the relatives of the prisoners) being gone, we guarded them (the Prisoners) as before to the Church, and after prayer, gave them to Pocahontas, the King's Daughter, in regard of her father's kindness in sending her; after having well fed them (the native prisoners), as all the time of their imprisonment, we gave them their bows, arrows, or what else they had, and with much content, sent them packing. Pocahontas also we requited, with such trifles as contented her. (Smith 1866, 74–75)

Importantly, no mention is made here of Smith's life being threatened by his dealings with the native people of Virginia. Indeed, it is not until Pocahontas briefly reappears in Smith's fourth published work in 1622, *New England's Trials*, that he enigmatically acknowledges that he is forever in her debt for extracting him from a difficult situation:

It is true in our greatest extremity, they (the native warriors) shot me, slew three of my men, and by the folly (cowardice) of them that fled, took me prisoner; yet God made Pocahontas, the King's Daughter, the means to deliver me. (Smith 1908 263)

It is this episode—where Captain John Smith claims that his life was spared through the courageous efforts of Pocahontas—that forms the very foundation of the romantic myth in question, because it is assumed by later writers that it was out of personal affection for Captain Smith that young Pocahontas put her own life at risk during what was intended to be a ceremonial execution.

The very first glimpse of this heroic rescue of Captain Smith by Pocahontas appears in a personal letter written by Smith to Queen Anne of England—the wife of King James I—in a letter dated 1616:

At the minute of my execution, she hazarded the beating out of her own brains to save mine; and not only that, but so prevailed with her father, that I was safely conducted to Jamestown. (Hillard 1902, 199)

In this important letter to the queen of England, Smith changes one significant detail. In his 1608, *True Relation* narrative, Smith estimates Pocahontas as being "a child of ten years old," but in his 1616 letter to Queen Anne, he describes her as "Pocahontas, the King's most-dear and well-beloved daughter, being but a child of twelve or thirteen years of age, whose compassionate and pitiful heart, of my desperate estate, gave me much cause to respect her" (Hillard 1902, 199).

Critics of Smith argue that the two alterations in Smith's 1616 letter to Queen Anne—an increase in Pocahontas's estimated age from ten to thirteen at the time of meeting Smith and the claim that she saved him from execution—were calculated to improve the queen's estimation of Pocahontas in anticipation of a private audience between the English royal couple and the young native princess. It is also possible that the myth of a romance between Smith and Powhatan's daughter might have begun when the queen read Smith's description of Pocahontas having "a compassionate and pitiful heart" concerning the life-threatening dangers then faced by the gallant English soldier.

Finally, in Smith's greatest narrative, the multivolume *Generall Historie of Virginia, New England and the Summer Isles*, the reader is exposed to the only detailed description of Smith's life-threatening adventure that culminates in his last-minute rescue by the compassionate princess, Pocahontas. Interestingly, he tells the vivid story entirely in the third person, as if he were an outside observer of himself and the actions surrounding him:

> At last they brought him (Captain Smith) to *Meronocomoco* (the primary native town), where Powhatan was their Emperor. Here more than two hundred of those grim courtiers stood wondering at him (Captain Smith), as if he had been a monster; 'til Powhatan and his train had put themselves in their greatest braveries. Before a fire, upon a seat like a bedstead, he (Powhatan) sat covered with a great robe, made of *rarowcun* (raccoon) skins, and all the tails hanging by. On either hand did sit a young wench of sixteen or eighteen years, and along each side of the house, two rows of men, and behind them as many women, with all their heads and shoulders painted red; many of their heads bedecked with the white down of birds; but everyone with something; and a great chain of white beads about their necks. At his (Captain Smith) entrance before the King (Powhatan), all the people gave a great shout. The Queen of *Appamattuck* was appointed to bring him (Captain Smith) water to wash his hands, and another brought him a bunch of feathers instead of a towel to dry them; having feasted him (Captain Smith) after the best barbarous manner they could, a long consultation was held, but the conclusion was, two great stones were brought before Powhatan; then as many as could laid hands on him (Captain Smith), dragged him to them (the stones), and thereon laid his head, and being ready with their clubs, to beat out his brains. Pocahontas, the King's dearest daughter, when no entreaty could prevail, got his head in her arms, and laid her own (head) upon his to save him from death; whereat the Emperor (Powhatan) was contented that he (Captain Smith) should live. (Smith 1908, 141)

This dramatic and perhaps fanciful scene—recorded and published by Captain Smith long after Pocahontas's death—has contributed, over the intervening four hundred years, most prominently in creating the public's understanding of the special relationship between the twenty-something Captain John Smith and Powhatan's teenage daughter. It is a scene that many critics, including some contemporaries of Smith, suspect as a fiction calculated to enhance Smith's reputation as a soldier and an adventurer. Beginning from this point, the key question is this: how did this colorful anecdote gradually evolve into a mythical romance story that culminates—according to some versions—in a marriage between the English captain and the Indian princess?

The ultimate responsibility for this romantic myth does not rest entirely with Captain Smith, who never personally expressed any romantic love for Pocahontas. Rather, the blame for its creation rests with those writers, historians, and storytellers who have, for many generations, retold, embellished, and published the tale of Princess Pocahontas and Captain John Smith, suggesting that theirs was more than a simple friendship based on mutual admiration and respect.

For example, as early as 1612, William Symonds, an English minister who wrote an important justification document for the Virginia Company, produced a book entitled *The Proceedings of the English Colonie in Virginia*, which provides his account of Pocahontas's negotiations with Captain Smith to free the native prisoners. Later in his narrative, Symonds denies a rumor already circulating among the Jamestown colonists that "Smith would make himself king by marrying Pocahontas" (Smith, Potts et al. 1612, 13–14).

Apparently, even during Smith's lifetime, gossip of this possibility among Jamestown residents was spreading. The colonists' suspicion of Smith's political ambitions may have been exacerbated by Powhatan's desire to offer Captain Smith the rank of subchief, or *werowance*, of the native village of Capahosic. Such a stratagem would have helped to solidify the alliance between the two opposing sides and theoretically place Smith in a subordinate relationship to Chief Powhatan, giving him some authority over the feisty English explorer. Indeed, some historians believe that the ceremony described by Smith in which he believed his life was being threatened by club-wielding warriors and possibly saved by Pocahontas was in reality a native ritual "intended to symbolize his death and rebirth as a member of the tribe" (Gleach 1997, 118–121).

Throughout the seventeenth and eighteenth centuries, the English and American reading public had already been exposed to many books and articles produced by authors such as John Ogilby, who wrote "The Relation of Captain Smith's Being Taken Prisoner by Powhatan, and of

His Being Delivered from Death by His Daughter Pocahonta" in 1671 (Ogilby, *America Being the Latest and Most Accurate Description of the New World*, London, 1671). Eighteenth-century naturalist Luigi Castiglioni's *Viaggio: Travels in the United States of North America, 1785–1787*, is another example; it tells how, as a prisoner of Powhatan, Captain Smith was about to be burned alive, but Pocahontas comes to his aid, pleading for mercy on his behalf and winning Smith's life and his heart. Together, they both escape from Virginia and relocate to England. After a brief time, Captain Smith "no longer showed her the affection that he manifested in America," whereupon "she became disgusted with him and the ingratitude with which she was treated" (Castiglioni 1983, 192). According to Castiglioni's version, Pocahontas then returns to the Jamestown Colony and marries John Rolfe on the rebound.

After the American Revolution, as the United States was beginning to expand its areas of settlement westward to realize the national goal of Manifest Destiny, the story of Pocahontas and John Smith became instrumental in proclaiming that the original inhabitants of North America, as early the first generation of settlement, had reached a mutual understanding, whereby European education and friendship had been offered by colonists and accepted by America's indigenous peoples. The story also posited that the newly arrived gifts of the Christian faith and the institution of Christian marriage had been acknowledged and received by Pocahontas, who dutifully renounced her pagan names, Pocahontas and Matoaka, in favor of the more conventional European and Christian name Rebecca Rolfe.

Pocahontas had, in the eyes of American colonists, finally seen the light and accepted a better way. One has only to look at the famous oval portrait of Pocahontas dressed in the lace and silk finery of an Elizabethan lady to understand the artistic implication as to whose culture should and would ultimately win out in the struggle for the continent. It was not by mere happenstance that the dominant iconic painting that graces the interior of the Rotunda of the United States Capitol is *The Baptism of Pocahontas* by John Gadsby Chapman. Painted in 1839 and installed in 1840, the image of Pocahontas kneeling before an Anglican altar and minister is a visual message for all Americans of what the "noble savage" should ideally become—submissive and Christian. It was painted near the end of the tragic and genocidal Trail of Tears episode that resulted from the Indian Removal Act, of May 28, 1830, a piece of congressional legislation demanding the federally enforced migration of native tribes from the southeastern United States to the Trans-Mississippi area and the Indian Territory (now Oklahoma).

It is no wonder that the subordination of one culture to the other, symbolically represented by the story of Pocahontas and John Smith, would grow increasingly popular throughout the 1800s and into the 1900s. A representative example of the increasing popularity of the myth is reflected in the number and variety of public entertainment that focused on the Pocahontas–John Smith story. Beginning in 1808, theatergoers at Philadelphia's Chestnut Street Theatre were introduced for the first time to the characters of Pocahontas and John Smith on stage in a musical play entitled *The Indian Princess, or La Belle Sauvage*, featuring a libretto by James Nelson Barker—loosely based on John Smith's 1624 *Generall Historie of Virginia* account as well as two other sources by American author John Davis, *Captain Smith and Princess Pocahontas: An Indian Tale* (1805) and *The First Settlers of Virginia* (1806), one of the first historical novels clearly portraying Captain John Smith and Pocahontas as a romantic couple.

But many theatrical productions were to follow in the wake of the initial success of *The Indian Princess* in Philadelphia. It was later introduced to the American public in New York City at the Park Theatre in January 1809, ultimately reaching theaters in the tidewater region of the Chesapeake. This play and other variations of it helped to keep the Pocahontas–John Smith myth before the public eye. The tendency of the majority of these plays was to present to American audiences the character of Pocahontas as a stereotypical "noble savage" who, in the end, would choose to embrace both Captain John Smith as well as the inevitability of the displacement of her people by means of "manifest destiny." What made James Nelson Barker's *The Indian Princess* unique from the other plays that followed was its musical score by Anglo-American actor and composer John Bray, who made it a "ballad-opera" with lyrics—melodically telling the Pocahontas–John Smith story with songs and choruses. This early nineteenth-century musical version enjoyed great theatrical success, with reviewers who praised it as a "chaste" and "elegant" play.

Even on the other side of the Atlantic, an English play entitled *Pocahontas: Or the Indian Princess* (bearing little resemblance to James Nelson Barker's production of a similar name) was performed at the Theatre Royal in London in 1820. Other similar plays followed in its wake: *Pocahontas, or the Settlers of Virginia* (1830); *Pocahontas* (1838); Robert Dale Owen's morality play *The Forest Princess* (1844); and *Po-ca-hon-tas: Or, the Gentle Savage* (1855). Each of these productions, in their own way, sought to present Pocahontas as an enlightened, kindhearted representative of the indigenous peoples of North America, who, for reasons best known to herself, rejected her own native way of life in favor of gallant Captain John

Smith and the European way of life he offered to her while welcoming the white colonists into her father's Virginian domain. The only contemporary resistance to this skewed interpretation of the Pocahontas myth was offered by American humorist Seba Smith (1792–1868), who wrote the humorous satire *Powhatan: A Metrical Romance in Seven Cantos* in 1841, which represented Powhatan as a heroic figure by refusing to give away his lands to the English. According to historian Alicia Puglionesi, Seba Smith stood alone in his critique of the nineteenth-century American public, bemoaning "how the embellishment of history *with a sentimental love story* had blinded the public to injustice happening in their own backyards" (Puglionesi 2019, 1).

The legend of the "Indian princess" was not confined to the stages of North America or England. Popular poems were composed that captured the imagination and inflamed the passions of a Victorian audience for the two lovers from two feuding nations. Renowned British author William Makepeace Thackeray (1811–1863) furthered the myth in his classic poem "Pocahontas," in which Captain John Smith is depicted as a noble knight surrounded by a "countless horde" of Indians, who, though threatened with a fiery death at the stake, is saved by brave Pocahontas:

"Pocahontas"
by William Makepeace Thackeray

Wearied arm and broken sword,
Wage in vain the desperate fight:
Round him press a countless horde,
He is but a single knight.
Hark! A cry of triumph shrill
Through the wilderness resounds,
As, with twenty bleeding wounds,
Sinks the warrior, fighting still.

Now they heap the fatal pyre,
and the torch of death they light;
Ah! 'tis hard to die of fire!
Who will shield the captive knight?
Round the stake with fiendish cry
Wheel and dance the savage crowd,
Cold the victim's mien, and proud.
And his breast is bared to die.

Who will shield the fearless heart?
Who avert the murderous blade?
From the throng with sudden start,
See there springs an Indian maid.
Quick she stands before the knight,
"Loose the chain, unbind the ring,
I am the daughter of the king,
And I claim the Indian right!"

Dauntlessly aside she flings
Lifted axe and thirsty knife;
fondly to his heart she clings, and her bosom guards his life!
In the woods of Powhattan,
Still 'tis told by Indian fires,
How a daughter of their sires
Saved the captive Englishman.
    (Thackeray 1889, 292)

In more recent times, perhaps the greatest impact on public assumptions concerning Pocahontas and her relationship with John Smith has come from the American film industry, which has consistently implied that the two people shared feelings of romantic affection. Popular cinematic images of Pocahontas and Captain Smith have been undeniably responsible for the maintenance of this mythical romance. Concerning this tendency, feature writer Steve Chagollan of the *New York Times* observes,

> Despite her status as a key figure in our nation's birth, the Powhatan princess—a mere ten- to twelve-year old when she first befriended the English explorer, Capt. John Smith, and the Jamestown settlers in 1607—has been mostly relegated to obscure B movies that relied more on legend than fact. The 1953 United Artists clunker "Captain John Smith and Pocahontas" veered so far off the tracks of history that it married the lead characters, serving up lines like, "It may well be that on the shoulders of that Indian girl will rest the whole future of Virginia." (Chagollan 2005)

Far more popular in the eyes of the American public, and thus far more influential in the perpetuation of the Pocahontas–John Smith myth, is Walt Disney's 1995 animated film *Pocahontas*. This film not only serves to further entrench the public's misunderstanding of the relationship between the two main characters, but it also makes no attempt to provide an accurate retelling of the tale in general. For example, instead of a Pocahontas of ten or eleven years, the film portrays her at the time of her first meeting with Captain Smith as "an exquisitely beautiful, fully formed woman with flowing black hair; almond-shaped eyes and just a hint of a nose, and Smith as a dashing adventurer with square jaw, Herculean build and blond surfer mane. It was 'Romeo and Juliet' without the tragic ending" (Chagollan 2005). Except that, in reality, the true story is indeed a tragedy.

Besides the inaccurate portrayal in age and physical appearance, there is the matter of their relationship, which is quickly addressed in the early stages of the production when Captain Smith encounters Pocahontas while exploring the area near Jamestown. Here, alone together in the wilderness, they quickly strike up a conversation, create a bond, and fall in love—in direct disobedience to Chief Powhatan's orders that all Englishmen are to be strictly avoided by all members of the tribe. In a later scene, after the level of hostility between natives and colonists has had the chance to develop, John and Pocahontas meet with Grandmother Willow and plan to end the conflict. At this juncture, the young lovers share a kiss that is witnessed from a distance by Pocahontas's intended husband, the warrior Kocoum, who attacks Captain John Smith in a jealous rage. While the story makes for excellent romantic fiction, Disney's writers have dramatically departed from what is known to be historically accurate.

Despite this failing in accuracy and historical integrity, Walt Disney's *Pocahontas*, released on June 16, 1995—a date claimed by Disney Studios as being Pocahontas's four hundredth birthday—won two Academy Awards, one Golden Globe, and one Grammy Award. By January 1996, the film had grossed over $141.5 million in the United States, being the fourth-highest-grossing film in North America for 1995. Worldwide, *Pocahontas* earned $346.1 million.

Moving well beyond Disney's animated romance, the 2005 historical drama *The New World* was described as a film "depicting the founding of the Jamestown, Virginia, settlement and inspired by the historical figures Captain John Smith, Pocahontas of the Powhatan tribe, and Englishman John Rolfe," written and directed by award-winning director Terrence Malick. This most recent version of the Pocahontas–John Smith myth places a teenage Pocahontas in direct contact with Captain Smith, a twenty-something soldier of fortune, who is captured by the Powhatan tribe while on a trading expedition and taken to their village for questioning. He is saved from execution by Pocahontas but remains a prisoner for an extended period of time, during which he comes to admire and respect the new way of life he is introduced to by "the naturals." In the course of his daily life in the village, Smith spends more time in the company of Pocahontas, and soon they are both deeply in love.

The passionate love affair between Smith and Pocahontas never results in marriage, however, and Smith eventually leaves Jamestown for England and the hope of leading a royal expedition to the East Indies. Pocahontas is deceptively told that John Smith has died on his return voyage, and after a time of extreme anguish, she meets and marries John Rolfe, converts to Christianity, takes the name Rebecca Rolfe, and has a son, Thomas. Throughout this transition, Pocahontas suffers from periods of deep depression for the loss of her "true love." Ultimately, she and Rolfe move back to England, where Pocahontas is briefly reunited with Smith, but she discovers that he is much changed from the man she once thought she loved. Now viewing John Rolfe as a better man than Smith, she resolves to return to Virginia with him but dies of pneumonia on the eve of her departure.

In many respects, this film is in keeping with many of the historical details of what is known of the Pocahontas story. The one major departure in *The New World* is the age of Pocahontas and the dominant theme of a passionate love affair between her and Captain Smith, which is a totally fictitious element to the story line. As a result, although the film does well in its attempt to replicate the world of early seventeenth-century Jamestown, Virginia, and the village life of the Powhatan people at *Werowocomomo*, Director Malick is clearly not interested in keeping Pocahontas ten years old or providing the viewer with an historically accurate assessment of the Pocahontas–Smith relationship. As a result, this film, like Disney's *Pocahontas*, only further perpetuates the myth and confuses the general public concerning the actual roles played by Pocahontas and Smith in American history.

What Really Happened

The reality of what happened in Jamestown between 1607 and 1610 is the tragic story of an ill-prepared group of colonists who were more interested in finding nonexistent precious metals than laboring to construct a fortified settlement and plant sufficient crops to sustain themselves in a wilderness environment. In the absence of sufficient quantities of corn and other essential supplies, trade with the sometimes hostile native peoples became necessary. This circumstance prompted Captain John Smith, a man designated by the London Company, to assume a leadership role in overseeing the construction of Jamestown between September 1608 and August 1609. In this capacity, he succeeded in overseeing the construction of a palisade fortification and simultaneously seeking out native settlements where trade for corn might take place. For the better part of that year, Smith and his scouts encountered native warriors who, if not hostile, would engage in trading small copper sheets, glass beads, and iron tools in exchange for baskets of native-grown corn.

Those primary source accounts in the form of journal entries are most often used by researchers for descriptions of trading activities, such as those written and published by Captain John Smith himself. These same journal entries provide the only direct perspective on what actually happened between Jamestown's colonists and the natives as well as what transpired between Captain Smith and Pocahontas. Fortunately, through his several publications, Captain John Smith still provides today's historians with a wide range of geographical information, observations on human behavior, and a fairly complete chronicle of events and activities that took place at Jamestown in the first three years of that colony's existence.

Not surprisingly, there are some of John Smith's contemporaries who expressed doubt concerning the veracity of some of his later observations, claiming that, as he rewrote and edited his recollections of his time at Jamestown, he had a tendency to elaborate and embellish the truth in an effort to make himself appear more heroic. This criticism is certainly true of his several accounts concerning Pocahontas, which became increasingly more detailed and colorful as time passed. Adding to the criticism of his contemporary English colleagues, there are the skeptical opinions of recent historians, anthropologists, and archaeologists, who generally consider Smith's accounts as being dotted with claims that do not ring true in light of known native customs and recent archaeological findings. That said, it appears that, with the exception of his embellishments, the greater part of Smith's writings are generally reliable, except in those few places where they clearly are not.

Finally, there is a substantial and skeptical body of information that has been passed down through many generations of the Mattaponi people, who are direct descendants of Powhatan's tribe. This native oral history archive, maintained by tribal historian Dr. Linwood Custalow, and appearing in Custalow's book *The True Story of Pocahontas, the Other Side of History*, agrees with some of what Captain Smith claims but differs with him on several important points.

First, the native Mattaponi version of the Pocahontas–John Smith myth calls John Smith's claim to have been saved by Pocahontas on two separate occasions "a fabrication" because Smith waited until 1624 to mention her involvement in protecting him. From the native perspective, it is suspicious that he failed to mention Pocahontas in his original published version (*A True Relation* 1608) of his encounter with Powhatan. It is also suspect that when Smith did describe Pocahontas's efforts to save his life, she could not refute his claims because she had died seven years earlier.

Second, according to tribal tradition, a ten-year-old female child would not have been allowed to be present at the ceremony of which Smith claimed to be a participant, nor was his life ever seriously threatened. Third, the Mattaponi oral history version also maintains that, in 1610, Pocahontas (or Matoaka), at the age of fourteen, was married according to tribal custom to Kocoum, the younger brother of the Potowomac chief Japazaw. The Mattaponi record maintains that Pocahontas and Kocoum produced a female child that was raised by the Patawomeck people and whose tribal name was Ka-Okee.

Finally, the native oral tradition maintains that Pocahontas told her sister, Mattachanna, and brother-in-law, Uttamatomakkin, that during her captivity at Jamestown she had been raped. Upon returning to Virginia, Mattachanna added her belief that Pocahontas's sudden death at Gravesend, England, was not the result of a natural illness, as many claimed, but was attributable to poisoning (Schilling 2014).

Smith's earliest writings on the founding of Jamestown refer to Pocahontas in a most matter-of-fact manner. They appear in *A True Relation*, published in London in 1608, which covers Smith's entire stay at Jamestown from 1607 to 1609. A remarkable fact is that throughout the entire text of *A True Relation*, Smith, a twenty-eight-year-old mercenary and soldier of fortune, only mentions Pocahontas once in a brief encounter to negotiate the release of some native prisoners—members of Powhatan's tribe—taken captive by Smith and his troop of militia:

> Powhatan, understanding we detained certain Savages (native warriors), sent his Daughter, a child of ten years old, which, not only for feature, countenance and proportion, much exceeding any of the rest of her people, but for wit, and spirit, the only Nonpareil (having no equal) of his country; this (daughter) he sent by his most trusted messenger, called Rawhunt, as much exceeding in deformity of person, but of a subtle wit and crafty understanding. He with a long circumstance told me how well Powhatan loved and respected me, and in that I should not doubt any way his kindness, he had sent his child, which he most esteemed, to see me, a deer and bread besides for a present. . . . His little Daughter he (Powhatan) had taught this lesson also; not taking notice at all of the Indians that had been

(our) prisoners (for) three days, until the morning that she saw their fathers and friends come quietly, and in good terms to entreat (negotiate) for their liberty. (Smith 1866, 73)

As previously mentioned, it is during this encounter with Pocahontas that Smith is impressed with her maturity and diplomatic skills, but he at no time describes her as anything more than "the King's Daughter," "his little Daughter," or "a child of ten years old." Clearly, although young, Smith respectfully viewed "the child" as having represented her father, the chief's interests, very well and rewarded her by releasing his prisoners into her custody.

Smith's entry continues:

In the afternoon, they (the relatives of the prisoners) being gone, we guarded them as before to the Church, and after prayer, gave them to Pocahontas, the King's Daughter, in regard of her father's kindness in sending her; after having well fed them, as all the time of their imprisonment, we gave them their bows, arrows or what else they had, and with much content, sent them packing. Pocahontas we also requited, with such trifles as contented her. (Smith 1866, 74)

The more famous incident involving Pocahontas and Captain Smith is where he claims to have been captured, feasted by his captors, and, in later versions, threatened with death by execution under the order of Pocahontas's father, Chief Powhatan. We know this event took place in the late fall of 1607, as the Virginia Colony was nearing the end of its food supply and was desperately low on foodstuffs. Captain Smith had been sent out of Jamestown in search of corn, game, and other essential consumables in the vicinity of the Chickahominy River, when he, his native guide, and his two English companions were suddenly attacked and Smith taken prisoner. Interestingly, Smith provides a vivid account of this incident in *A True Relation*, but as has been noted by many historians, in this first version, he inexplicably omits any mention of being threatened with death or of being rescued by Pocahontas.

First, Captain John Smith is captured:

During the boiling of our victuals, one of the Indians I took with me, . . . the other Indian I left with Master Robinson and Thomas Emry, with their matched lighted in order to discharge a piece (matchlock musket), for my retreat at the first sight of any Indian. But within a quarter of an hour I heard a loud cry, and a howling of Indians, but no warning piece; supposing them surprised, and that the Indians had betrayed us, presently

I seized him (his guide) and bound his arm fast to my hand with a garter, with my pistol ready bent to be revenged; he advised me to fly, and seemed ignorant of what was done, but as we went discoursing, I was struck with an arrow on the right thigh, but without harm; upon this occasion I espied two Indians drawing their bows, which I prevented in discharging a French pistol. By the time that I had charged again (reloaded) three or four more did the like for the first fell down and fled at my discharge . . . they did not like; my hinde (Native guide) I made my barricade who offered not to strive. Twenty of thirty arrows were shot at me, but short. Three or four times I had discharged my pistol ere the king of Pamaunck called Opeckankenough with 200 men, environed (surrounded) me each drawing their bow, which done, they laid them upon the ground, yet without a shot; by hinde (guide) treated betwixt them and me of conditions of peace. He discovered me to be the Captain. My request was to retire to the boat; they demanded my arms, the rest (of his companions) were slain; only me they would reserve; the Indian importuned me not to shoot. In retiring being in the midst of a low quagmire, and minding them more than my steps, I stepped fast into the quagmire, and also the Indian in drawing me forth; thus surprised, I resolved to try their mercies. My arms I cast from me, until which non durst approach me; being seized upon me they drew me out and led me to the king. (Smith 1866, 26)

Next Captain Smith is brought before Chief Powhatan after a long journey:

Arriving at Werawocomoco, their Emperor (Powhatan) proudly lying upon a bedstead a foot high upon ten or twelve mats, richly hung with many chains of great pearls about his neck, and covered with a great covering of raccoons. At his head sat a woman, at his feet another, on each side sitting upon a mat upon the ground were ranged his chief men on each side of the firs, ten in a rank, and behind them as many young women, with each a great chain of white beads over their shoulders, their heads painted in red, and he (Powhatan) with such a grave and Majestical countenance, as drove me into admiration to see such "state" in a naked savage. He kindly welcomed me with good words, and great platters of sundry victuals, assuring me his friendship, and my liberty within four days; he much delighted in Openchancanough's relation of what I had described to him, and oft examined me upon the same. (Smith 1866, 33)

What follows is an account of the exchange of information that takes place between Captain Smith and Powhatan (or Wahunsenacawh) in his dwelling surrounded by his "courtiers" of subchiefs and warrior captains. Smith is warned about all the fierce and powerful tribes to the north, west, and south. The account concludes with Powhatan offering Smith an opportunity to move Jamestown Colony closer to his capital town of Werawocomoco and a religious ceremony, which he describes:

> Their religion and ceremony I observed was thus; three or four days after my taking seven of them into the house where I lay, each with a rattle began at ten o'clock in the morning to sing about the fire, which they environed (surrounded) with a circle of meal, and after, a foot or two from that, at the end of each song, laid down two or three grains of wheat, continuing this order until they have included six or seven hundred in a half circle, and after that two or three more circles in like manner a hands-breadth from another. That done, at each song, they put betwixt every three, two or five grains, a little stick, so counting as an old woman her "Pater noster." (Smith 1866, 41–42)

The ceremony continued:

> One disguised with a great skin, his head hung round with little skins of weasels, and other vermin, with a crown of feathers on his head, painted as ugly as the Devil, at the end of each song will make many signs and demonstrations, with strange and vehement actions; great cakes of deer suet, deer and tobacco he casts into the fire. Until six o'clock in the evening, their howling would continue ere they would depart. Each morning in the coldest frost, the principal to the number of twenty of thirty, assembled themselves in a round circle, a good distance from the town, where they told me they there consulted where to hunt the next day; so fat they fed me, that I much doubted that they intended to have sacrificed me to the *Quiyoughquosicke*, which is a superior power they worship. A more uglier thing cannot be described; one they have for chief sacrifices, which also they call *Quiyoughquosicke* to cure the sick, a man with a rattle and extreme howling, shouting and singing and such violent gestures, and antic actions over the patient will suck out blood and phlegm from the patient out of their unable stomach, or any diseased place, as no labor will more tire them. (Smith 1866, 42–43)

In the end of the 1608 version, after three or four days living at Werawocomoco as Chief Powhatan's prisoner, Captain Smith is finally sent back to Jamestown—without being threatened with death. No mention of Pocahontas is made, no life is threatened, and absolutely no potential romantic relationship between a ten-year-old girl and a twenty-eight-year-old man has been in any way described in Smith's *A True Relation*.

The same account, but in more flamboyant detail, is repeated in Smith's 1624 book, *The Generall Historie of Virginia*. It is this version of the story of Smith's capture and imprisonment—strangely told by Smith in the third person—that is essentially responsible for the creation of the romantic myth of Pocahontas and Captain John Smith, as in the end, she affectionately protects him with her own life—a situation never mentioned in Smith's 1608 account.

> At last they brought him to *Meronocomoco*, where was Powhatan their emperor. Here more than two hundred of those grim courtiers stood wondering at him, as he had become a monster; 'til Powhatan and his train had put themselves in their greatest braveries. Before a fire upon a seat like a bedstead, he sat covered with a great robe, made of raccoon skins, and all the tails hanging by. On either hand did sit a young wench of 16 or 18 years, and along on each side of the house, two rows of men, and behind them as many women, with all their heads and shoulders painted red; many of their heads bedecked with the white down of birds; but everyone with something and a great chain of white beads about their necks. At his entrance before the King, all the people gave a great shout. The Queen of *Appamattuck* was appointed to bring him water to wash his hands, and another brought him a bunch of feathers, instead of a towel to dry them; after feasting him after their best barbarous manner they could, a long consultation was held, but the conclusion was, two great stones were brought before Powhatan; then as many as could laid hands on him, him to them, and thereon laid his head, and being ready with their clubs, to beat out his brains. Pocahontas, the King's dearest daughter, when no entreaty could prevail, got his head in her arms, and laid her own upon his to save him from death; whereat the Emperor was contented he should live. (Smith 1908, 141)

In comparing the two accounts of the same event, contemporary historians disagree. Most take the position that in all probability a ceremony—as described in both variations—did take place. Its purpose was to honor Captain Smith by bringing him into a closer relationship with Powhatan, elevating him to the rank of a subordinate chief known as a *werowance*. This possibility is agreed upon by Native American scholars who also point out that at such solemn occasions as a werowance initiation ceremony, ten-year-old Pocahontas (or Matoaka) would have been excluded, as according to tribal custom, children were not allowed to attend such events. It would therefore appear that, in all probability, although Smith and Pocahontas were certainly well acquainted as a result of Smith's friendly relationship with Powhatan as an adopted member of the tribe, it is unlikely that the ten-year-old girl would have brought a tribal ceremony to a standstill, especially if Smith's life was in no way threatened.

To the bitter end, however, the swashbuckling Captain Smith steadfastly maintained in his other writings, such as *New England's Trials* (1622) and even in personal correspondence to great ladies, that he owed the debt of his life, on at least two separate occasions, to his young friend Pocahontas. A good example of this practice appears in a published letter to "the Lady Francis, Duchesse of Richmond and Lenox," in which the adventurer writes,

> Yet my comfort is, that heretofore honorable and virtuous ladies, and incomparable (but amongst themselves, have offered me rescue and protection in my greatest dangers; even in foreign parts, I have felt relief from that sex. The beauteous Lady Tragabigzanda, when I was a slave to the Turks, did all she could to secure me. When I overcame the Bashaw of Nalbrits in Tartaria, the charitable Lady Callamata supplied my necessities. In the utmost of many extremities, that blessed Pokahontas, the Great King's daughter of Virginia, oft saved my life. When I escaped the cruelty of Pirates and most furious storms a long time alone in a small boat at sea, and driven ashore in France, the good Lady Madam Chanoyes bountifully assisted me. And so verily these my adventures have tasted the same influence from your Gracious hand. (Ashton 1883, 271)

The question therefore remains, if the two main characters of this famous legend were not lovers and not married, as many people have assumed, what was the nature of their relationship? One source that sheds light upon this question is supplied by one of Captain Smith's fellow adventurers at Jamestown, Richard Potts, in a published testimonial defending the actions of Smith in making friends with Chief Powhatan and his daughter and trading supplies for Indian corn to save the colony in 1607 and 1608. Smith was suspected, criticized, and accused by some in the company of advancing his own political agenda:

> Some prophetical spirit calculated that he (John Smith) had the savages in such subjection, he would have made himself a king, by marrying Pocahontas, Powhatan's daughter. It is true that she was the very "nonpareil" of his kingdom, and at most not past thirteen or fourteen years of age. Very oft she came to our fort, with what she could get for Captain Smith, that ever loved and used the Country well, but her especially, he ever much respected; and she so well requited (returned) it, that when her father intended to have surprised him, she by stealth in the dark of night, came through the wild woods and told him of it. But her marriage could have in no way entitled him by any right to the kingdom, nor was it ever suspected that he had ever such a thought, or more regarded her. (Smith, Potts et al. 1612, 113)

The phrase "but her especially, he ever much respected, and she so well requited it" touches upon the special nature of the relationship between these two people and the friendship they shared, not as lovers but as people who admired and respected each other as equals. This touches upon the fundamental nature of the relationship that has, over many years been interpreted as a love affair, but it transcends in some ways the contemporary expectations of how a man and woman might relate in friendship. To clarify, there is a passage found in a letter written by Captain John Smith to Princess Queen Anne of Great Britain in which he describes Pocahontas as a respected ally in his attempt to colonize Virginia:

Most admired Queen,
That some ten years ago being in Virginia, and taken prisoner by the power of Powhatan their Chief King, I received from this Great Savage exceeding great courtesy, especially from his son, Nantaquaus, the most manliest, comliest, boldest spirit, I ever saw in a Savage and his sister, Pocahontas, the King's most dear and well-beloved daughter, being but a child of twelve or thirteen years of age, whose compassionate and pitiful heart, of my desperate estate, gave me much cause to respect her; I being the first Christian this proud king and his grim attendants ever saw; and thus enthralled in their barbarous power, I cannot say I felt the least occasion of want that was in the power of those, my mortal foes to prevent, notwithstanding all their threats. After about six weeks fattening amongst those savage courtiers, at the minute of my execution, she hazarded the beating out of her own brains to save mine, and not only that, but so prevailed with her father, that I was safely conducted to Jamestown, where I found about thirty-eight miserable poor and sick creatures, to keep possession of all those large territories of Virginia, such was the weakness of this poor Commonwealth, as had the savages not fed us, we would directly have starved. And this relief, most Gracious Queen, was commonly brought us by this Lady Pocahontas, notwithstanding all these passages when inconstant Fortune turned our Peace to War, this tender Virgin, would still not spare to dare to visit us, and by her, our jars have been oft appeased, and our wants still supplied; were it the policy of her father thus to employ her, or the ordinance of God thus to make her His instrument, or her extraordinary affection to our Nation, I know not; but of this I am sure; when her father with the utmost of his policy and power sought to surprise me, having but eighteen with me, the dark night could not affright her from coming through the irksome woods, and with watered eyes gave me intelligence, with her best advice to escape his fury; which, had he known, he had surely slain her. Jamestown, with her wild train, she as freely frequented as her father's habitation; and during the time of two or three years, she next under God, was still the instrument

to preserve this colony from death, famine and utter confusion, which if in those times had once been dissolved, Virginia might have remained as it was at our first arrival unto this day. Since then, this business having been turned and varied by many accidents from that I left it at, it is most certain after a long and troublesome war after my departure, betwixt her father and our colony, all which time she was not heard of, about two years after she herself was taken prisoner, being so detained near two years longer, the colony was by that means relieved, peace concluded, and at last rejecting her barbarous condition, was married to an English Gentleman, with whom at this present, she is in England; the first Christian ever of that Nation, the first Virginian ever to speak English, or had a child in marriage by an Englishman, a matter surely, if my meaning be truly considered and well understood, worthy of a Prince's understanding. (Hillard 1902, 201)

Smith concludes,

Thus most gracious Lady, I have related to your Majesty, what at your best leisure our approved Histories will account you at large, and done in the time of your Majesty's life, and however this might be presented to you from a more worthy pen, it cannot from a more honest heart, as yet I never begged anything of the state, or any, and it is my want of ability and her exceeding desert, your birth, means and authority, her birth, virtue, want and simplicity, doth make me thus bold, humbly to beseech your Majesty to take this knowledge of her, though it be from one so unworthy as myself, and the rather being of so great a spirit, however her stature; if she should not be well received, seeing that this Kingdom, may rightly have a Kingdom by her means; her present love to us and Christianity, might turn to such scorn and fury as to divert all this good to the worst of evil, where finding so great a Queen should do her some honor more than she can imagine, for being so kind to your servants and subjects, would so ravish her with content, to endear her dearest blood to effect that, your Majesty and all the King's honest subjects most earnestly desire: and so I humbly kiss your gracious hands. (Hillard 1902, 201)

The implication here is that Smith is entreating the queen of England to pay kind royal attention to this newly arrived Christian princess of Virginia in the hope and expectation that it might be possible to better and more peaceably establish the colony with assistance from Pocahontas. In this respect, it seems possible that Captain Smith, besides ingratiating himself to the queen, is also seeking to take full advantage of the recent conversion of Pocahontas from savage princess to English gentlewoman, implying that the conquest and settlement of Virginia would be much easier for England with the cooperative assistance of an Anglophile Indian princess lending her approval to facilitate the takeover.

Captain Smith next attempts to explain the nature of the special relationship that he maintains with Pocahontas, even after their reunion in England. To accomplish this, he confides to the queen a revealing and intimate conversation with Pocahontas:

> Being about this time prepared to set sail for New England, I could not stay to do her that service I desired, and she well deserved; but hearing she was at Branford with divers of my friends, I went to see her. After a modest salutation, without any word, she turned about, obscured her face, as not seeming well contented; and in that humor her husband, with divers others, we all left her (for), two or three hours, repenting myself (not) to have writ(ten) for she could speak English. But not long after, she began to talk, and remembered me well, what courtesies she had done; saying: 'You did promise Powhatan what was yours would be his, and he the like to you; you called him Father being in his land a stranger. And by the same reason so must I do you. (Webster 1840, 219)

Here Pocahontas is insisting that, in the same way that John Smith in his werowance ceremony pledged to be a "son" to Powhatan and Powhatan reciprocated by pledging support for Smith, she be allowed to call Smith her father now that she is a stranger living in his homeland. This implies that Pocahontas viewed herself as a loyal daughter to Captain Smith, not his lover.

Captain Smith here explains to Queen Anne that although he understands and would excuse Pocahontas's desire to be regarded as his daughter, according to the custom and manners of his culture, he could not allow such a familial relationship to be recognized between them because he was merely a commoner and she was a princess. In his view, such a relationship would be highly inappropriate, especially in England, where one's social rank mattered. But Pocahontas pushes back at Smith:

> With a well-set countenance she said, "Were you not afraid to come into my father's country, and caused fear in him and all his people—but me; and fear you here that I should call you father? I tell you then, I will, and you shall call me child, and so I will be forever and ever your Countryman! They did tell us always that you were dead, and I knew no other, until I came to Plymouth (England). Yet Powhatan did command *Uttamattomakkin* (Powhatan's political advisor travelling with Pocahontas) to seek you,

and know the truth, because your Countrymen will lie much." (Webster 1840, 219)

In his letter to the queen, Captain Smith now ends his verbatim narrative of his conversation with Pocahontas with the poignant phrase "your countrymen lie much" and shifts to an explanation as to exactly who "Uttamattomakkin" is, why he was angry at King James, and why he travels with Princess Pocahontas (Webster 1840, 219). Smith finally concludes by observing that, in his opinion and that of others, Pocahontas's conversion to Christianity could well have been a blessing from God in that she was a supremely accomplished gentlewoman whose pro-English sentiment would have been a tremendous advantage to England's efforts to establish a colonial empire in the New World had she lived:

> The small time I stayed in London, divers Courtiers and others, my acquaintances, have gone with me to see her, and generally concluded, that they did think God had a great hand in her conversion, and they have seen many English ladies worse favored, proportioned and behaviored, and as since I have heard, it pleased both the King and Queen's Majesty honorably to esteem her, accompanied with that honorable Lady the Lady De la Ware and that honorable Lord her husband, and divers other persons of good qualities, both publically at the masks (masked balls) and otherwise, to her great satisfaction and content, which doubtless she would have deserved—had she lived to arrive in Virginia. (Hillard 1902, 204)

The concluding paragraph indicates that while the bulk of the letter was written to the queen during Pocahontas's 1616 residency in England, for whatever reason, the letter was not concluded until after Pocahontas's death in March 1617. The excerpt of the letter quoted from here appears in "The Fourth Book" of John Smith's *The General History of Virginia*. It is important as a source that reveals Captain John Smith's perspective concerning his relationship with his devoted Virginia princess. Her stunned reaction to being reconciled to a close friend she thought long dead has the ring of truth and is quite understandable under the circumstances. Her reprimand of Smith and his behavior concerning his treatment of her father likewise seems plausible. But most insightful is her desire to be to Smith in his homeland of England what Smith was supposed to be to her father in Virginia, not a lover but rather a daughter, a devoted child, combined with a sincere wish "to be for ever and ever your Countryman." This deep and sincere desire for filial connectivity is, as best as we may ascertain from the primary sources left behind, the truth about the unique relationship between Pocahontas and Captain John Smith.

Further Reading

Ashton, John. 1883. *The Adventures and Discourses of Captain John Smith*. Oxford: Cassell.
Barbour, Philip L. 1971. *Pocahontas and Her World: A Chronicle of America's First Settlement in Which Is Related the Story of the Indians and the Englishmen, Particularly Captain John Smith, Captain Samuel Argall, and Master John Rolfe*. London: Robert Hale.
Castiglioni, Luigi. 1983. *Viaggio: Travels in the United States of North America, 1785–1787*. Syracuse, NY: Syracuse University Press.
Chagollan, Steve. 2005. "The Myth of the Native Babe: Hollywood's Pocahontas." *New York Times*, November 27, 2005. Accessed July 6, 2020. https://www.nytimes.com/2005/11/27/movies/the-myth-of-the-native-babe-hollywoods-pocahontas.html.
Custalow, Linwood, and Angela L. Daniel. 2007. *The True Story of Pocahontas: The Other Side of History: From the Sacred History of the Mattaponi Reservation People*. Golden, CO: Fulcrum Pub.
Gleach, Frederic W. 1997. *Powhatan's World and Colonial Virginia*. Lincoln: University of Nebraska Press.
Hillard, George Stillman. 1902. *Captain John Smith*. New York and London: Harper and Brothers.
Hoobler, Dorothy, and Thomas Hoobler. 2007. *Captain John Smith: Jamestown and the Birth of the American Dream*. Hoboken, NJ; Chichester: John Wiley & Sons.
Milton, Giles. 2000. *Big Chief Elizabeth: The Adventures and Fate of the First English Colonists in America*. 1st American ed. New York: Farrar, Straus and Giroux.
Ogilby, John. 1671. *America Being the Latest and Most Accurate Description of the New World*. London: Printed by the author.
Price, David A. 2003. *Love and Hate in Jamestown: John Smith, Pocahontas, and the Heart of a New Nation*. New York: Knopf.
Puglionesi, Alicia. 2019. "How a Romanticized Take on Pocahontas Became a Touchstone of American Culture." History News, April 4, 2019. Last Modified April 4, 2019. https://www.history.com/news/how-early-american-stage-dramas-turned-pocahontas-into-fake-news.
Rountree, Helen C. 1990. *Pocahontas's People: The Powhatan Indians of Virginia through Four Centuries*. The Civilization of the American Indian Series, Vol. 196. Norman: University of Oklahoma Press.

Schilling, Vincent. 2014. "The True Story of Pocahontas: Historical Myth versus Sad Reality." *Indian Country Today*, April 5, 2014.

Smith, John. 1866. *A True Relation of Virginia*. Cambridge, UK: John Wilson and Sons.

Smith, John. 1908. *The True Travels, Adventures and Observations*. Cambridge, UK: Cambridge University.

Smith, John, Richard Potts, et al. 1612. *The Proceedings of the English Colonie in Virginia*. Oxford: Joseph Barnes.

Thackeray, William Makepeace. 1889. *The Complete Works of William Makepeace Thackeray: Christmas Stories; Ballads, and Other Poems; Tales*. Boston, MA and New York: Houghton, Mifflin.

Townsend, Camilla. 2005. *Pocahontas and the Powhatan Dilemma: An American Portrait*. New York: Hill and Wang.

Webster, M. M. 1840. *Pocahontas: A Legend*. Philadelphia: Herman Hooker.

Woolley, Benjamin. 2008. *Savage Kingdom: The True Story of Jamestown, 1607, and the Settlement of America*. First Harper Perennial edition. New York: Harper Perennial.

3

Puritans and Pilgrims Are the Same People

What People Think Happened

There is a common misconception that the American Pilgrims (or Separatists) who settled at Plymouth, Massachusetts, in 1620 and the American Puritans (reformed Anglicans) who settled at Salem and Boston, Massachusetts, in 1628–1630 were essentially the same group of people. While it is true that both distinctly American religious groups are descended from the Elizabethan Puritan movement, by the time colonization in North America began, they had split into two very different factions of reformed Protestantism. For this reason, to assume that Pilgrims were essentially the same as the Puritans living in New England is entirely wrong and misleading.

That this is a widespread myth in contemporary American society is entirely understandable because both groups have much in common: (1) Both American Puritans and American Pilgrims were originally offshoots of the Church of England, and they objected to that church's manner of administration and conduct on many levels. (2) Both groups are English in origin. (3) Both groups ultimately traveled to present-day Massachusetts to establish coastal colonies for what they regarded as their "religious freedom" for themselves. (4) Both groups were reformed Protestant sects following the teachings of French reformer John Calvin (1509–1564) and thus were both known theologically as Calvinists. (5) Both groups were profoundly intolerant of Roman Catholicism and eschewed the use of religious liturgy, vestments, candles, incense, stained glass, and church organs and the use of Latin in their worship services. (6) Both groups referred to their place of community worship not as a "church" but rather as a "meetinghouse," presided over by a religious leader known as a "pastor" or "reverend" but never by a "priest." (7) Both believed in extemporaneous prayer and mandatory church attendance for all community members. (8) Neither group celebrated nor observed religious holidays, including Easter and Christmas. (9) Neither engaged in prayer to saints or allowed the placement of religious paintings, statues, icons, or images of saints or divine beings in their places of worship. (10) Both groups believed that the institution of marriage is a legal contractual agreement between two people of the opposite sex that does not require the participation of a clergyman and that, when married, the custom of wearing wedding rings is not required. (11) Both groups agreed that the male is the ruler of the home with his wife as his helpmate and that every family should observe a time for daily scripture reading as well as a time of daily family prayer led by both parents but under the spiritual guidance of the father of the household. Based on the aforementioned shared common characteristics, it appears that the American Pilgrims (or Separatists) and Puritans are the same.

However, as similar as these two groups may appear to be at first, there were some serious social and political differences that set them apart as two distinct religious groups, each with its own independent practices and beliefs, which kept them at a distance from each other until 1689, when the Massachusetts Bay Colony and the Plymouth Colony were politically unified into the Colony of Massachusetts under the royal governorship of Sir William Phips.

Once the two colonies were finally united by King William and Queen Mary to create a larger and more diverse royal crown colony, the sharp distinctions that once separated Pilgrim from Puritan quickly began to fade, until, ultimately, by the turn of the nineteenth century, writers and even theologians were unable to clearly distinguish one from the other. By 1700, they were both collectively referred to as "New England Puritans," despite the fact that by that time both groups had been merged together into the Congregational Church denomination. This joining of Puritan and Pilgrim/Separatist was possible because separation from the Church of England was essentially a dead issue by 1700. With the merger of the two colonies—Massachusetts Bay and Plymouth Colony—and the two distinct religious groups into one, the myth that the American Puritans and Pilgrim/Separatists were always the same group was born, and it would continue to grow over the next three hundred years.

How It Became Popular

The origin of this common misunderstanding is derived from a public perception that could not have developed in the first half of the seventeenth century when the presence, impact, and memory of the great leaders of the American Puritans and American Separatists was still alive. Foremost among these dynamic leaders was Governor John Winthrop (1587–1649), the devout Puritan leader who gently but deliberately kept the colonists of Massachusetts Bay Colony at a safe distance from his Pilgrim counterpart, Governor William Bradford (1590–1657), and his Separatist followers in Plymouth Colony. And yet, even with their two colonies' economic competition and political differences, the Puritan and Pilgrim colonies managed to cooperatively work together on issues involving their safety and mutual best interests. These cooperative ventures included joining forces to fight and win the Pequot War (1637) and King Phillip's War (1675–1676). Such a mutually beneficial alliance between Puritan and Pilgrim tended to publicly obscure the theological and political differences between them.

The degree to which Pilgrims and Puritans occasionally joined and worked together further clouds the reality of their essential differences as two distinct religious groups over time. For example, during the winter of 1628–1629—prior to the arrival of Governor John Winthrop in June 1630—Puritan deputy governor John Endicott (1600–1665), the resident leader of the newly arrived Massachusetts Bay Colony at Salem (or Naumkeag), found it necessary to petition the Pilgrims/Separatists at Plymouth for supplies of food and medicine. This was done despite his direct instructions from Massachusetts Bay Company governor Matthew Craddock in London to avoid any dealings with the Separatists at Plymouth Colony. To the pragmatic Endicott, the immediate emergency of malnutrition and sickness among his people logically outstripped the political agenda of his board of directors in the comfort of the Inns of Court back in London. They understood the need for a sharp separation between Puritans and Pilgrims—working together was, for the Massachusetts Bay Company, potentially political suicide.

The reason for this was that the Puritan leaders of the newly formed Massachusetts Bay Company felt that if news of cooperation between the Pilgrims of Plymouth Colony and Anglicans of Massachusetts Bay

Company were to leak back to England, the company's loyalty to the king and his Church of England might be called into question. Such a violation, in their view, might then lead to their royal charter from King Charles I of England being revoked, and that simply should not happen.

Nonetheless, Governor William Bradford, the Separatists at Plymouth Colony, and their physician, Doctor Samuel Fuller (1580–1633), responded to Endicott's plea for help, loaded up their one-mast shallop, and transported an essential supply of food and medicine to Salem. In this respect, although still separated by political and religious differences, the Pilgrim Separatists were responsible for literally saving the fledgling Puritan Colony of Massachusetts Bay. This was only the first of many occasions when Massachusetts Puritans and Plymouth Pilgrims/Separatists, although representing different perspectives, worked together as allies and friends. Interestingly, although generally known as a profoundly inflexible Puritan, John Endicott was entirely won over by Plymouth's generosity and Bradford's kindness—to the degree that Endicott desired to establish a friendship with William Bradford. Thus, Endicott sent the governor of the Pilgrim colony a letter apologizing for his previous negative views of the Pilgrim/Separatists and expressing appreciation for Bradford's help during the past winter's crisis. It is clearly a call to unite the two groups, expressing a desire to end the current feelings of factionalism between Puritan and Pilgrim, acknowledge their kinship as fellow Christians, and work harmoniously together to further God's Kingdom in New England. The letter begins as follows:

> Naumkeag, May 11, Anno 1629
> Right Worthy Sir:
>
> It is a thing not usual that servants to one master (God) and of the same household (God's elect) should be strangers; I assure you, I desire it not, nay to speak more plainly, I cannot be so to you. God's people are all marked with one and the same mark, and sealed with one and the same seal, and have for the main, one and the same heart, guided by one and the same spirit of truth. And where this is, there can be no discord, nay here must needs be sweet harmony. And the same request (with you) I make unto the Lord, that we may, as Christian brethren be united by a heavenly and unfeigned love, bending all our hearts and forces in furthering a work beyond our strength, with reverence and fear, fastening our eyes always on Him that only is able to direct and prosper all our ways. (Endicott 1847, 27)

In the next paragraph, Endicott explains that based on his private discussions with Dr. Samuel Fuller, he has changed his opinion of the character and mode of worship practiced by the Pilgrims and now feels comfortable associating with them:

> I acknowledge myself much bound to you for your kind love and care in sending Mr. Fuller among us, and rejoice much that I am by him satisfied touching your judgements of the outward form of God's worship. It is, as far as I can gather no other than (what) is warranted by the evidence of truth. And the same which I have professed and maintained ever since the Lord in mercy revealed Himself unto me. Being far from the common report that hath been spread of you touching that particular. (Letter from Governor John Endicott to Governor William Bradford, May 11, 1629; Endicott 1847, 27)

Regarding this observation, John Endicott says that among the Puritans, there were rumors about the Pilgrims being very strict and rigid Separatists, and he is pleased to discover that those criticisms are unfounded. Endicott quickly became an advocate for Plymouth among the leaders of the Bay Colony and took a much more supportive position than the more politically astute Governor John Winthrop, who, as a lawyer from the Inns of Court, understood the negative implications of associating with another colony whose reputation and claim to territory were not as highly esteemed back in England. For the next sixty years, the political division between these two distinct groups remained while ties of intermarriage, military alliances, and migration across colonial boundaries created the illusion that Puritans and Pilgrims were, at least in New England—if not in Europe—one and the same people.

Ultimately, a closer bond developed between the people of Massachusetts Bay Colony and the Pilgrims of Plymouth to the extent that the differences that once separated them diminished and the common characteristics they shared, especially in their devotion to the religious teachings of Calvinism, brought the two distinct groups closer together until their two colonies, their land and governments, were finally merged under the new 1691 Charter of Massachusetts Bay issued by King William and Queen Mary following the Glorious Revolution. The charter states,

> The Charter of Massachusetts Bay—October 7, 1691
>
> William and Mary by the Grace of God King and Queen of England, Scotland, France and Ireland, . . . We would be graciously pleased by Our Royal

Charter to Incorporate Our Subjects in Our said Colony and to grant and confirm into them such powers, privileges and Franchises as in our Royal Wisdom should be thought most conducing to Our Interest and Service and to the Welfare and Happy State of our Subjects in New England, and We being graciously pleased to gratify Our said Subjects and also to the end (that) Our good subjects within Our colony of New Plymouth in New England aforesaid may be brought under such a form of government as may put them in a better condition of defense and considering as well the granting unto them as unto Our Subjects in the said Colony of Massachusetts Bay Our Royal Charter with reasonable powers and privileges will much tend not only to the safety but to the Flourishing estate of Our subjects in the said parts of New England. . . . And We do by these rights and presents Unite, Erect and Incorporate the same into One Real Province by the name of Our Province of the Massachusetts Bay in New England. (Thorpe 1909, 1870–1874)

With the legal and geographical boundaries that once separated the Pilgrims from the Separatists gone, the myth of unity between the two former colonies could begin to take hold and develop, and it did. The American people do not like nuance and subtleties. If two entities or groups in all visible respects appear the same, to most people they are. The myth of the Puritans and the Pilgrims as the same group began when those key characteristics that, in the 1620s, initially distinguished them from each other vanished in less than one hundred years of their arrival on the shores of New England. Without those differences—the desire for total colonial control of both church and state and the ethical need for complete separation from the Church of England—virtually everything else they shared as Massachusetts Calvinists, living and worshipping together, was visible for the outside observer to evaluate. And they essentially appear to be the same.

What Really Happened

In reality, the colonizing efforts of New England were undertaken by *three distinct groups* in the early seventeenth century, all of whom shared some similarities but nearly as many differences.

Secular Planters

The first group was actually composed of various groups of secular businesspeople who were nominal adherents to the Church of England and whose primary motivation to come to New England was economic—land, lumber, fur, and fish. This group included the fishing communities on the Isles of Shoals and Cape Ann as well as those who settled along the coasts of what would later become the Provinces of Maine and New Hampshire. This group was encouraged and largely sponsored through the efforts of Sir Fernando Gorges (1565–1647); his son, Captain Robert Gorges (1595–1629); and John Mason (1600–1672).

Separatists

The second colonizing group was composed of those commonly known today as "Pilgrims" but to their own time were called "Separatists." These were religious nonconformists who had completely broken with the Church of England, despairing of ever cleansing it of its corrupt and nonbiblical practices. They subsequently left England to practice a more fully reformed faith based on the teachings of French reformer John Calvin. After suffering persecution and arrest in England, they sought a European refuge in more religiously tolerant Holland.

The first known congregation of Separatists left London for Amsterdam in 1593, followed by several other groups, the last in 1608. They left their various employments, lands, and personal possessions in the vicinity of Scrooby, England, and finally settled in Leiden in 1609. After over ten years in exile from England, the Leiden Separatist congregation, now under the leadership of Rev. John Robinson (1576–1625), decided to relocate to North America in 1620. Rev. Robinson would stay and die in Leiden, a victim of a virulent plague that killed eight thousand residents (one in every five people in the city).

The complex motivations for this decision for the Pilgrims to migrate from Holland to America were, according to Bradford, (1) "the hardness of the place" that is poor living and working conditions; (2) the long-term exposure to the difficulties of work life in Holland caused many to suffer as "old age began to steal on many of them; and their great and continual labors, with other crosses and sorrows, hastened it before the time"; (3) Separatist children were working exceptionally hard, and "that which was more lamentable, and of all sorrows most heavy to be borne, was that many of their children, by these occasions and the great licentiousness of the youth in that country, and the manifold temptations of the place, were drawn away by evil examples into extravagant and dangerous courses, getting the reins off their necks and departing from their parents"; (4) by 1619, the Dutch treaty with Spain was about to end, and the possibility of a renewed religious war—known as the Thirty Years' War—loomed, or as Bradford said, "Like skillful and beaten soldiers were fearful to either be entrapped or surrounded by their enemies so as they should neither be able to fight or fly. And therefore thought it better to dislodge betimes to some place of better advantage and less danger if any such could be found"; and (5) finally, the need to spread the Calvinist Christian faith to others: "Lastly, and which was not the least, a great hope and inward zeal they had of laying some good foundation, or at least to make some way thereunto, for the propagating and advancing the gospel of the Kingdom of Christ in those remote parts of the world" (Bradford 1967, 23–25).

The Pilgrim/Separatist motivation was to find a safe place where they might practice their faith safely and raise their families in the Calvinist doctrine as devout Christians, and there was a general sense that if English authorities would grant them permission to settle in "northern Virginia" such desirable conditions might be possible. What they never intended was to establish, as John Winthrop described, a "City upon a Hill"—a model society of Calvinist theocracy as a working example of how the nations of the world should live. That was a distinctly Puritan idea (Langdon 1966).

Puritans

The third group responsible for colonizing New England was composed of the nonseparating Puritans, who were sent to New England under the auspices of the Massachusetts Bay Company, at that time based in London, England. Unlike the Separatists that settled Plymouth, theirs was a well-organized, well-financed, and well-planned endeavor supported by thousands of members of the English middle and upper-middle class, who steadfastly wanted to colonize New England while retaining their reputation as loyal English subjects. This was because the English monarch, since the days of King Henry VIII, was the head of the Church of England, and one's loyalty as a subject depended on one's loyalty to the state church.

Thus, the unique position held by England's Puritans was that although they strongly disagreed with the corrupt practices of the Church of England, they were willing to endure them for the time being in the hope and expectation of gradually and eventually purifying the Anglican Church from within. Throughout the Great Migration of Puritans to America between 1630 and 1640, most Puritans on both sides of the Atlantic would never risk the public outcry by officially withdrawing from the established Anglican Church.

For Puritans, turning one's back on the Church of England was not simply an act of conscience—as it was for the Separatists. Rather, it was legally considered an *act of treason* to betray and reject one's king as well as one's church. In this way, Puritans are distinct from the Separatists who publicly rejected their king and church and deliberately broke the King's Peace by violating the law against independent worship and were forced to live their lives in exile in either Holland or New England. The Puritans, mindful of their positions in English society, avoided breaking the King's Peace, and while many chose to remain in England, many others chose to migrate to New England, where royal authority and the Church of England were three thousand miles away. In New England, they could recreate the Church of England in the image of John Calvin and essentially practice a fully reformed and purified faith without publicly risking their reputation as loyal subjects of the king or breaking the law. The Separatists could not do this.

Puritans versus Separatists

It is this difference that set the Massachusetts Bay Puritans at odds with their Calvinist brethren, the Separatists/Pilgrims of Plymouth. Or as Harvard historian Perry Miller writes,

> The great body of Puritans, whether they were working for a Presbyterian or Congregational purification of England, were horrified by the Separatists. These endangered the cause (of reformed faith) by seeming to prove to the (English) Government that Puritanism was really what the government said it was—subversive, anarchical, disloyal. The solid Puritans were not trying to achieve *mere* toleration as against an established church; they had *no notion whatsoever that religious liberty was feasible or desirable within society.* They—whether of the Presbyterian or Congregational faction—were scheming and plotting for the day when they would oust the bishops and rule at Canterbury and York. Whichever of them won was predetermined to suppress the other, with methods as ruthless as those of King James and Charles, and also to deal even more severely with such dissidents as dared to attempt a separation. (Miller 1956, 3–4)

Puritans sought control, total control, of English society—its government and its church—first in the Massachusetts Bay Colony and later in England, after the English Civil War (1642–1651). With the beheading of King Charles I (1600–1649) and the seizure of Parliament, the Puritans achieved total control, albeit temporarily. Separatists never had the desire, the power, or the numbers needed to set their goals so high. They kept their control within the modest boundaries of Plymouth Plantation, and the laws they established, not "contrary to the laws of England," were strictly in agreement with the teachings of Holy Scripture. But Harvard professor and historian Perry Miller, in his classic comparative assessment between Pilgrim and Puritan, observes,

> So the little band who eventually landed and suffered at Plymouth in 1620 are not quite representative. The large and well organized body who settled Massachusetts Bay in 1630, though committed to the Congregational idea, stoutly maintained that they were not, and never had been Separatists. This difference made for some distinctions between the characters of the two plantations (colonies), yet in another sense the Separatists, by the fact of having withdrawn, were able to concentrate upon the *essence* of Puritanism. (Miller 1956, 4)

What Miller is saying is that the humble and transparently honest Pilgrims/Separatists did not need to struggle to maintain a façade of religious loyalty to the Church of England; they were officially and totally outside the pale when they landed in New England. They had already made their break with the king's church, and now they were free to concentrate on living a reformed spiritual life without the intellectual and political sleight of hand necessarily resorted to by the Puritans in Massachusetts Bay Colony, who used their vast geographical distance from England to surreptitiously launch a truly reformed "congregational" church in New England. It would be a church completely devoid of "papist trappings" and fully independent of the troublesome influence of the archbishop of Canterbury. This the Puritans would do while officially and publicly maintaining that they were still loyal adherents to the Anglican faith. In this respect, Puritans and Pilgrims could not have been further apart.

By 1630, the year of Governor Winthrop's arrival, the American Puritans had achieved in New England what they had been unable to achieve in Old England—total control of church and state. Unlike their Separatist neighbors, they also had a well-thought-out visionary and strategic plan of action. It is clearly articulated in Governor John Winthrop's first sermon delivered on the deck of his flagship, the *Arabella*, on or about June 12, 1630, the day the Puritan fleet arrived at Salem, Massachusetts. With him on his vessel, Winthrop carried the newly issued Massachusetts Bay Charter bearing the signature of King Charles I—granting the area known as the Massachusetts Bay Colony to the elite Puritan oligarchy of the Massachusetts Bay Company, now relocated from their headquarters in London to New England—a convenient three thousand miles from the English church and English king. No similar charter was given by the king to Plymouth Colony; their settlers had to struggle to secure permission to live at New Plymouth, and that was essentially all they wanted. So, what did the Puritans want? The answer is revealed in John Winthrop's classic sermon delivered on board the *Arabella*:

A Model of Christian Charity

God Almighty in his most holy and wise providence hath so disposed of the condition of mankind, as in all times some should be rich some poor, some high and eminent in power and dignity; and others mean and in subjection.

The reason hereof:

1st Reason.

First to hold conformity with the rest of His world, being delighted to show forth the glory of his wisdom in the variety and difference of the creatures, and the glory of His power in ordering all these differences for the preservation and good of the whole, and the Glory of His greatness, that as it is the glory of princes to have many officers, so this great king will have many stewards, counting himself more honored in dispensing his gifts to man by man, than if he did it by his own immediate hands.

2nd Reason.

Secondly, that He might have the more occasion to manifest the work of his Spirit; first upon the wicked in moderating and restraining them, so that the rich and mighty should not eat up the poor and despised rise up against and shake off their yoke. Secondly, in regenerate, in exercising His graces in them, as in the great ones, their love, mercy, gentleness, temperance, etc., and in the poor and inferior sort, their faith, patience obedience, etc.

3rd Reason.

Thirdly, that every man might have need of others, and from hence they might be all knit more nearly together in the bonds of brotherly affection. From hence it appears plainly that no man is made more honorable than another or more-wealthy, etc., out of any particular and singular respect to himself, but for the glory of his Creator and the common good of the creature, Man. Therefor God still reserves the property of these gifts to Himself as Ezekiel 16:17, He therefore call wealth, His gold and His silver, and Proverbs 3:9, He claims their service as His due, "Honor the Lord with thy riches", etc.—All men being thus (by Divine Providence) ranked into two sorts, rich and poor; under the first are comprehended all such as are able to live comfortably by their own means duly improved; and all others are poor according to the former distribution.

Question: What rule must we observe and walk by in cause of community of peril?
Answer:
The same as before, but with more enlargement toward others and less respect towards ourselves and our own right. Hence it was that in the primitive Church they sold all, had all things in common, neither did nay man say that which he possessed was his own. Likewise, in their return out of captivity, because the work was great for the restoring of the church and the danger of enemies was common to all, Nehemiah directs the Jews to liberality and readiness in remitting their debts to their brethren, and disposing liberally to such as wanted and stand not upon their own dues which they might have demanded of them. Thus did some of our forefathers in times of persecution in England, and so did many of the faithful of other churches, whereof we keep an honorable remembrance of them; and it is to be observed that both in Scriptures and latter stories of the churches that such as have been most bountiful to the poor saints, especially in those extraordinary times and occasions, God hath left them highly commended to posterity.

Thus stands the cause between God and us. We are entered into covenant with Him for this work. We have taken out a commission. The Lord hath given us leave to draw our own articles. We have professed to enterprise these and those accounts, upon these and those ends. We have hereupon besought Him of favor and blessing. Now if the Lord shall please to hear us, and bring us, in peace, to the place we desire, then hath he ratified this covenant and sealed our commission, and will expect a strict performance of the articles contained in it; but if we shall neglect the observation of these articles, which are the ends we have propounded, and dissembling with our God, shall fall to embrace the present world and prosecute our carnal intentions, seeking great things for ourselves and our posterity, the Lord will surely break out in wrath against us, and be revenged on such a people, and make us know the price of the breach of such a covenant.

Now the only way to avoid this shipwreck, and to provide for our posterity, is to follow the counsel of Micah, to do justly, to love mercy, to walk humbly with our God. For this end we must knit together, in this work as one man. We must entertain each other in brotherly affection. We must be willing to abridge ourselves of our superfluities, for the supply of others' necessities. We must uphold a familiar commerce together in all meekness, gentleness, patience and liberality. We must delight in each other; make others' condition our own; rejoice together; mourn together, labor and suffer together, always having before our eyes our commission and community in the work, as members of the same body. So, shall we keep the unity of the spirit in the bond of peace. The Lord will be our God, and delight to dwell amongst us, as His own people, and will command a blessing upon us in all our ways, so that we shall see much more of His wisdom, power, goodness and truth than formerly we have been acquainted with. We shall find that the God of Israel is among us, when ten of us shall be able to resist a thousand of our enemies; when he shall make us a praise and glory that men shall say of succeeding plantations, "may the Lord make it like that of New England."

For we must consider that we shall be as a city upon a hill. The eyes of all people are upon us. So that, if we shall deal falsely with our God in this work we have undertaken, and so cause him to withdraw His present help from us, we shall be made a story and a by-word through the world. We shall open the mouths of enemies to speak evil of the ways of God and all professors for God's sake. We shall shame the faces of many of God's worthy servants, and cause their prayers to be turned into curses upon us till we be consumed out of the good land whither we are going.

And to shut this discourse with the exhortation of Moses, that faithful servant of the Lord, in his last farewell to Israel, Deuteronomy 30. "Beloved there is now set before us life and death, good and evil, in that we are commanded this day to love the Lord our God, and to love one another, to walk in his ways and to keep his commandments and his ordinance and his laws, and the articles of our Covenant with Him, that we may live and be multiplied, and that the Lord our God may bless us in the land whither we go to possess it. But is our hearts shall turn away, so that we will not obey, but shall be seduced, and worship other gods, our pleasure and profits, and serve them; it is propounded unto us this day, we shall surely perish out of the good land whither we pass over this vast sea to possess it.

> There-fore let us choose life,
> That we and our seed may live,
> By obeying His voice and cleaving to Him,
> For He is our life and our prosperity.

(Source: John Winthrop, "A Model of Christian Charity," in *A Library of American Literature: Early Colonial Literature, 1607–1675*, Edmund Clarence Stedman and Ellen MacKay Hutchinson, eds. (New York: 1892), pp. 304–307.)

The preceding sermon, written by the leader of the New England Puritan migration to New England, lays out several basic characteristics of the sect that sets it apart from other nonconformist groups, such as the Pilgrims.

First, they acknowledge the God-ordained concept of nondemocratic hierarchy. God's creation shows us that there is order in nature, from the greatest to the least. Likewise, Puritan society must consist of those who know who they are and where God expects them to fit into the social order—gratefully accepting their preordained place, doing what God intended for them to do.

Second, as God's chosen people—"the Elect"—they have a promise, or covenant, with God, as did the ancient Children of Israel, and they are obligated to keep that covenant sacred, honoring Him in all things. If they are faithful to God in keeping their covenant with Him, he will bless their enterprise in New England and prosper their endeavor to establish a godly commonwealth. Conversely, if they do not keep faith with God and fail to maintain their covenant with Him, God will withdraw his hand of blessing, all their efforts will fail, and they will become a laughingstock throughout the world.

Finally, as the eyes of the world are now upon them, they, "the Elect," are to serve as a prototypical example—like a city on a hill—to the rest of mankind for how a Puritan commonwealth and a community of reformed Christian people should be governed. For this reason, they must live godly lives because failure in the eyes of the world is not an option.

Historian Edmund Morgan affirms this assessment in saying to Governor John Winthrop, "The purpose of New England was to show the world a community where the laws of God were followed by church and state—as nearly as fallible human beings could follow them" (Morgan 2007, 161).

Implied within the text of "A Model of Christian Charity" is the belief that an aristocratic system is God's system—ordained by Him because it is the natural predatory order of God's creation. Next, Winthrop infers that doctrinally the Calvinist Congregational way is the only acceptable way for a godly community to live and that toleration or compromise with other communities of believers is not an acceptable option. This belief would, at least during the ascendancy of the Puritan oligarchy in Massachusetts, ultimately lead to state-enforced public morality and state-enforced religious intolerance for all other nonconforming persons or religious groups (i.e., Quakers, Baptists, Separatists, etc.).

This inflexible policy of intolerance in the infant Massachusetts Bay Colony was evidenced in the 1630s by the enforced removal of Rev. Roger Williams to Narragansett Bay. Roger Williams, who arrived in the Massachusetts Bay Colony in 1631, fresh from England, was an avowed Separatist of the most intense variety who, during his brief time in Massachusetts Bay Colony, refused to pastor any church not willing to publicly reject the Church of England—demanding that all Puritan congregations publicly renounce the Church of England, or, as he expressed it, referring to the members of the Boston congregation, "I durst not officiate to an unseparated people, as upon examination and conference, I found them to be" (Rev. Roger Williams, quoted in Morgan 2007, 104).

This somewhat arrogant demand was considered politically outrageous to most Massachusetts Bay Puritans, and it undid much of the earlier goodwill established between Puritan John Endicott and his friend Pilgrim/Separatist William Bradford during the disastrous winter of 1628–1629. With John Winthrop, and others even less flexible, now in charge of the "Bay Colony," it was a dangerous position to take, reflecting the radical nature of separatism. Consequently, the split between the two groups would remain sharp and irreconcilable much longer than necessary.

Interestingly, it seems that Roger Williams' separatism was even too radical for the Pilgrims at Plymouth, where he traveled after leaving Massachusetts Bay. Governor Bradford found him to be "a man Godly and zealous, having many precious parts, but very unsettled in judgement" (William Bradford quoted in Reich 2011, 74). This unsettled radical Separatist finally made himself unwelcome even among his kindred Separatists, or as Bradford concludes, "He began to fall into some strange opinions, and from opinion to practice; which caused some controversy between the (Plymouth) church and him, and in the end some discontent on his part, by occasion whereof he left them somewhat abruptly" (Gov. William Bradford, quoted in Morgan 2007, 106). Added to this was Williams's claim that the Massachusetts Bay Charter issued to the Massachusetts Bay Company was invalid because King Charles I of England did not properly own the land he was giving away and his claim that he did was a public lie.

Ultimately, the leaders of Massachusetts Bay Colony had no choice but to warn Williams away into exile along Narragansett Bay or, alternatively, to send him in chains back to England, where his traitorous opinions would, in all likelihood, place him in prison or lead to his death. He wisely fled, negotiated the sale of land from the Narragansett people, and established what would later be known as the Colony of Rhode Island. Here, he would, in time, create a sanctuary for religious dissenters and dissidents like himself whose opinions would not be tolerated in the Puritan colonies or even in Plymouth.

Roger Williams's excommunication from the Massachusetts Bay Colony was soon followed by the banishment of Rev. John Wheelwright, Captain John Underhill, Anne Hutchinson, and all their families and followers—casualties of the controversy in Boston.

It is interesting that the policies were first articulated by Governor John Winthrop on the deck of the *Arabella* before any passengers of his fleet had even disembarked. But it underscores that, from the beginning, the vision of a "City upon a Hill" for the Puritan Commonwealth of Massachusetts Bay was never to be a welcome beacon for the religious minorities and dissidents of the world. Rather, it was meant to be a prototype community of Calvinist doctrine, "a society where the perfection of God would find proper recognition among imperfect men" (Morgan 2007, 138).

In a similar but less ostentatious way, in 1620, the Pilgrims prepared a less complex document to define their Separatist community. It was drawn up and signed by all adult male passengers aboard their flagship, *The Mayflower*. It would become a famous political statement that would simply outline their desires and plan for Plymouth Colony. It has since 1620 famously become known as "The Mayflower Compact," one of America's first citizen-composed constitutional documents. Instead of pietistic rhetoric, it humbly articulates the hopes and expectations of a much different plantation than Massachusetts Bay. The one shared common characteristic is their devotion to Calvinism and the belief that each was fulfilling the predestined will of God in establishing two colonies whose guiding principles of social conduct were firmly grounded in both the teachings of John Calvin and Holy Scripture.

The Mayflower Compact

In the Name of God, Amen

We whose names are underwritten, the loyal subjects of our dread Sovereign Lord King James, by the Grace of God of Great Britain, France, and Ireland King, Defender of the Faith, etc.

Having undertaken, for the Glory of God and advancement of the Christian Faith and Honor of our King and Country, a Voyage to plant the First Colony in the Northern Parts of Virginia, do by these presents solemnly and mutually in the presence of God and one of another, Covenant and Combine Ourselves into a Civil Body Politic, for our better ordering and preservation and furtherance of the ends aforesaid; and by virtue hereof to enact, constitute and frame such just and equal Laws, Ordinances, Acts, Constitutions and Offices from time to time, as shall be thought most meet and convenient for the general good of the Colony, unto which we promise all due submission and obedience. In witness whereof we have hereunder subscribed our names at Cape Cod, the 11th of November, in the year of the reign of our Sovereign Lord King James, of England, France and Ireland the eighteenth and of Scotland the fifty-fourth. Anno Domini 1620. (Bradford 1967, 75)

Here is the other side of the division between Puritan and Pilgrim, and it is a simpler, humbler vision. No mention is made of an expectation of being seen by the eyes of the world or to become a "City upon a Hill" that mankind may emulate. The Pilgrims are much less ambitious in their scale of what they hope to accomplish in their new American home: "to plant the First Colony in the Northern Parts of Virginia" and "to Covenant and Combine Ourselves into a Civil Body Politic" and, finally, "to enact, constitute and frame such just and equal Laws, Ordinances, Acts, Constitutions and Offices from time to time as shall be thought most meet and convenient for the general Good of the Colony" (Bradford 1967, 75).

The fact is that this small band of Pilgrim Separatists was originally only authorized to settle a coastal area north of Jamestown, but closer to the Dutch colony of New Netherlands, nearer to the mouth of the Hudson River. Instead, they made a conscious decision to remain near to where they first made landfall, at the end of Cape Cod, and established their colony of New Plymouth inside Cape Cod Bay. This choice of location was not authorized by the Virginia Company, whose jurisdiction only went to the northern boundary of the Virginia Grant. It was intentionally selected to provide the Pilgrim Separatists with the freedom to worship in a fully reformed Congregational manner without the interference of Anglicans from Virginia.

In addition, the group of settlers at Plymouth was a mixture of saints and strangers, that is, both reformed Separatists and an almost equal number of nonseparating members of the Church of England. Membership was only possible if a colonist could testify to the indwelling of the Holy Spirit and the gift of grace to be regarded as a member of the elect and a member of the congregation. But attendance at worship service each Sabbath was required of everyone, whether a church member or not. In other words, although the initial plan in Holland was to establish a truly Separatist colony, in reality, English people—some Separatists, some not—all lived, worked, and worshipped collectively in Plymouth Colony.

Plymouth's loosely administered church and government were as unlike Massachusetts Bay Colony as could be imagined. In terms of *financial resources*, the Puritans were primarily drawn from the middle and upper-middle class with a smattering of lesser nobility, while the Pilgrims were from the lower to middle levels of English society. Related to this was *better education*. Puritans in general were better educated with a very high literacy rate. Not surprisingly, they placed a high priority on the education of their children, establishing the first public school in New England at Boston Latin School and New England's first college at Harvard in Cambridge in 1636.

Generally, the Pilgrims were not well educated, except for their leadership—Bradford, Carver, and Winslow. Neither did they possess the resources nor inclination to establish a college to train their ministers. The Puritans felt strongly that their religious instruction should come from a university-trained minister—often from Cambridge University until Harvard was established—while the Pilgrims went for years without a pastor, and often lay preaching and simple Bible study were the best they could expect in their religious services. It was this theological disparity and lack of academic status that truly set the two groups apart for the first thirty years of their coexistence.

A partial healing of the long-standing split between Puritan and Pilgrim ultimately took place in 1668 when the Plymouth Congregation called Rev. John Cotton Jr., the Harvard-educated son of Rev. John Cotton Sr. and the preeminent Puritan minister of Boston, to serve as the pastor of the Plymouth Congregational church. His coming "gave the (Plymouth) church the stamp of respectability; no one could doubt his commitment to orthodox Puritanism. Cotton's presence proved beyond the shadow of a doubt what had long since become apparent; that as John Robinson had predicted, the issue of separatism was dead" (Langdon 1966, 100). When Plymouth Colony and Massachusetts Bay Colony were finally joined politically in 1691, all vestiges of the division that had for so long stood between Puritan and Pilgrim were ultimately erased.

Further Reading

Bangs, Jeremy Dupertuis, and New England Historic Genealogical Society. 2004. *Pilgrim Edward Winslow: New England's First International Diplomat: A Documentary Biography*. Boston, MA: New England Historic Genealogical Society.

Bradford, William. 1967. *Of Plimoth Plantation*. Edited by Samuel Eliot Morison. New York: Random House.

Bremer, Francis J. 1994. *Shaping New England: Puritan Clergymen in Seventeenth-Century England and New England*. Twayne's United States Authors Series, TUSAS 631. New York: Twayne.

Coffey, John, and Paul Chang-Ha Lim, eds. 2008. *The Cambridge Companion to Puritanism*. Cambridge Companions to Religion. Cambridge, UK, and New York: Cambridge University Press.

Endicott, Charles M. 1847. *Memoir of John Endicott*. Salem, MA: Observer Office.

Fraser, Rebecca. 2017. *The Mayflower: The Families, the Voyage, and the Founding of America*. 1st U.S. ed. New York: St. Martin's Press.

Goss, K. David. 2012. *Daily Life during the Salem Witch Trials*. Santa Barbara, CA: Greenwood.

Langdon, George D. 1966. *Pilgrim Colony: A History of New Plymouth, 1620–1691*. New Haven, CT: Yale University Press.

Miller, Perry. 1956. *The American Puritans*. Garden City, NY: Doubleday-Anchor Books.

Morgan, Edmund S. 2007. *The Puritan Dilemma: The Story of John Winthrop*. 3rd ed. Library of American Biography. New York: Pearson Longman.

Morone, James A. 2003. *Hellfire Nation: The Politics of Sin in American History*. New Haven, CT: Yale University Press.

Reich, Jerome R. 2011. *Colonial America*. New York: Routledge.

Ryken, Leland. 1990. *Worldly Saints: The Puritans as They Really Were*. Grand Rapids, MI: Academie Books.

Schmidt, Gary D. 1999. *William Bradford: Plymouth's Faithful Pilgrim*. Grand Rapids, MI: Eerdmans Books for Young Readers.

Stedman, Edmund Clarence, and Ellen MacKay Hutchinson, eds. 1892. *A Library of American Literature: Early Colonial Literature, 1607–1675*. New York: Charles L. Webster and Company.

Thorpe, Francis Newton. 1909. *The Federal and State Constitutions, Colonial Charters, and Other Organic Laws of the State, Territories, and Colonies Now or Heretofore Forming the United States of America*. Washington, DC: Government Printing Office.

Winship, Michael P. 2018. *Hot Protestants: A History of Puritanism in England and America*. New Haven, CT: Yale University Press.

4

The First Thanksgiving Was a Shared Harvest Celebration

What People Think Happened

The American people and many outside the American culture have a long-standing image of what constitutes the national holiday known as Thanksgiving. To the great majority, this holiday is a uniquely American tradition. It was established by the Pilgrim Fathers, who, after a devastating time of famine and sickness between 1620 and 1621, finally enjoyed a plentiful harvest. After gathering their crops, the Pilgrim colonists decided to celebrate with a feast of thanksgiving to which they invited their Native American neighbors, Chief Massasoit and the Wampanoag (or Pokanoket) people. They sat in friendship together, ate wild turkey, and collectively thanked God for his providential deliverance. This first thanksgiving established in the 1620s in Plymouth Colony was the only first celebration of an annual tradition passed down each year from that time to the present.

The grains of truth contained within these mythical pearls of American history are supported by early seventeenth-century sources, such as Edward Winslow's letters describing the actual event and references by Governor William Bradford in his history of the colony, *Of Plimoth Plantation*. In fact, throughout the past three hundred years, this image has been reinforced by the writings of such diverse persons as Rev. Cotton Mather, Governor Thomas Hutchinson, and most especially Victorian writer and editor Sarah Josepha Hale. To these writers, and many others, the image of the Pilgrims and native people breaking bread and dining together is as essential to our understanding of the American historical legacy as our images of the Boston Tea Party, the signing of the Declaration of Independence, and the surrender of Lee at Appomattox. In reality, however, the greatest part of this First Thanksgiving picture is factually distorted and, in many ways, misunderstood.

The misunderstanding largely stems from the fact that most present-day Americans view the First Thanksgiving as the initial example of mutual friendship and acceptance between the English colonists and Native Americans. In reality, the gathering represented the beginning of an essential military alliance—agreed upon by Governor William Bradford and the Wampanoag's Chief Massasoit in 1621—that was established for the self-preservation and mutual protection of both groups. It was not, as is now perceived, a gathering of Christians and non-Christian native people for the purpose of collectively thanking the Judeo-Christian deity for an abundant supply of food at the end of the first planting season.

In actuality, the present contemporary image of Pilgrims and native people worshipping, sharing a harvest feast, and thanking God together for his bounty is profoundly wrong on several levels—both social and theological. The fact that this image now represents an important part of the myth of Thanksgiving reflects what may only be described as wishful thinking on the part of many contemporary Americans and a justifiable rationale for resentment on the part of present-day native peoples.

On top of this widespread, common misunderstanding, our current myth of the First Thanksgiving has—over the past century and a half—traditionally served the American population as the first identifiable example of the spiritual and cultural superiority of the Pilgrim Fathers in that this imagined "Christian feast of thanksgiving and brotherhood" introduced native people to a "better way" whereby they might live. What is often overlooked is that the Pilgrim Separatists were among the most intolerant of all Puritan subgroups; they preferred to become an exiled and persecuted minority by leaving religiously intolerant England rather than worship with their fellow English subjects. Later, they would leave religiously tolerant Holland rather than allow their children to be exposed to the cultural diversity of Leiden and Amsterdam. The Separatists preferred to risk their lives in an untamed wilderness so that they might isolate themselves in worship from all those who were not, in their view, members of God's Elect. For them, worshipping God with non-Separatist Christians was sometimes necessary but far from ideal, and worshipping with non-Christian natives was unacceptable.

How It Became Popular

As to how the Thanksgiving myth infiltrated the American mind-set, there are many contributing factors, and some go back to before the settlement of Plymouth Colony.

For New England's Puritans, the practice of days of public thanksgiving with prayer, worship, and feasting as well as days of public humiliation with fasting originated with biblical references in the Old Testament. The rulers of ancient Israel declared public days of thanksgiving for deliverance from their enemies and days of fasting and prayer to seek God's forgiveness. Such community activities were held spontaneously at different times in response to varying circumstances and God's intervention in the lives of the Israelites.

By the seventeenth century, the Jewish religious calendar was already filled with regularly scheduled religious holidays—established to thank God for his faithfulness to the Children of Israel—such as Passover, Purim, and Hanukah. Imitating this practice, the "New Israel," that is, New England's Puritans, followed a similar custom of communally begging God's forgiveness for their sins and giving thanks for God's deliverance and protection.

The Plymouth Separatists, also known as Pilgrims, while refusing to celebrate Christmas and Easter—as those holidays were both pagan in origin and Roman Catholic by tradition—were nonetheless inclined to offer God their thanks for his care and faithfulness in overcoming adversity. But such celebrations were generally spontaneous; at no time did they set a specific day annually for this purpose.

In English tradition, under Queen Elizabeth I, subjects were accustomed to Thanksgiving celebrations and worship services. A recent historian's text observes that, at this time, "the clergy often read thanksgiving prayers, and under Elizabeth it became customary to draft new ones for every blessed occasion; the end of an epidemic, the Armada's defeat, or some bloody massacre inflicted on the Irish" (Bunker 2010, 65). Thus, it seems clear that the English people in general, and the Pilgrims in particular, all had long experience with official church observances of thanksgivings in England. It was common practice.

It is also worth noting that the London Company, later known as the Virginia Company, instructed the thirty-eight English colonists who arrived at Virginia Colony on board the ship *Margaret* in 1619 to acknowledge God's provision by holding a day of thanksgiving. This event, although not widely remembered historically, actually predates the first Plymouth Thanksgiving by two years.

Importantly, the actual date of the first observance took place in October 1621. This constituted a three-day feast at Plymouth, but its details and underlying purposes are vague. Some scholars have even speculated that it may have taken place as early as July of that year—essentially negating the whole image of a "harvest festival." It was not until November 15, 1636, that the *Plymouth Colony Records* established a new regulation that would officially "allow our Governor (William Bradford) and Assistants, to command solemn days of humiliation by fasting, etc., and also for thanksgiving as occasion shall be offered" (XI, 18).

In fact, while such occasions as "thanksgiving days" might be occasionally so declared, it does not appear that there was any official, regularly scheduled attempt on the part of the first generation of Pilgrims to annually celebrate a specific Day of Thanksgiving. Historically, such celebrations in Plymouth only happened on an "as needed basis." So, how then did the "myth of the First Thanksgiving" start?

There were two distinct events that happened at Plymouth that, over the succeeding four centuries, gradually coalesced in the popular imagination. The first feast, as previously described, took place in 1621 and involved Massasoit and his native people in large numbers. The second event occurred on July 30, 1623, with no mention of direct native participation. Both events have come to be generally regarded as Plymouth Colony "thanksgivings" by historians of seventeenth-century New England culture, but only the 1623 gathering is detailed by Governor William Bradford in his *Of Plimoth Plantation* narrative. This gathering is described as having been specifically established to give thanks to the Lord for deliverance of the colony from a harsh summer drought and an abundant harvest.

Both of these events, remembered by the participants and through the retelling of the "tale of the Pilgrims," gradually came to be merged into a single all-encompassing thanksgiving celebration—the one acknowledged today. Whereas neither the 1621 nor the 1623 celebrations represented cultural ideals by later social standards, when combined, they came closer to them. The first contributed native people as guests, and the second included devout and thankful Plymouth colonists focusing on a celebration of God's faithfulness in miraculously ending the 1623 summer drought. It became an ecumenical celebration of mixed faiths and cultures worthy of a modern Unitarian convention, but it was hardly accurate according to the Separatist, Calvinist belief system of the early seventeenth century.

The gradual transition of the holiday of Thanksgiving away from the public memory of these original Plymouth events was begun by Governor John Winthrop in 1637, when he and the government of Massachusetts Bay Colony officially declared a general Day of Thanksgiving. However, this Thanksgiving was not to celebrate a native alliance nor a bountiful harvest but, rather, to acknowledge God's faithfulness in granting military victory to the Massachusetts militia in its bloody struggle against the Pequot nation—an event known historically as the Pequot War. Thus, within less than two decades of settlement, two New England Calvinist colonies, Massachusetts Bay and Plymouth, were joined together in the American practice of observing days of thanksgiving. What soon became evident is that the underlying purpose of such celebrations could and did change dramatically in much the same way that earlier Elizabethan thanksgivings varied according to events worthy of praise for God's deliverance.

Over the next several hundred years, many declarations and commentaries were produced by ministers and political leaders urging Americans to be thankful for their many and varied blessings. These sermons and publications, combined with periodic episodes of historical amnesia, began to gradually blur and alter the story of the original Thanksgiving. Ultimately, the idea of a public time given over to a day of general prayer and thanksgiving ceased being strictly confined to the religious denomination of the Puritans, that is, the Congregational Church. With the introduction of other newly arrived religious sects—Quakers, Baptists, Anglicans, and others—Thanksgiving Days eventually became an interdenominational Christian holiday in the colony of Massachusetts, which after 1692 included the former Plymouth Colony as well.

The gradual transition of Thanksgiving to a more widespread and popular holiday for the people of Massachusetts in general began when Lieutenant Governor Thomas Hutchinson, the man credited with bringing William Bradford's journal *Of Plimoth Plantation* to England, followed Bradford's Plymouth example by issuing a public declaration in 1769:

> By the Honorable Thomas Hutchinson, Esq., Lieutenant Governor and Commander-in-Chief over His Majesty's Province of the Massachusetts Bay in New-England.
> A Proclamation for a Public Thanksgiving.
> Forasmuch as it has pleased Almighty God to bestow upon us many and great public Mercies in the Course of the present Year, which call for our

> most grateful Acknowledgements . . . more especially for that it has pleased Him to prolong the invaluable Life of our Sovereign Lord the King and to continue the Blessing and Peace to His Majesty's Dominions; to prevent the Spread of a malignant, contagious Distemper with which some of the Towns in This Province have been threatened; and to give us favourable Seasons, and a plentiful Harvest: I Have therefore thought fit; by and with the Advice of His Majesty's Council, to Appoint Thursday the Sixteenth Day of November next to be observed as a Day of Public Thanksgiving throughout the Province. And I recommend to the Religious Societies of every Denomination to offer up their devout Praises to Our Most Bountiful Benefactor for these and all other (of) His Mercies conferred upon us; and to accompany their Praises with fervent Prayers that we may evidence the Gratitude of our Hearts by the Obedience of our Lives, and may so order our Conversation aright as to see the further Salvation of God. And all servile Labor is forbidden on the said Day.
> T. Hutchinson (Hutchinson 1769)

Could this announcement have had a political motive? Very possibly, it did. It certainly may well have been partially prompted by recent political developments in the Massachusetts colony, beginning with the Stamp Act in 1765 and concluding with the Townsend Duties that went into effect in November 1767. This in turn led to a widespread boycott of British goods by 1768, when extensive and violent public protests resulted in the arrival of two thousand British troops to occupy Boston in 1769. Governor Hutchinson seems to be trying to convince the local population that things are not that bad, and they ought to take time away from their daily activities to thank God for his blessings. What better way to reflect on such things than to observe an officially sanctioned Day of Thanksgiving? The Boston Massacre, which took place four months later, in March 1770, certainly discouraged Bostonians from experiencing the general "thankfulness" that Governor Hutchinson was hoping to achieve in an official capacity.

This is not to say that, by the mid-eighteenth century, New Englanders generally did not practice the annual custom of setting aside a day each year for a thanksgiving celebration. They did, and as noted previously, it was usually set in the late fall, often in November. The New England Thanksgiving of the mid-eighteenth century was largely based on the simple belief that it honored the traditional practice—established by the Pilgrims—of thanking God for a bountiful harvest. But, as with Governor Hutchinson's proclamation, the political figures of the era wished to reshape the holiday and endow it with more political significance.

Moving even further away from the original intent of the Plymouth model of Thanksgiving, in 1777, following the victory of American forces at the Battle of Saratoga, the U.S. Congress suggested that a national day of thanksgiving be set aside to thank God for the victory. Commander in Chief George Washington therefore agreed and proclaimed December 18, 1777, as the first national Day of Thanksgiving of the newly independent United States of America.

This set a precedent for Congress to regularly establish a Day of Thanksgiving for the American people, not for harvests or peaceful pursuits but for political and military victories. For example, on October 11, 1782, while meeting in Philadelphia, Congress passed a proclamation proclaiming the following:

> It being the indispensable duty of all nations, not only to offer up their supplications to Almighty God, the Giver of all Good, for His gracious assistance in a time of distress, but also in a solemn and public manner, to give him praise for His goodness in general, and especially for great and signal interpositions of His Providence in their behalf. Therefore the United States in Congress assembled, taking into their consideration the many instances of Divine Goodness to these States in the course of this important conflict in which they have been so long engaged: the present happy and promising state of public affairs and the events of the war in the course of the year now drawing to a close (1782); particularly the harmony of the public councils which is so necessary to the forces of the public cause, the perfect union and good understanding which has hitherto subsisted between them and their Allies notwithstanding the artful and unwearied attempts of the common enemy (England) to divide them; the success of the arms of the United States; and those of their Allies; and the acknowledgement of their independence by another European power whose friendship and commerce must be of great and lasting advantage to these States—do hereby recommend to the Inhabitants of these States in general to observe and request the several States to interpose their authority in appointing and commanding the observation of Thursday, the 28th day of November next as a day of Solemn Thanksgiving to God for all His mercies; and they do further recommend to all ranks to testify their gratitude to God for His goodness by a cheerful obedience to His laws, and by promising each in his station, and each by his influence the practice of true and undefiled religion which is the great foundation of public prosperity and national happiness.
>
> Done in Congress in Philadelphia, the eleventh day of October in the Year of our Lord, one thousand-seven-hundred and eighty-two, and of the Sovereignty and Independence (of the United States), the seventh (year). (Hanson 1782)

The Treaty of Paris officially ending the American Revolution took place in September 1783, less than a year later. The date of this celebration was followed by more days of thanksgiving proposed by the representatives of the Congress through 1784. By this time, the national Day of Thanksgiving—at least outside New England—had transitioned from a simple and prayerful acknowledgment of God's bounty to a celebration of national military prowess and God's granting the former colonies ultimate victory over their common enemy, Great Britain.

By 1789, congressional representative Elias Boudinot from New Jersey presented a resolution requesting that Congress persuade newly elected President Washington to declare a national Thanksgiving observance in honor of the creation of the new United States Constitution. Congress agreed and passed the resolution, whereupon President Washington issued a presidential proclamation on October 3, 1789, designating Thursday, November 26, as a national Day of Thanksgiving in the following manner:

> Whereas it is the duty of all nations to acknowledge the providence of Almighty God, to obey his will, to be grateful for his benefits, and humbly to implore his protection and his favor, and Whereas both Houses of Congress have by their joint Committee requested me "to recommend to the People of the United States a day of public thanks-giving and prayer to be observed by acknowledging with grateful hearts the many signal favors of Almighty God, especially by affording them an opportunity peaceably to establish a form of government for their safety and happiness." Now therefore I do recommend and assign Thursday, the 26th day of November next to be devoted by the People of these States to the service of that great and glorious Being, who is the beneficent Author of all the good that was, that is, or that will be. That we may then all unite in rendering unto him our sincere and humble Thanks, for his kind care and protection of the People of this country previous to their becoming a Nation, for the signal and manifold mercies, and the favorable interpositions of his providence, which we experienced in the course and conclusion of the late war, for the great degree of tranquility, union and plenty, which we have since enjoyed, for the peaceable and rational manner in which we have been enabled to establish constitutions of government for our safety and happiness, and particularly the national One (Constitution) now lately instituted, for the civil and religious liberty with which we are blessed, and the means we have of acquiring and diffusing useful knowledge, and in general for all the great and various favors which he hath been pleased to confer upon us. (Saunders 1893, 116)

Far from avoiding any potential ideological controversies concerning the introduction of a theological justification for the national holiday of general thanksgiving, Washington concludes with a direct, unequivocal statement merging religion and the newly established state by encouraging all citizens to collectively petition God for the forgiveness of their sins, promoting the "practice of true religion" in the following manner:

> And also that we may then unite in most humbly offering our prayers and supplications to the Great Lord and Ruler of Nations and beseech him to pardon our national and other transgressions, to enable us all, whether in public or private stations, to perform our several and relative duties properly and punctually, to render our national government a blessing to all the People, by constantly being a government of wise, just and constitutional laws, discreetly and faithfully executed and obeyed, to protect and guide all Sovereigns and Nations (especially such as have shown kindness to us) and to bless them with good government, peace and concord. To promote the knowledge and practice of true religion and virtue, and the increase of science among them and Us, and generally to grant unto all Mankind such a degree of temporal prosperity as He alone knows to be best. (Saunders 1893, 116–117)

What is intriguing about this declaration is the many additional reasons offered by President Washington as to why such a day of thanksgiving should be observed. Thanks for a bountiful harvest is left unmentioned—unless his phrase "union and plenty" is construed to mean agricultural produce and not monetary gain.

Instead, in Washington's statement, the reasons for a Day of Thanksgiving were (1) the Almighty's care of the American people prior to the outbreak of the Revolution, (2) His assistance to them in achieving political independence from England, and (3) His help in establishing the new constitutional government.

Despite the zealous efforts of Washington and Congress to politicize the traditional holiday of Thanksgiving in 1789, their interpretation of the celebration generally failed to be accepted nationally. Not one to be discouraged, Washington submitted—during his second term of office—yet another proposal for a national Thanksgiving holiday in February 1795.

This time, Washington suggested that the nation should be thankful to God for the federal government's recent defeat of a group of excise-tax-evading backcountry Pennsylvania farmers in the recently concluded Whisky Rebellion. This attempt, like the previous proposal, ultimately failed to achieve national acceptance. But the campaign to establish a nationally recognized Thanksgiving holiday continued at the federal level.

Like Washington, Presidents John Adams and James Madison both attempted to create a national interest in a federally sponsored Thanksgiving holiday, but both similarly failed to do so. Each president gave his own justification for Thanksgiving to the American people.

For President John Adams, the idea of a celebratory Thanksgiving came from penitence and mourning for the sins of the young Republic. For the second president, the time of Thanksgiving was a time for the American people to express their acknowledgement "of the Governing Providence of a Supreme Being and of the accountableness of men to Him as the searcher of hearts and righteous distributer of rewards and punishments" (Adams 1969, 172).

Adams, who was well known for his somewhat dour and somber character, believed that, in light of the political and national crisis of 1799 facing the United States—that is, the so-called XYZ Affair and the undeclared war with France—the people of the United States needed to repent their sins and ask for God's protection and forgiveness to survive the "hostile designs and insidious acts of a foreign nation (France)."

Or, as President Adams said,

> For these reasons I have thought proper to recommend, and do hereby recommend accordingly, that Thursday, the 25th day of April next, be observed throughout the United States of America as a day of solemn humiliation, fasting and prayer; that the citizens on that day abstain as far as may be from their secular occupations, and devote their time to the sacred duties of religion in public and in private; that they call to mind our numerous offenses against the Most High God, confess them before Him with the sincerest penitence, imploring his pardoning mercy, through the Great Mediator and Redeemer, for our past transgressions, and that through the grace of His Holy Spirit we may be disposed and enabled to yield a more suitable obedience to His righteous requisitions in time to come. (Adams 1969, 1973)

For Adams, a national day of prayer and fasting with almost no public celebration was exactly what was needed to put the United States back on the safe and righteous path with God. Like Washington, his predecessor, Adams did not mince words regarding the importance of religious faith to the American people as an essential means of achieving a desired political objective. In this respect, he paralleled the kings of ancient Israel,

Queen Elizabeth I, and even Governor William Bradford—all of whom called upon their people to petition the Lord with prayer to avert a looming national crisis, such as the Spanish Armada or the Plymouth drought of 1623.

Adams concluded,

> That He would interpose to arrest the progress of that impiety and licentiousness in principle and practice so offensive to Himself and so ruinous to Mankind; that He would make us deeply sensible that "righteousness exalteth a nation, but sin is a reproach to any people." (Adams 1969, 1973)

Finally, almost as an afterthought, Adams did manage to insert a passage in his proclamation calling for a national thanksgiving celebration with the caveat that above all it must be "fervent":

> And I do also recommend that with these acts of humiliation, penitence and prayer, fervent Thanksgiving to the Author of all Good be united, for the countless favors which He is still continuing to bestow upon the people of the United States, and which render their condition as a nation eminently happy when compared with the lot of others. (Adams 1969, 1974)

A mere decade and a half later, on November 16, 1814, President James Madison, a Virginian with none of the staunch Puritan background of John Adams, attempted to resurrect Thanksgiving with a slightly different focus. During the War of 1812, Madison issued a new presidential proclamation calling the people of the nation to appeal to God for deliverance and forgiveness for their sins and recognition of His blessings upon them:

> The two Houses of the National Legislature having by a joint resolution expressed their desire that in the present time of public calamity and war a day may be recommended to be observed by the people of the United States as a day of public humiliation and fasting and of prayer to Almighty God for the safety and welfare of these States, His blessing on their arms, and a speedy restoration of peace, I have deemed it proper by this proclamation to recommend that Thursday, the 12th of January next be set apart as a day on which all may have an opportunity of voluntarily offering at the same time in their respective religious assemblies their humble adoration to the Great Sovereign of the Universe, of confessing their sins and transgressions, and of strengthening their vows of repentance and amendment. (Richardson 1896, 558)

Following this time of national repentance, Madison asks for a balanced time of national thanksgiving for the blessings God had bestowed on the nation:

> They will be invited by the same solemn occasion to call to mind the distinguished favors conferred on the American people in the general health which has been enjoyed, in the abundant fruits of the season, in the progress of the arts instrumental to their comfort, their prosperity, and their security, and in the victories which have so powerfully contributed to the defense and protection of our country, a devout thankfulness for all which ought to be mingled with their supplications to the Beneficent Parent of the Human Race that He would be graciously pleased to pardon all their offenses against Him; to support and animate them in the discharge of their respective duties; to continue to them the precious advantages flowing from political institutions so auspicious to their safety against dangers from abroad, to their tranquility at home, and to their liberties, civil and religious; and that He would in a special manner preside over the nation in its public councils and constitutes authorities, giving wisdom to its measures and success to its arms in maintaining its rights and in overcoming all hostile designs and attempts against it; and finally, that by inspiring the enemy with dispositions favorable to a just and reasonable peace its blessings may be speedily and happily restored. (Richardson 1896, 558)

Interestingly, President Madison followed this with a second thanksgiving proclamation on March 4, 1815, for the restoration of peace with England. Decidedly less ominous and more in keeping with the spirit of gratitude evidenced by William Bradford, this thanksgiving proclamation exclusively focused on the blessings of God upon the nation as a whole:

> The Senate and House of representatives of the United States have, by a joint resolution, signified their desire that a day may be recommended to be observed by the people of the United States with religious solemnity as a day of thanksgiving and of devout acknowledgements to Almighty God for His great goodness manifested in restoring them to the blessings of peace. No people ought to feel greater obligations to celebrate the goodness of the Great Disposer of Events of the Destiny of Nations. His kind providence originally conducted them to one of the best portions of the dwelling place allotted for the great family of the human race. (Richardson 1896, 561)

The reason for this sudden outpouring of public thanksgiving by President Madison was twofold: (1) the signing of the Treaty of Ghent on December 24, 1814, and (2) the overwhelming victory of Andrew

Jackson's American forces over the British army at the Battle of New Orleans on January 8, 1815.

The final realization and redefining of the national myth of Thanksgiving came about gradually during the decades following Adams and Madison, as emerging popular American writers such as Joseph Sylvester Clark and Nathaniel Hawthorne used their imaginations to create a stereotypical image of hearth and home and, in the process, sentimentalized the concept of the Thanksgiving feast and its symbolic meaning.

Joseph S. Clark (1800–1861), in his very influential 1831 historical short story "The History of the Pilgrims: Or a Grandfather's Story," provides his young readers with a fictional and venerable New England grandfather who relates the moralistic story of the Pilgrims to his grandchildren in a manner that combines both fact with fiction, including verbatim dialogue allegedly spoken by the Pilgrims.

Interestingly this work was produced by Clark a full decade before the original manuscript written by Governor William Bradford was rediscovered in the bishop of London's library at Fulham Palace in London during the 1840s. *The History of the Pilgrims* presents a historical tale with the authority of an authoritative historical narrative told with a distinctively Protestant moralistic motivation, but in its accuracy—in the absence of some essential primary sources—it was flawed with myth. He begins by breaking his guiding principle concerning the importance of accurate history:

> The principles and practices of our forefathers, and the remembrance of God's dealings with them, should be carefully preserved and handed down to posterity, that the generations to come may know them, even the children which shall be born, who shall arise and declare them to their children; that they may set their hope in God, and not forget the works of God, but keep his commandments. (Clark 1831, 13)

In Clark's somewhat distorted version of the Pilgrim story, the important 1621 three-day celebratory gathering with Wampanoag sachem Massasoit and his warriors, as described in a letter by colonist Edward Winslow, is entirely missing:

> The fall of the year was now coming on, and the settlers mindful of their last winter's sufferings, began to repair their houses. They gathered in a good harvest of Indian corn, but their English grain was very poor. However, they got large quantities of fowl and fish during the autumn, by which they were much refreshed. (Clark 1831, 100)

Instead, as his version of the First Thanksgiving, Clark provides the following anecdote from the 1623 drought that nearly devastated the crops of the Plymouth Colony:

> The Pilgrims, too, were in great extremities at this time, but God did not forsake them. Amid all their difficulties with the natives they were also suffering for want of food. They expected supplies from England, but none came. They now began to feel that they could no longer look to others for help, but must depend upon their own labor and the blessing of God for a living. In the spring of 1623 they planted more corn than ever before. But by the time they had finished planting, their victuals were wholly spent. Many a time when they had taken one meal, they knew not where they should find the next. Every morning they had need to pray, "Give us this day our daily bread."; and God always answered this prayer in one way or another. They had one boat left, and a fishing net, with which they caught bass; when these failed, they dug clams for a living. In the month of June their hopes of a harvest were nearly blasted by a distressing drought, which withered up their corn, and made the grass look like dry hay. When Hobamak [sic] saw their cornfields in this sad state he appeared to be much alarmed for the Pilgrims, and feared that they would lose all their corn and perish with hunger. "The Indians," said he, "can live in any way; but the English must starve if the corn is cut off."
>
> In their distress the Pilgrims set apart a day for fasting, humiliation and prayer to seek help from God; and continued their religious exercises *eight of nine hours*. God heard their fervent prayers and sent them an answer [which] filled everyone with admiration. Although the morning of their fast day was clear, and the weather very hot and dry during all the forenoon, yet before night it began to rain and gentle showers continued to fall for many days, so that the ground became thoroughly soaked, and the drooping corn revived.
>
> "This was a most remarkable answer to prayer," said I, "and reminds us of God's promise, 'while they are yet speaking, I will hear.'"
>
> Mr. Allerton: True. The providence of God was so cleanly seen, that the Indians said to the Pilgrims, "Now we see that the Englishman's God is a good God, for He has heard you, and sent you rain without storms, and tempests, and thunder, which usually come with our rain and break down our corn—surely your God is a good God." (Clark 1831, 116–118)

Once again, the reader is prompted to wonder how a native witness to the rain might be so accurately quoted. In his journal, even Bradford only acknowledges his impression that "He (God) was pleased to give them a gracious and speedy answer, both to their own and the Indians' admiration" (Bradford 1967, 131).

Clark continues,

> Mr. Allerton: "Our pious fathers did not soon forget this kindness of God. At a convenient time they set apart a day for public thanksgiving and praised their heavenly benefactor for his goodness, as heartily as they had prayed for his mercy!" (Clark 1831, 118)

Clark's book was distributed through the Massachusetts Sabbath School Union and thus reached the minds and imaginations of many Massachusetts children who shared the stories with their families from the 1830s onward.

By 1840, in his collection of short stories, *The Snow Image and Other Twice-Told Tales*, New England author Nathaniel Hawthorne submitted to the reading public a classic tale of a family's harvest celebration in "John Inglefield's Thanksgiving" replete with symbolic significance and colorful moralistic Hawthorne imagery.

But the holiday held a special place in the heart of this great Victorian author. In his personal journal for Thanksgiving in 1842, Hawthorne recorded his thoughts from his home in Concord:

> This is Thanksgiving Day! A good old festival, and my wife and I have kept it with our hearts, and besides have made good cheer upon our turkey, and pudding, and pies and custards, although none sat at our board but our two selves. There was a new and livelier sense, and I think that we have, at last, found a home. (Hawthorne 1870, 2:107)

But it would not be until 1863, under the administration of Abraham Lincoln, in the midst of the Civil War, that Thanksgiving would finally achieve not a replication of William Bradford's original time of prayerful thanksgiving but national status and general acceptance as a holiday of national unity at a time of national fragmentation. This would come about in large part through the influence of author Sarah Josepha Hale, editor of the very popular magazine *Godey's Ladies Book*.

What Really Happened

To begin, it is worth noting Governor Bradford's entry in *Of Plimoth Plantation* where he describes the events surrounding the first harvest season (1621) in the colony and "First Thanksgiving" following the first year's "starving time":

> They began now to gather in the small harvest they had, and to fit up their houses and dwellings against the winter, being all well recovered in health and strength and had all things in good plenty. For as some were thus employed in affairs abroad, others were exercised in fishing, about cod and bass and other fish, of which they took good store, of which every family had their portion. All the summer there was no want. And now began to come in store of fowl, as winter approached, of which this place did abound when they came first (but afterward decreased by degrees). And besides waterfowl, there was great store of wild turkeys, of which they took many, besides venison, etc. Besides they had about a peck of meal a week to a person, or now since harvest, Indian corn to that proportion. Which made many afterwards write so largely of their plenty here to their friends in England, which were not feigned, but true reports. (Bradford 1967, 93–94)

Here, in the most important primary source relating the story of Plymouth Colony, there is no mention of a celebratory gathering of Pilgrim families, Native American guests, or even the need to thank God for his generous provision in providing the colony a bounteous harvest. In reality, very little is said by Bradford or those who attended the first Thanksgiving until a single letter appears, written on December 11, 1621, by Edward Winslow, a prominent member of the Plymouth Colony, who gives a more detailed account:

> Our harvest being gotten in, our Governor (Bradford) sent four men on fowling, that so we might in a more special manner *rejoice together*, after we had gathered the fruit of our labours. They four in one day killed as much fowl as, with a little help besides, served the Company almost a week. At which time, amongst other recreations, we exercised our arms, many of the Indians coming amongst us, and amongst the rest their greatest king, Massasoit with some 90 men, whom for three days *we entertained and feasted*. And they went out and killed five deer which they brought to the plantation and bestowed on our Governor (Bradford) and upon the Captain (Standish) and others. (Dexter 1865, 133)

Even in this more detailed eyewitness account of the so-called First Thanksgiving at Plymouth, the closest Edward Winslow gets to identifying "giving thanks" as a reason for the community event is the specific desire for the colonists to "rejoice together" in celebration of a bountiful harvest. The clear implication is that enjoyment and recreation for the celebrants was the primary purpose of this multiday gathering, and among those who enjoyed the event were their Native American neighbors who were "entertained and feasted" and actually contributed food supplies to the party by bringing a large amount of venison to the banquet.

The image of this 1621 feast, based on the very modest descriptions of it drawn from the only two available primary sources—Bradford and Winslow—is that it constituted a three-day festival of entertainment, including militia drilling, weapon demonstrations, hunting, eating, and drinking, primarily done for the enjoyment of the Plymouth colonists and their native guests. No mention is made in either description of worship, prayer, or public thanksgiving to God, and yet, in many secondary sources, this gathering of natives and colonists is frequently regarded as "the first thanksgiving at Plymouth."

Much later, in late July 1623, William Bradford tells of a second episode far removed from the earlier celebratory gathering. This event did not revolve around the creation of a native-colonial alliance but the avoidance of possible agricultural disaster through God's miraculous "Divine Intervention":

> I may not omit how, notwithstanding all their great pains and industry, and the great hopes of a large crop, the Lord seemed to blast, and take away the same, and to threaten further and more sore famine unto them. By a great drought which continued from the third week in May, 'til about the middle of July, without any rain and with great heat for the most part, insomuch as the corn began to wither away though it was set with fish (as fertilizer), the moisture whereof helped it much. Yet at length it began to languish sore, and some of the drier grounds were parched like withered hay, part whereof were never recovered. (Dent 1920, 63)

The 1623 drought was a natural event that might well have become a turning point in the evolution of the Plymouth Colony, resulting in starvation not only for the English colonists but also their native neighbors, as both groups depended heavily upon corn as the principal staple of their diet. Bradford continues his narrative,

> Upon which they set apart a solemn day of humiliation, to seek the Lord by humble and fervent prayer, in this great distress. And He was pleased to give them a gracious and speedy answer, both to their own and the Indians' admiration that lived amongst them. For all the morning, and the greatest part of the day, it was clear weather and very hot, and not cloud or any sign

of rain to be seen; yet toward evening it began to overcast, and shortly after to rain with such sweet and gentle showers as gave them cause of rejoicing and blessing God. (Dent 1920, 63)

Such an immediate answer to prayer, while miraculous in itself, deserved a detailed description in the mind of Governor Bradford to underscore the wonder and divine nature of such a supernatural occurrence. Appropriately, he goes on to paint a vivid verbal image of the full impact of the miracle on the community of English settlers at Plymouth:

It came without either wind or thunder or any violence, and by degrees in that abundance as that the earth was thoroughly wet and soaked and therewith. Which did so apparently revive and quicken the decayed corn and other fruits, as was wonderful to see, and made the Indians astonished to behold. And afterwards the Lord sent them such seasonable showers, with interchange of fair warm weather as, through His blessing, caused a fruitful and liberal harvest, to their no small comfort and rejoicing. For which mercy, in time convenient, they also set apart *a day of thanksgiving*. (Dent 1920, 64)

We do not know when that "time convenient" finally came because Bradford offers no record of the event. It is also worth noting that throughout Bradford's text, no description of what would happen at a "thanksgiving day" is provided. Bradford does not indicate whether food would be consumed or, indeed, whether the day took place at all. He certainly implies that it did happen and that the emphasis was on public rejoicing and thanking God for his mercy in delivering Plymouth Colony from drought. This is the only rationale for Bradford's day of thanksgiving in 1623. Bradford does not indicate that future thanksgiving days would be observed at a specific time or day annually. Such events as thanksgiving days happened on an as needed basis, when it was "convenient" for the entire community and for specific reasons. In Bradford's account, the prayer and praise of the colonists are clearly those activities that deserve to be emphasized—all of the Elect in Plymouth Colony understood this.

The question is, to what extent did the early Plymouth settlers divide their thanksgiving celebrations between worship activities and the consumption of food? The answer, based on contemporary sources, is that thanksgiving days customarily placed a strong emphasis on spiritual activities such as praise and worship, with food consumption occupying a position of secondary importance. An example of this practice is shown in an early account of a community Thanksgiving celebration held in the Plymouth Colony town of Scituate thirteen years later, on December 22, 1636:

> In yt Meeting House, beginning some halfe an hour before nine & continued until after twelve oclocke, yt day being very cold, beginning wt a short prayer, then a psalme sang, then more large in prayer, after that another Psalme, & then the Word taught, after that prayer,—& then a psalme . . . and this then followed by an afternoon of merry-making with a dinner where the poorer sort being invited by the richer. (Scituate, Plymouth Colony, *First Church Record*)

This last-mentioned charitable aspect, helping the less fortunate—that is, caring for the "poorer sort"—has continued on as an important part of the early "thanksgiving celebrations." For example, in the *Connecticut Courant* published on December 1, 1766, a description of a Thanksgiving holiday in Boston provides insight: "Yesterday was observed here a Day of general Thanksgiving. On this occasion, large Collections were made in many or most of the Churches in Town for the Relief of the Poor and Indigent, to enable them the better to provide against the Inclemency of the approaching (winter) Season" (Anonymous, *Connecticut Courant*, December 1, 1766). Thus, even before the United States was established as an independent nation, the idea of a Thanksgiving holiday was part of the late fall seasonal calendar in New England at least—even if Christmas was not observed.

The real problem outside of New England was lack of general acceptance and unanimity for the Thanksgiving holiday. Some states would have it in November and some not at all. Others states would have a Thanksgiving time at another time of the year, such as summer. But by the time of the Civil War, it seemed that the nation was torn regionally and fragmented politically, with little sense of national cohesiveness. What was needed in the minds of many was a uniquely American holiday that would bring a divided nation together. Some believed that such a thanksgiving holiday, if shared by all Americans on precisely the same day, with all citizens collectively thanking God for His faithfulness and blessings, might result in a nationally unifying event.

It would take a New Englander, New Hampshire–born Sarah Josepha Hale, a woman not influenced by the political exigencies of the presidential administrations, to finally establish a national Thanksgiving holiday that would become popular outside New England. For her time, she was one of the nation's most influential female writers and one who recognized American thanksgiving celebrations as having a deep connection to the nation's Puritan roots. Hale's simple request, written on September 28, 1863, to President Abraham Lincoln, then in the midst of a devastating Civil War, was instrumental in helping to bring about the establishment of a national Thanksgiving Holiday:

> Sir-
>
> Permit me, as Editress (editor) of the "Ladies Book," to request a few minutes of your special time, while laying before you a subject of deep interest to myself and—I trust—even to the President of our Republic, of some importance. This subject is to have the day of our annual Thanksgiving made a National and fixed Union Festival.
>
> You may have observed that, for some years past, there has been an increasing interest felt in our land to have the Thanksgiving held on the same day, in all the States; it now needs National recognition and authoritative fixation only, to become permanently, an American custom and institution.
>
> Enclosed are three papers (being printed, these are easily read) which will make the idea and its progress clear, and show also the popularity of the plan.
>
> For the last fifteen years, I have set forth this idea in the "Lady's Book," and placed the papers before the Governors of all the States and Territories—also I have sent these to our Ministers abroad, and our Missionaries to the heathen—and Commanders in the Navy. From the Recipients I have received, uniformly the most kind approval. Two of these letters, one from Governor (now General) Banks and one from Governor Morgan are enclosed. Both gentlemen as you will see, have nobly aided to bring about the desired Thanksgiving Union.
>
> But I find there are obstacles not possible to be overcome without legislative aid—that each State should, by statute, make it obligatory on the Governor to appoint the last Thursday of November, annually, as Thanksgiving Day;—or, as this way would require years to be realized, it has occurred to me that a proclamation from the President of the United States would be the best, surest and most fitting method of National appointment.
>
> I have written to my friend, Hon. William H. Seward, and requested him to confer with President Lincoln on this subject. As the President of the United States has the power of appointments for the District of Columbia and the territories; also for the Army and Navy and all American citizens abroad who claim protection from the U.S. Flag—could he not, with right as well as duty, issue his proclamation for a Day of national Thanksgiving for all the above classes of persons? And would it not be fitting and patriotic for him to appeal to the Governors of all the States, inviting and commanding these to unite in issuing proclamations for the last Thursday in November as the Day of Thanksgiving for the

people of each State? Thus the Great Union Festival of America would be established.

Now the purpose of this letter is to entreat president Lincoln to put forth his Proclamation, appointing the last Thursday in November (which falls this year on the 26th) as the National Thanksgiving for all those classes of people who are under the National Government particularly, and commending this Union Thanksgiving to each State Executive; thus, by the noble example and action by the President of the United States, the permanency and unity of our great American Festival of Thanksgiving would be forever secured.

An immediate proclamation would be necessary, so as to reach all the States in season for State appointments, also to anticipate the early appointments by Governors.

Please excuse the liberty I have taken.
With profound respect,
Yours truly,
Sarah Josepha Hale,
Editress of the "Lady's Book" (Hale 1863)

What is not mentioned here is that Sarah Josepha Hale had petitioned every American president since Franklin Pierce in her tireless Thanksgiving campaign. The response from all of these—except Abraham Lincoln—was negative. Thanksgiving was generally regarded as an occasional holiday, only appropriate in times of crisis and great blessing, but by mid-1863, the nation—despite military victories at Vicksburg and Gettysburg in July—was in desperate need of overcoming the national crisis and joining together in a unifying holiday of thanksgiving. For these reasons, Lincoln quickly responded with assistance from Hale's friend Hon. William H. Seward. With this statement, the Thanksgiving Holiday would be established throughout the nation as a federal holiday:

Washington, D.C.
   October 3, 1863
   By the President of the United States of America
   A Proclamation
   The year that is drawing towards its close, has been filled with the blessings of fruitful fields and healthful skies. To these bounties, which are so constantly enjoyed that we are prone to forget the source from which they come, others have been added, which are so extraordinary in nature, that they cannot fail to penetrate and soften even the heart which is habitually insensible to the ever watchful providence of Almighty God. In the midst of a civil war of unequalled magnitude and severity, which has sometimes seemed to foreign States to invite and to provoke their aggression, peace

has been preserved with all nations, order has been maintained, the laws have been respected and obeyed, and harmony has prevailed everywhere, except in the theatre of military conflict; while that theatre has been greatly contracted by the advancing armies and navies of the Union.

Needful diversions of wealth and of strength from the fields of peaceful industry to the national defense, have not arrested the plough, the shuttle or the ship; the axe has enlarged the borders of our settlements. And the mines, as well of iron and coal as of the precious metals have yielded even more abundantly than heretofore. Population has steadily increased, notwithstanding the waste that has been made in the camp, the siege and the battlefield; and the country, rejoicing in the consciousness of augmented strength and vigor, is permitted to expect continuance of years with large increase of freedom.

No human counsel hath devised nor hath any mortal hand worked out these great things. They are the gracious gifts of the Most High God who, while dealing with us in anger for our sins, hath nevertheless remembered mercy. It has seemed to me fit and proper that they should be solemnly, reverently and gratefully acknowledged as with one heart and one voice by the whole American People.

I do therefore invite my fellow citizens in every part of the United States, and also those who are at sea, and those who are sojourning in foreign lands, to set apart and observe the last Thursday of November next, as a day of Thanksgiving and Praise to our beneficent Father who dwelleth in the Heavens.

And I recommend to them that while offering up the ascriptions justly due to him for such singular deliverances and blessings, they do also, with humble penitence for our national perverseness and disobedience, commend to His tender care all those who have become widows, orphans, mourners or sufferers in the lamentable civil strife in which we are unavoidably engaged, and fervently implore the interposition of the Almighty Hand to heal the wounds of the nation and to restore it as soon as may be consistent with the Divine purposes to the full enjoyment of peace, harmony, tranquility and Union.

In testimony whereof, I have hitherto set my hand and caused the Seal of the United States to be affixed. Done at the City of Washington, this Third Day of October, in the year of our Lord one-thousand-eight-hundred and sixty-three; and of the Independence of the United States the Eighty-eighth.

By the President: Abraham Lincoln

William H. Seward, Secretary of State (Lincoln 1894, 151)

With this document, the very first nationally recognized holiday of Thanksgiving was finally and officially established in the American calendar and transformed from a predominantly New England harvest feast to an observance of national gratitude for the general blessings of God bestowed upon the American people. No longer merely a replication of the original Pilgrim celebration of God's miraculous provision of food and the needful essentials of life, in the intervening 150 years, it would become an amalgam of national gratitude for conquest, military victories, industrial productivity, successful trade, growing wealth and increased population. At the same time, the American people would gradually misremember the two distinct thanksgiving events that started it all: a 1621 harvest feast that brought Separatists and their native neighbors together in friendship and a 1623 "miracle" where God harkened to the prayers of Plymouth's elect and responded with a miraculous downpour of life-giving rain. This then is the myth and reality of the contemporary American Thanksgiving, a holiday rooted in the past and altered by tradition, political exigencies, and cultural expectations that now have more to do with modern political correctness than with historical reality.

Further Reading

Adams, John, and Adams, Charles Francis. 1969. *The Works of John Adams: Official Letters, Messages, and Public Papers*. Vol. 7. Freeport, NY: Books for Libraries Press.

Anonymous. *Connecticut Courant*, December 1, 1766.

Bradford, William. 1967. *Of Plymouth Plantation with Introduction by S. E. Morison*. New York: Modern Library Edition.

Bunker, Nick. 2010. *Making Haste from Babylon: The Mayflower Pilgrims and Their World: A New History*. 1st American ed. New York: Alfred A. Knopf.

Clark, Joseph Silvester. 1831. *The History of the Pilgrims*. Boston, MA: J. R. Marvin.

Dent, J. M. 1920. *Chronicles of the Pilgrim Fathers*. New York: E. P. Dutton & Co.

Dexter, Henry Martyn, ed. 1865. *Mourt's Relation or Journal of the Plantation at Plymouth*. Boston, MA: J. K. Wiggin.

Hale, Sarah Josepha. 1863. "A Letter from Sarah Josepha Hale to Abraham Lincoln on September 28, 1863." WikiSource. Accessed July 6, 2020. https://en.wikisource.org/wiki/Letter_to_Abraham_Lincoln_from_Sarah_Josepha_Hale.

Hanson, John. 1782. "Congressional Thanksgiving Day Proclamation." October 11, 1782. Exeter, NH: n.p.

Hawthorne, Nathaniel. 1870. *Works of Nathaniel Hawthorne.* Boston, MA: Houghton, Mifflin and Company.

Hutchinson, Thomas. 1769. "A Proclamation from the Governor Declaring a Day of Thanksgiving." October 23, 1769. Boston, MA: Richard Draper.

Lincoln, Abraham. 1894. *Complete Works.* Vol. 9. Harrogate, TN: Lincoln Memorial University.

Plymouth Colony. Scituate. *First Church Records*, December 1636.

Richardson, James Daniel, comp. 1896. *A Compilation of the Messages and Papers of the Presidents, 1789–1897.* Vol. 1, *1789–1817.* Washington, DC: Government Printing Office.

Saunders, Frederick. 1893. *Addresses, Historical and Patriotic.* New York: E. B. Treat.

Winslow, Edward. 1622. *Mourt's Relation.* London: G. Mourt.

5

Manhattan Island Was Purchased for $24

What People Think Happened

Manhattan Island, the heart of New York City and its most famous borough, is the highest-prized piece of real estate in the world. One would be hard pressed to find a square foot of buildable land on this island for under $1,000. The entire area of Manhattan is 636.1 million square feet. One can easily do the math. Amazingly, it is commonly thought that at some early point in history, the entire island was purchased by a group of Dutch colonists from local Native Americans for a sum of $24 or that the natives were paid in cheap trinkets amounting to that price tag. Wasn't it the best real estate deal ever? Others, however, may point out that the value of the purchased land would be more correctly estimated in Dutch guilders because the U.S. dollar simply did not exist at that time in history.

Stories about the establishment and early history of major centers of population are always cherished. Any city that firmly exists on the map also strives to locate its origin on the historic time line. Once established, such a point seems to gain additional reverence in each subsequent generation of dwellers as a legendary common past becomes more and more distant. Of course, one is not presumed to fully believe in all aspects of a foundational myth, but it is best when the values embodied by such a myth are relatable and sustainable. The oft-quoted sum of $24 that was supposedly paid to the resident native people for the island of Manhattan remains unchanged in printed accounts from different time periods, even as the inflation of U.S. currency can be observed over an individual's lifetime.

However, this monetary phenomenon does not stop most of us from believing in the foundational myth of New York because this story has exactly what we want and expect to see. When it comes to the early beginnings of the business capital of the world, this myth possesses all the key ingredients: a financial transaction, an amazing bargain, and a show of ingenuity—with a hefty dose of trickery and just a hint of dishonesty—that allowed the original Dutch traders to make something out of nothing when the moment was right. It is up to each one of us to decide whether the recognizable (if stereotypical) ethos of today's Big Apple should be admired or disdained. But is this ethos actually rooted in history?

How It Became Popular

In May 1839, a law was passed in the New York State Senate authorizing the governor to send a state-appointed agent to England, Holland, and France for the purpose of "procuring the originals or copies of all such documents in the archives and offices of those governments relating to or in any way affecting the colonial history of our State" (New York (State). Legislature. Senate. 1844, 1). Among the prerequisite skills for this task was fluency in the Dutch language and an in-depth knowledge of the history of the New York Colony and its predecessor, the New Netherlands Colony.

Understandably, it took some time to locate a suitable candidate, but by 1841, Governor William H. Seward had nominated John Romeyn Brodhead (1814–1873) for this position of the state agent. Brodhead was an ideal choice, having graduated from Rutgers University with a degree in history, and his fluency in the Dutch language was rooted in his family's lineage. Most importantly, he had already worked for the American delegation in The Hague and was familiar with Dutch governmental institutions. Brodhead proved to be a diligent archival researcher, producing many volumes of transcriptions of seventeenth-century manuscripts filled with valuable information related to the early colonial history of the United States in general and the colony of New York/New Netherlands in particular.

The budget for Brodhead's colonial research project was approved by a vote of the New York State Senate and set at an impressive $4,000. This sum is even more remarkable in light of the recent financial crisis known as the Panic of 1837 (some states in the Union even faced bankruptcy as a result). Regardless of the monetary uncertainty then faced by New York State and its government, a high priority was placed on Brodhead's work, and even more project-related disbursements were anticipated through the 1840s.

The underlying rationale for Brodhead's activities was state pride motivated by a desire on the part of New York State, as the only major colony of the thirteen colonies originally established by a *non-English* European government, to be able to offer its citizens a state archive of historical materials tracing the colony all the way back to its founding as a Dutch fur trading settlement in 1626.

This massive research project was already nearing its completion when public officials back home in New York decided to examine Brodhead's prolific output with the main purpose of ascertaining its relative worth as well as the feasibility of further support for the mission. The State Senate's select committee went so far as to order a translation of some chapters from the manuscript collection supplied by Brodhead. The committee's resulting assessment presented at the next meeting, on February 3, 1844, was astonishingly devastating:

> As a collection of documents, designed to perpetuate and preserve valuable information, for the benefit of future generations, the committee must say that they are of trifling value, compared with the enormous price at which they have been procured. (New York (State). Legislature. Senate. 1844, 7)

Although this pronouncement may well have been politically motivated, the committee's assessment is an example of a shortsighted approach to the importance and use of historical primary sources. The Senate's select committee simply failed to see any value in documents that were not directly related to the history of the state, even though they provided much evidence about colonial economic, political, and military affairs of the time. The committee members' disappointment in Brodhead's work was that it did not, in their opinion, bring to light anything new about New York's past but instead offered "very little, however, but what is perfectly familiar to every school boy" (New York (State). Legislature. Senate. 1844, 5). Or, as the report concludes,

> Occasionally may be found a document which appears to be of some value as illustrative of our early history: but even many of these have long since been well known and understood from the different histories of our country. (New York (State). Legislature. Senate. 1844, 3)

It is therefore deeply ironic that this report by the New York State select committee offered to posterity, as a representative example of how unimportant and generally worthless the Brodhead collection of documents was, an official report addressed to the officers of The Hague concerning developments at the newly established colonial port of New Amsterdam in 1626.

On page 155 of volume I may be found the following:

> High and Mighty Lords, at the Hague: Yesterday arrived the vessel the 'Arms of Amsterdam:' she left New-Netherlands on the 23d of Sept. from the river Mauritius (the Hudson), bringing advices that our people there live wisely and peacefully. Their wives also bear children, and they have bought the island of Manhattan from the savages for the sum of sixty guilders. They have already sowed grain in the middle of May and gathered it in the middle of the month of August, and the samples I send you are taken from the harvest of wheat, rye, barley, oats, buck-wheat, canary seed, beans and flax.
>
> The cargo of the above mentioned vessel consists of 7,246 beaver skins; 850 otter skins; 34 little rat skins; a great many oak caulkins and nut trees.
> P. SCHAGEN.
> Amsterdam, Nov. 5, 1626.—[Copy of the original remaining in the Royal Dutch Archives at the Hague.]

The report continues,

> This document no doubt was interesting to the honest denizens of Holland, whose sons and daughters had emigrated to the new country. It brought them the important intelligence that children could be raised in the new world, and that the earth produced abundance to sustain them.
>
> They must have been gratified also to know that their descendants in the New-World were disposed to obey the command of the great law giver, when he said "be fruitful and multiply and replenish the earth;" and it may perhaps be well enough to perpetuate this information in our archives for the benefit of future generations. (New York (State). Legislature. Senate. 1844, 4–5)

The vitriolic tone of the committee's evaluative report leaves no doubt that Schagen's letter was included as evidence of the triviality and uselessness of the documents collected by Brodhead. As such, the text was perhaps found amusing but offered little else to members of the committee.

For the writers of the report, it would have been contrary to their purpose to display any interest in the curious bit of information about the actual price—sixty guilders—paid for the island of Manhattan; they must have surely noticed how insignificant it was. They did not have to convert sixty guilders to a modern monetary equivalent because even the other representative "specimens" of John Brodhead's transcripts, prepared for the committee, included references to salaries paid to the Dutch West India Company officers in New Netherlands in the thousands of guilders as well as massive disbursements of money for the colony authorized in Amsterdam.

The outcome of the meeting was somewhat anticlimactic. The authors of the report expressed their hope that Brodhead would be able to procure more valuable documents during the rest of the mission while collecting historic sources in England and France; "otherwise, the State will receive a very trifling equivalent for this outlay of the public funds" (New York (State). Legislature. Senate. 1844, 4–5). It is reasonable to conclude that Brodhead was notified of the committee's dissatisfaction, but the bulk of his work had already been finished.

Precisely at the same time when members of the committee expressed their skepticism in Brodhead's findings, the news about the document detailing the purchase of Manhattan was already spreading throughout the country. Peter Schagen's original letter was published in January 1844 by the *Northern Light*, a monthly periodical in Albany, New York. The document (translated independently from the version circulated among the committee members) was prefaced with a short note that stated that the island was purchased for sixty guilders, or twenty-four dollars. As it was a common practice at that time, the curious article was republished by many other newspapers, including the *New York Daily Tribune*, the *Hartford Currant*, the *Cleveland Herald*, and the *Daily National Intelligencer* (Washington, DC). The text of the original document that had been procured by Brodhead could only have been obtained for publication by someone privy to the ongoing work of the state's agent oversees. Such an individual (or a group of people) would have also shared a genuine interest in the history of the State of New York combined with understanding of the immense value represented by Brodhead's findings.

The person whose name inevitably comes up in this connection is Edmund Bailey O'Callaghan (1797–1880). Irish born and Paris educated, this doctor, politician, and, subsequently, journalist settled in Albany at the end of the 1830s. O'Callaghan became a frequent contributor to the *Northern Light* and developed such a strong interest in the history of New York that he eventually abandoned his medical practice to concentrate on academic research. In January 1842, the *Northern Light* began to publish

O'Callaghan's "Notes on the New Netherlands." Although the brief notice about Peter Schagen's letter that appeared in the January 1844 issue was anonymous, it is logical to suspect that the doctor turned historian was somehow connected to its publication. "Notes on the New Netherlands," published in the same issue, were already very much advanced in their chronological scope to accommodate new information about the early days of the colony. It would not have made sense to fit Schagen's report into this narrative.

It is curious, however, that the author of "The Notes" shows the same proclivity to supply the reader with estimated dollar amounts when talking about Dutch guilders. In the exact issue of the *Northern Light* in which Peter Schagen's letter was published, "Notes on the New Netherlands" equate a fine of one thousand guilders to $400 and a sum amounting to fourteen hundred guilders is said to be equal to $560. In the same article, however, three hundred guilders were converted to $30, but this was most likely an error. In most cases, O'Callaghan consistently used the 2.5 conversion rate—the same rate that would be responsible for equating sixty guilders with $24.

Everything seems to point to the fact that E. B. O'Callaghan was either the author of the note about the purchase of Manhattan or was closely involved in its publication. However, there is more to consider. When John Brodhead's mission was complete and all of his findings arrived in the United States, it was none other than E. B. Callaghan who was picked as the curator, translator, and editor of this multivolume collection of historic documents. The reference to $24 is absent from this invaluable academic work (Broadhead 1853–1858). It was also not included in the book's apparatus supplementing the translation of Peter Schagen's letter. More curiously, the footnote that appears in the committee's report already cited above was omitted when the report appeared among the book's introductory materials.

Nevertheless, O'Callaghan was the first historian to mention the price paid for Manhattan in a published book. The first volume of his *History of New Netherlands: Or, New York under the Dutch*, appeared in 1846 and stated that Manhattan was "purchased from the Indians, who received for that splendid tract the trifling sum of sixty guilders, or twenty-four dollars" (O'Callaghan 1846, 104). It is likely that O'Callaghan considered it useful to provide a modern U.S. currency equivalent for the sake of contemporary readers in a book that was nothing but a pioneering effort to explore the history of the Dutch colony. He had more lofty hopes for the multivolume edition of primary sources that was likely remain in use for years to come, so the dollar amounts were dropped from this academic work.

As far as the actual translation of Peter Schagen's letter that was included by O'Callaghan in "Documents Relative to the Colonial History of the State of New-York" (Broadhead 1853–1858), it is different from the version published in the *Northern Light*.

However, this fact does not diminish the likelihood of O'Callaghan being the author of both texts. Comparing the text of his "Notes on the New Netherlands" with similar passages in *History of New Netherlands* reveals O'Callaghan's habit of making substantial revisions, often just for the sake of better style.

Needless to say, if the note in the *Northern Light* was written by someone other than O'Callaghan, its publication only became possible as a result of someone's familiarity with Brodhead and his work in progress. Could it have been Brodhead himself who submitted one of his most curious findings while still traveling overseas? Whether this is plausible or not, he certainly did not see any problem stating in his *History of the State of New York*, published in 1853, that Manhattan was purchased for "about twenty-four dollars of our present currency" (Brodhead 1853, 164).

Intricacies aside, it appears at the moment that the earliest printed statement about the $24 deal between the Dutch colonists and members of a Native American tribe occurred in 1844 on the pages of the *Northern Light*. However, the first complete translation of the document that served as a basis for this story entered the public record as a part of the New York State Senate proceedings. It took a little over a year before the purchase of Manhattan was once again brought up before the Senate. John R. Brodhead's mission came to its conclusion, and a final report was presented by the Select Committee on the Colonial Agency. This new report began with a lengthy preamble in praise of the careful and reverent preservation of "the monuments of history." The two-page introduction may have been brought about by the arrogant attacks in the previous year's select committee report. Nevertheless, it seems that new report agreed with the committee's evaluation in correctly identifying one of the most significant documents found during his mission—Peter Schagen's letter:

> The document alluded to, although brief, enables us to show the existence of the colony still earlier than the correspondence with Governor Bradford. The attention of the Legislature has already been called to it, in a report made to this body during the last session, but for a very different purpose, and in an incomplete and inaccurate translation; it is therefore reproduced here. (New York (State). Legislature. Senate. 1845, 5–6)

This report, which contained a superior translation of the letter, the publication of the same letter in the *Northern Light* as well as the books by E. B. O'Callaghan and John Brodhead were the starting points of the $24 myth. Textbooks of the late nineteenth century were eager to continue using this bit of information, but for many Americans interested in their country's history, it was the painting by William Ranney (1813–1857) that provided information about this historic event. In 1858, the *National Magazine* used an engraving of Ranney's "Manhattan Purchase" to illustrate the story of the Dutch colony known as New Amsterdam. As if the picture was not vivid enough, the magazine supplied a written description of the scene, including this passage: "The red men, in their savage attire, with their squaws and children, are engaged in examining, with wonder and delight, the trinkets and European clothes given them as the consideration for the purchase" (Noyes 1858, 445).

The idea that the transaction was carried out using primarily cheap trinkets soon became commonplace, further devaluing the deal as far as the Native Americans were concerned. From now on, the phrase "twenty-four dollars' worth of trinkets" became indelibly associated with the purchase of Manhattan. Considering how many tourists from around the world visit New York City every day of the year, this myth probably has earned a prize for being told most often and in the most number of languages.

PRIMARY DOCUMENT
THE LETTER BY P. SCHAGEN

The myth of the Manhattan purchase for $24 provides us with a unique opportunity to observe how a very brief historical document can receive different interpretations over a short period of time. Within years of Peter Schagen's discovery, it was seen in two different ways: as a rather useless curiosity and as a very important document confirming much of what has been already known, but still presenting new information, about the establishment of New Amsterdam. However, it was a seemingly innocuous footnote that rapidly grew well beyond the context of the document, giving fodder to politically and racially charged sentiments.

To the High and Mighty Lords of the States-General at The Hague:

My Lords,—There arrived here yesterday the ship called the 'Arms of Amsterdam,' which sailed from the river Mauritius, [the Hudson,] in New-Netherland, on the 23d of September. Report is brought that our people there are diligent, and live peaceably; their wives have also borne them children. They have purchased the island of Manhattan from the Indians for the sum of sixty guilders;* it contains 11,000 morgens† of land. They have sown all kinds of grain in the middle of May, and reaped in the middle of August. I send you small samples of the summer grains, as wheat, rye, barley, oats, buckwheat, canary seed, beans and flax.

The cargo of the ship consists of 7,246 beaver skins,
178½ otter "
675 " "
48 mink "
36 cat-lynx "
33 mink "
34 small rat "

together with a considerable quantity of oak timber and nut-wood.

"Commending your High and Mighty Lordships to the favor of the Almighty,
I am your High Mightinesses' humble servant,
P. SCHAGEN."
"At Amsterdam, Nov. 5th, anno 1626."

The historical value and interesting character of this document, cannot fail to strike any one who is capable of appreciating the first efforts to introduce the arts of civilized life into a new and widely extended domain, which has since grown from these small beginnings into a large and flourishing commonwealth, excelling in population and resources some of the monarchies of the old world.

---

* About twenty-four dollars.
† A morgen is nearly two acres.

Source: New York (State). Legislature. Senate. 1845. "In Senate. Report." *Documents of the Senate of the State of New York* 3 (11) (May 5, 1845): 5–6.

What Really Happened

So far, we have established that mid-nineteenth-century historians (whether O'Callaghan, J. R. Brodhead, or someone else) were responsible for introducing the amount of $24 into the popular Manhattan purchase narrative. The original Dutch document, of course, referred to sixty guilders instead. At the time when the deal was struck, there was no such thing as a U.S. dollar, as the United States of America would not be created for another century and a half. Therefore, we can be certain that the 2.5 conversion rate could not have originated from researching contemporary records of currency exchange. Before we discuss the actual value of the resulting sum, let's look into the process used to come up with this figure.

The logic behind the conversion rate of 2.5 can be easily reconstructed. Information about currency exchange rates from the mid-1840s may be found in contemporary periodicals. It appears that the value of Dutch guilders to the U.S. dollar in the 1840s remained stable, around ten guilders for $3.90. A simple calculation provides us with the value of sixty guilders at about $23.40. Rounding this figure up in favor of the seller gives us the very $24 that we see in accounts of the purchase of Manhattan to this day. The resulting conversion rate is 2.56, which is not suitable for quick calculations. It would have seemed harmless to a historian to use 2.5 instead, enabling one to convert guilders into dollars effortlessly, even without resorting to paper and pencil.

In all likelihood, this is exactly what O'Callaghan did for all the many instances when he supplied dollar equivalents of colonial Dutch amounts and transactions. At least at one point, this method failed him. In the February 1843 installment of "Notes on the New Netherlands," he inexplicably suggested $21 (not $20) as an equivalent of fifty guilders after correctly comparing twenty guilders to $8 just a few sentences prior.

While the math certainly works, the intrinsic problem with the assertion of a $24 purchase price for Manhattan is that an exchange rate current at the time of the initial publications was used to provide insight into historic data and circumstances. It is indeed useful for a reader to know how to relate various measures and currencies to what is current and comparable. However, while units of weight and measures are fairly objective and can always be converted to some generally accepted standard, it is notoriously difficult to show the value of money because the relative value of currency was and still is in a constant state of flux. Moreover, money is a complex phenomenon that exhibits varying characteristics and dynamics in different economic environments. Any direct conversion between historic and modern currencies is simply inapplicable.

For purposes of historic research, there are different approaches that can be implemented. It is common, for example, to look at prices of consumer staples and food stocks. Sometimes even salaries and daily or monthly wages for well-known occupations are used to the same effect. The market prices of gold and silver can often generate good clues. Depending on the exact computational approach, researchers can end up with different results because monetary units can never fully represent the underlying economic situation—which so often depends on time and place. Regardless of the process, we tend to assume that when historians provide us with such helpful figures and statistics, they use methods that may be replicated, if not verified.

In our particular example, the process for arriving at $24 can easily be repeated; however, the methodology itself is worthless in the strict academic sense. The amount of sixty guilders in 1626 simply did not equal the value of sixty guilders in 1844. Converting this amount to mid-nineteenth-century U.S. dollars added another dimension to the problem by creating a set price tag directly tied to the value of the two currencies in 1844—a completely arbitrary point in time—and diminishing its worth at the rate of the U.S. dollar's inflation. It is really unfortunate that the historians' flawed attempt to give their readers a better sense of an important real estate deal in the seventeenth century came to be seen as a valid piece of information.

As we acknowledge that the $24 price tag used by O'Callaghan and Brodhead in the mid–nineteenth century is inadmissible and irrelevant, even for that time, the question remains about the actual worth of the transaction that supposedly took place in 1626. Modern historians have made many attempts to arrive at the actual value of what was paid for Manhattan in 1626 currency by using the prevailing price of silver, the seventeenth-century cost of consumer goods, and even soldiers' salaries. The resulting figures range from $100 (in 1892) to as much as $5,000 (in 2008 currency). Without attempting to give any firm numbers, let's try to form a framework to help us understand this real estate deal.

Although we know from the primary source that no money exchanged hands, it should be presumed that whatever the Native Americans received as payment for Manhattan could have been purchased for sixty guilders. Sticking strictly to real estate prices, there is evidence that the cost of agricultural land in the Netherlands in the first half of the seventeenth century varied between two hundred and one thousand guilders per morgen (Bieleman 2010, 88). Peter Schagen approximated that the size of the island was eleven thousand morgens (a somewhat imprecise traditional Dutch unit of area measurements). At the time of the purchase, Manhattan may not have been suitable for agriculture; nevertheless, the price of $60/11,000 = 0.005$ guilders per morgen seems like a bargain.

The average price of agricultural land in the Netherlands in 2002 was 40,150 euros per hectare (Eurostat n.d.). This particular year is useful because it marks the transition from the Dutch guilder to new European Union (EU) currency, with the set rate of 2.20371 guilders per euro. Consequently, the price of one hectare in 2002 was a whopping 88,479 guilders. Let's assume that one morgen equals 0.8516 hectares. As a result, the price of a morgen that year was well over 75,000 guilders (it is important to consider that land in the Netherlands is historically expensive). During the same year, the price of land in Romania was 278.22 euros per hectare, or roughly 522 guilders per morgen (144 times cheaper than the price of the same amount of land in the Netherlands). This is a stunning discrepancy, especially keeping in mind that the Netherlands and Romania at that point in time were close to becoming united within one economic space (Romania joined the EU in 2007). In 1626, how much would an island halfway across the globe be valued at in the eyes of the Dutch?

Let's presume, hypothetically, that in 1626 the expected difference between the price of land in the Netherlands and in North America amounted to approximately 144 times (the same ratio that we observed looking at recent data for two countries in Europe). The cost of land in Manhattan would then be calculated at no lower than just over one guilder per morgen. The price for the entire eleven thousand morgens (the size of Manhattan, according to Schagen) would be a five-digit figure—perhaps fifteen thousand guilders? It is, of course, a far cry from sixty guilders. However, let's be mindful of the original meaning of the term *morgen*. It used to denote an area that a single person could plow during one morning of work. When someone purchased land in the Netherlands in 1626, paying between two hundred and one thousand guilders, this land was acquired for the specific purpose of cultivating it.

This was simply not a viable plan for the island on the Hudson purchased from Native Americans. Hundreds of Dutch peasants equipped with contemporary agricultural tools (in turn requiring hundreds of horses to operate) would not have been readily available even if the land in North America were ready for plowing. Once adjusted for lack of infrastructure, extreme remoteness, and generally limited usability, what would have been a fair price for Manhattan in 1626? It seems that any well-informed guess would not surpass the price of just a few ordinary bulbs during the Tulip Mania that took place in 1636–1637, when a single "onion" could fetch hundreds or thousands of guilders.

It is hardly contestable that the price of Manhattan in 1626 could not have represented anything other than a fraction of the price normally paid for agricultural land in the Netherlands. Yet, sixty guilders still seems like a particularly low offer. Was it indeed a trifling amount of money? The documents collected by John R. Brodhead in Europe have many references to financial transactions, fees, and fines. One of particular interest to us is the "Report on Garrisoning Fort Casimir, on the Delaware River" (Brodhead 1853–1858, 1: 81). This document details the cost of maintaining a garrison at Fort Casimir, specifying the salaries of different groups of military personnel. According to the report, the monthly salary of a captain was fifty guilders, a lieutenant had to be content with thirty guilders, and a soldier received a compensation of eight guilders.

It may be tempting to use the basic pay of today's active duty soldier to calculate the worth of sixty guilders in 1626, thus easily arriving at thousands of dollars. It is more important, however, to understand that the purchasing value of money during different historic times is not as straightforward as we would like it to be. Moreover, if it seems for one moment that through some calculations one can come to believe that the price paid for Manhattan was indeed substantial, it only remains to consider that the whole thing can be turned around—every Dutch lieutenant could afford to buy himself a few islands on a yearly basis. Such was not the case, however (otherwise much of the East Coast of the United States would be controlled by descendants of the Fort Casimir garrison).

Dutch colonists were not systematically buying all available land in the New World. High demand would have been the only factor that could drive up the price of Manhattan. Because the demand was negligible or nonexistent, the price of sixty guilders was good and fair as far as the colonial administration was concerned. They were able to strike a deal for the price of probably no more than an acre of arable land back home.

Let's now turn to the other side of this transaction. Were the Native Americans equally happy with the deal? Will it suffice to concede that while the dollar figure permeating American textbooks and popular historical literature was not obtained through proper research, does the actual gist of the story remain unchanged? Did the Native Americans really receive nothing but a few cheap trinkets for a piece of land that the Dutch already knew to be of considerable value?

We have already discussed the complexities of comparing the value of money during different historical periods. It is equally difficult to gauge how much something could be worth to individuals immersed in an entirely different culture. Had members of the indigenous tribe opted to receive their payment in European silver coins, this wish would have most likely been granted, especially given the insignificance of the sum.

However, they apparently preferred to receive their payment in kind, which means that the Native Americans who sold Manhattan for sixty guilders' worth of goods actually received what they wanted (even if the amount was not significant enough). As no paperwork from this deal has survived, it is impossible to ascertain the precise terms and get a glimpse of exactly what happened. Fortuitously, there is a more detailed account of a very similar transaction: the purchase of Staten Island. It is found in an early English translation of a letter by Cornelius Melyn, in which he explains what is known to him about the purchase of Staten Island.

According to Melyn, the island was purchased by Governor Peter Minuit for some "duffles, kettles, axes, hoes, wampum, drilling awls, Jews harps, and diverse other small wares" (Melyn 1914, 124). Among these items, only wampum could possibly be seen as "trinkets" by members of the public in the nineteenth century. These beads, made from seashells, were typically strung together and measured by the fathom and were a common form of currency used at the time by both the native inhabitants of the Eastern Woodlands and the European newcomers (and thus hardly to be interpreted as trinkets). For several decades, wampum was even considered a legal tender in some American colonies (Cronon 2003, 102). Consequently, it would be fair to say that some money actually exchanged hands during the purchase of Staten Island. Other than that, there is no reason to believe that the items featured in that sale could be characterized as trinkets. More importantly, none of these items were a novelty (as one might think after viewing William Ranney's painting). On the contrary, by the 1620s, Native Americans were becoming more and more dependent on European-made products. To receive a fair amount of such objects might have seemed a good deal.

It is more than likely that when the Dutch paid for Manhattan, the actual itemized list of goods offered for the island contained many of the same types of objects. But would it have been a fair amount for the Dutch to offer in exchange for the use of a large island forever?

The real estate along the Eastern coastline of North America in the early seventeenth century appears to have been a buyer's market. European colonial powers had the forefront of the entire continent within their reach, and they were free to choose which parts of it to develop and how to obtain ownership rights. The sellers of ancestral homelands oftentimes did not know or understand the reasons why certain areas were more sought-after by the newcomers from Europe. And no one could have anticipated the strange and unfortunate turns that history would take in the next fifty to one hundred years.

Amid this uncertainty, any trade deal had the potential to seem like a good bargain to both sides. The Dutch obtained a piece of paper that they could later produce to the English, and the indigenous tribes received valuable tools and consumer goods in return. It is, of course, difficult to disregard the apparent imbalance between the price paid and the size of the purchased territory, but was this imbalance obvious to the Native Americans?

The purchase of Manhattan (as well as other similar transactions) marked the meeting point of two different civilizations whose ideas about landownership were not perfectly aligned, and the resulting deals reflected this divide. Researchers have previously suggested that the European notions of owning, buying, and selling land was incomprehensible to the de facto owners of land in the New World. Perhaps, indigenous tribes did not understand that they were selling Manhattan and not simply allowing the Dutch to use it on a temporary basis? To accept this theory fully would mean failing to recognize the level of cultural attrition already in play by this time. Whatever customs and habits native tribes had prior to their contacts with Europeans, they were quickly learning more about the European way of doing business. Apart from that, it must also be acknowledged that indigenous tribes of the American Northeast certainly had their established ways of managing land resources and exercising ownership.

It would have been convenient for Europeans to claim that Native Americans had no rights to their land because they had no written and codified laws, no government, and no commercial activity able to sustain landownership. This view was most notably expressed by John Locke in his book *Two Treatises of Government*. Such a position effectively legitimized appropriating any and all land occupied by Native Americans. In actuality, ownership does not always depend on legal formalities.

In our particular case, common ownership could be described as "an organic aspect of fishing, hunting, grazing, or wood-cutting communities" (Greer 2012, 368). The land in the parts of North America that were actively being colonized in the seventeenth century was held in ownership in the form of commons by the tribes residing in those areas. A distinction could often be made between inner and outer commons, signifying the cleared and cultivated areas, as opposed to the wilderness used for hunting and gathering. However, even the resources of the outer commons would have been subject to regulations, responsible use, and careful management. To some extent, this prevailing form of ownership exercised by the indigenous peoples of North America was acknowledged by the colonists, who, in turn, also formed their own inner and outer commons, still evidenced in the layout of many towns and cities.

On the other hand, Native Americans were not accustomed to the European practice of enclosures, which resulted in stricter rules of use, exclusivity, and transferability. The idea that someone could claim sole proprietorship of a piece of land in all perpetuity was counterintuitive to the more organic way in which collective ownership was exerted. For example, in such a model, "different groups sometimes lay claim to overlapping areas for distinct foraging purposes" (Greer 2012, 371). It is unavoidable that sale agreements between Native Americans and the colonists were conducted against the background of different landowning practices. Consequently, these treaties were subject to revisions and adjustments. It may appear to us that Native Americans totally subscribed to the European model of landownership. However, the Dutch had to make reluctant concessions to certain expectations harbored by the native peoples.

Cornelius Melyn, for instance, soon after confirming with the native tribes the fact that Staten Island had been purchased fair and square by Governor Minuit, his predecessor, discovered that the sale apparently came with a curious unwritten proviso:

> The Year following arriving in New Netherland & being come on Staten Island I (ye sd. Cornelius Melyen) caused ye Indians to be askt whether they were not well recompenced by Minnewit for sd. Island, They gave me for Answer, yt they had sold it to sd. Minnewit & were paid for it, but that it was their custome, when a New Governr came to such a place, that there should be a Gratuity given them; thereby to continue the friendship between ye Indians & or nation, which I did to ye great content & Satisfaction of them all. (Melyn 1914, 124)

Cornelius Melyn also relates how, in 1649, the Indians began to talk about buying Staten Island from them on the grounds that "ye Island by reason of ye war, by killing, burning & driving us off, was become theirs again, and therefore thought that there must be a new bargain made." Melyn categorically refused to do so, saying that "ye Dutch will not pay twice for any thing, which they have once bought, but if they will once more have a small gift gratis to maintain good friendship as had been done before I would give it them, whereunto (after mature deliberation among themselves) they resolved" (Melyn 1914, 125).

These are just a couple of instances from what is sometimes described as "the sales of Staten Island." An important takeaway here is that apart from being a buyer's market, real estate on this end of the Atlantic Ocean remained very volatile and was understood as such by both parties (albeit for different reasons). The Dutch would have been wary of the hardships implied by developing an area so far from their homeland while facing constant threats from the native population and other European powers. The indigenous tribes most likely saw the arrival of a new group as one of many similar events in their collective history, bringing opportunities for trade and military alliances. Holistic principles of common landownership would have permitted that a newly arrived "tribe" at least be considered as a future neighbor and ally, although this status depended on their survival and adaptation. It is rather unthinkable that in the unlikely event of a complete failure of Europeans to make a home in America the local groups would have heeded any hard boundaries and "private property" signs. In time, the appropriation of land by Europeans came to be understood as clearly defined expansionism with irreversible effects that were harmful to the native inhabitants.

As we discuss the perception of the Manhattan purchase by the Native Americans, it is worthwhile to mention what seems to be a folkloric interpretation of this event. In the absence of firsthand written testimonies, there is the account recorded by John Heckewelder (1743–1823), who was a missionary particularly interested in America's indigenous nations. His informant was "an intelligent Delaware Indian" who related the tradition about the first arrival of "men in white skin" (Heckewelder 1876, 77). Although the account was first made public in 1819. Heckewelder indicated that the story was told to him many years prior. His missionary work among the Indians began in the 1770s, which would mean that several generations separated the account from eyewitness reports.

While there are many details in the narrative that most likely stem from storytelling conventions, it has much to say about the first contacts between Native Americans and Europeans "in the country, situated between New England and Virginia" (Heckewelder 1876, 71). The story begins with a group of Indians observing a large house floating in the water. There was just enough time to gather the chiefs and most of the population to witness this curiosity before the apparent ship came close to shore and a canoe was sent from it, carrying a remarkable man in red garments trimmed with silver laces. The locals perceived this stranger to be the great Mannito (the supreme deity) and offered him and his entourage every manner of hospitality. In turn, the visitors provided an inebriating drink of which the Indians partook, enjoying "the most delicious sensations." While the party progressed, the guests went to their vessel and brought back many presents, such as "beads, axes, hoes, and stockings such as the white people wear" (Heckewelder 1876, 71).

The Dutch then explained that they were planning to go home, but they would return next year and would want to have a little land "to sow seeds, in order to raise herbs and vegetables to put into their broth." They indeed came back the very next year, with more presents, and there was much mutual rejoicing, which was marked by a humorous side story. The Indians had not known what to do with hoes and axes, which had been provided to them without handles. Perceiving them to be objects of value, they hanged them on their necks as ornaments. The stockings were used as tobacco sacks. The Dutch laughed and then proceeded with a demonstration: a tree was cut down, the ground was hoed up, and stockings were properly put on. The Indians joined in the laughter.

As familiarity turned into a sort of friendship, the white men asked for a small patch of land: no bigger than what a hide of a bullock would cover. This reasonable request was granted, but the outcome was remarkable, as the newcomers cut the hide in a circular fashion, creating a thin rope. The land that this hide encompassed was much larger than had been anticipated. Amazed by this, the Indians did not contend the result because they still had plenty of land.

> The white and red men lived contentedly together for a long time, though the former from time to time asked for more land, which was readily obtained, and thus they gradually proceeded higher up the Mahicannittuck, until the Indians began to believe that they would soon want all their country, which in the end proved true. (Heckewelder 1876, 75)

Parts of this story certainly sound implausible, especially the trick with the bullock's hide, which in mainstream European culture stems from Virgil's account about the purchase of Carthage by Queen Dido (Book I of the *Aeneid*). Either the Dutch indeed wanted to recreate this classical story or the Native Americans later embellished the event using a similar myth from their own oral tradition. It is far more important to note that the acquisition of land was part of the amicable exchange between the two groups. The "presents" helped cement their relationship, while the actual granting of the land was an answer to a need as opposed to a merely expressed wish of an acquisition. The gradual nature of the takeover is also notable, as it makes clear that the territorial expansion, at least during its initial stages, was conditioned upon the growing demands of the newcomers. The pattern of interaction suggested by the Native American account is compatible with the principles of landownership by North

American communities, and the Dutch in the story, at least outwardly, seem to respect the indigenous people's property rights, until it becomes clear that the eventual displacement of local tribes is the goal of the colonists' endeavors.

All these considerations allow us to conclude that at the moment when the Manhattan deal was struck, it did not appear too bad or imbalanced to Native Americans, and with good reason. They received valuables in exchange for their decision, but they did not agree to surrender anything for all perpetuity—the deal, as far as they were concerned, was subject to further revisions. They may have been aware or unaware of European real estate practices, but they operated within their own tradition. Indigenous landowners felt that they could prevail in their interpretation of the sale later on.

The sale of Manhattan, often seen as a groundbreaking event in American history, is more likely a representative episode of a complicated relationship between the Dutch and the Native Americans in which both sides looked for temporary gains rather than grand deals that would be talked about by future generations. The Dutch worked toward establishing a strong social and military presence in the colony, mindful of the age-old principle that "possession constitutes nine-tenths of the law." The Native Americans carefully tried to remain a force to be reckoned with in the face of a vastly more technologically superior power. Neither side could be sure about the future and simply hoped to be on the winning side.

Consequently, the Dutch were only prepared to pay the lowest possible price for the land that was infinitely less desirable compared to what they were used to in the Netherlands. In turn, the Native Americans hardly expected to be paid a fortune, especially given their approach to possessing land; although they considered such ownership to be real and tangible, it was also organic and fluid, as all things in life. The two parties of the deal had their own presuppositions going into the deal. Only with time, this transactional encounter was revealed to heavily benefit the colonists, with their legalistic view of real estate. It is possible, however, that the excited tone of Peter Schagen's letter foreshadowed this eventual outcome.

From the historiographic point of view, the myth of the $24 purchase can serve as a reminder that when history is told, even using actual available sources, simple interpretive mistakes can thwart the understanding of events for centuries to come. Carelessly performed currency conversion of a figure found in an obscure letter has taken on a separate life, unchallenged by inflation and rational reasoning. It played well into conflicting mythologies and could be used to demonstrate any number of lessons of history.

It is impossible to combat such presuppositions as well as both racist and patronizing attitudes toward indigenous people of the Americas simply on the grounds of a single debunked myth. Still, having a more accurate understanding of the facts behind the myth should help us build the foundation for a healthier understanding of history.

Further Reading

Anbinder, Tyler. 2016. *City of Dreams: The 400-Year Epic History of Immigrant New York*. Boston, MA: Houghton Mifflin Harcourt.

Bieleman, Jan. 2010. *Five Centuries of Farming: A Short History of Dutch Agriculture, 1500–2000*. Mansholt Publication Series. Vol. 8. Wageningen, Netherlands: Wageningen Academic Publishers.

Brodhead, John Romeyn. 1853. *History of the State of New York*. Vol. 1. New York: Harper & Brothers.

Brodhead, John Romeyn, comp. 1853–1858. *Documents Relative to the Colonial History of the State of New-York*. 15 vols. Translated and edited by E. B. O'Callaghan. Albany, NY: Weed, Parsons and Company.

Burrows, Edwin G., and Mike Wallace. 2000. *Gotham: A History of New York City to 1898*. First issued as an Oxford University Press paperback. Oxford: Oxford University Press.

Cronon, William. 2003. *Changes in the Land: Indians, Colonists, and the Ecology of New England*. Rev. ed. New York: Hill and Wang.

Eurostat. n.d. "Agricultural Land Prices by Region—Historical Data (until 2009)." Accessed November 25, 2019. https://appsso.eurostat.ec.europa.eu/nui/show.do?dataset=apri_lprc_h.

Greer, Allan. 2012. "Commons and Enclosure in the Colonization of North America." *American Historical Review* 117 (2): 365–386

Heckewelder, John. 1876. *History, Manners, and Customs of the Indian Nations Who Once Inhabited Pennsylvania and the Neighbouring States*. Philadelphia: n.p.

Jackson, Kenneth T., and New-York Historical Society, eds. 2010. *The Encyclopedia of New York City*. 2nd ed. New Haven, CT: Yale University Press; New York: New-York Historical Society.

Jacobs, Jaap. 2005. *New Netherland: A Dutch Colony in Seventeenth-Century America*. Vol. 3 of *The Atlantic World*. Leiden, Netherlands: Brill.

Loewen, James W. 2007. *Lies across America: What Our Historic Sites Get Wrong*. New York: Simon & Schuster.

Melyn, Cornelius. 1914. "Melyn Papers 1640–1699." *Collections of the New-York Historical Society for the Year 1913.* Vol. XLVI. New York: New-York Historical Society.

New York (State). Legislature. Senate. 1844. "In Senate. Report." *Documents of the Senate of the State of New York* 1 (42) (February 3, 1844).

New York (State). Legislature. Senate. 1845. "In Senate. Report." *Documents of the Senate of the State of New York* 3 (11) (May 5, 1845).

Noyes, J. O. 1858. "The Dutch in New Amsterdam." *National Magazine* 12 (May 1858).

O'Callaghan, E. B. 1846. *History of New Netherland; or, New York under the Dutch.* New York: D. Appleton & Company.

Oldboy, Felix. 1890. *The Island of Manhattan, a Bit of Earth.* New York: n.p.

Reitano, Joanne R. 2010. *The Restless City: A Short History of New York from Colonial Times to the Present.* 2nd ed. New York: Routledge.

Scheltema, Gajus, Russell Shorto, and Heleen Westerhuijis. 2013. *Exploring Historic Dutch New York: New York City, Hudson Valley, New Jersey, Delaware.* Mineola, NY: Dover Publications. Accessed May 4, 2020. https://www.hoopladigital.com/title/12239307.

Scobey, David M. 2003. E*mpire City: The Making and Meaning of the New York City Landscape.* Philadelphia: Temple University Press.

Shorto, Russell. 2005. *The Island at the Center of the World: The Epic Story of Dutch Manhattan and the Forgotten Colony That Shaped America.* New York: Vintage.

Verney, Jack. 1994. *O'Callaghan: The Making and Unmaking of a Rebel.* Carleton Library Series 179. Ottawa: Carleton University Press.

Weslager, C. A., and Kalmar Nyckel Foundation. 1990. *A Man and His Ship: Peter Minuit and the Kalmar Nyckel.* Wilmington, DE: Kalmar Nyckel Foundation.

6

Witches Were Burned in Salem

What People Think Happened

Few events in American history are surrounded by more myth and misconception than the Salem witch trials of 1692–1693. The reason for this general misunderstanding can be found in the negative modern perception of Puritan New England. Almost any strange practice and belief attributed to these religious *zealots* is readily accepted by the general public today. People believe that the Puritans only wore black clothing punctuated with buckles, white collars, and cuffs; that they spent virtually all their time in prayer and Bible reading; that they were generally intolerant of any ethnic group or religious belief other than their own; and that they were generally harsh, unnecessarily nasty, and unmerciful in their dealings with transgressors and others. The facts are much more complex.

Although the Puritans indeed sought to establish their presence in the New World in a manner that best accommodated their own religious practices and cultural habits, the reality of this new harsh environment called for adaptability and dynamic approaches to challenges. This was reflected in the daily lives of New England communities as well as their interactions with the neighbors. The resulting subtleties may be hard to convey to a general public so heavily prejudiced against the Puritans, and the Salem witch trials provide a good example of just how persistent this negative perception can be. Despite clear and well-documented historic facts, it is all too common for modern Americans to believe that the condemned individuals were burned at the stake, ascribing this most barbaric practice to the community that arguably laid the foundations of American society.

The fact that the accused witches in Salem were hanged, not burned, is probably not the strongest evidence of the Puritans' relative tolerance and mercy in their treatment of individuals who appeared to be in opposition to their belief system and ostensibly presented a danger to their community. However, it is worth noting that in sixteenth- and seventeenth-century continental Europe, for example, individuals found guilty of religious crimes such as heresy or witchcraft could expect an ecclesiastical court to condemn them to a fiery death. This execution practice was quite common throughout the Italian and German states and, indeed, throughout the Holy Roman Empire, France, Spain, Austria, and Switzerland.

In comparison, England (from the reign of Queen Elizabeth I and for all years thereafter) primarily executed individuals by only two methods: beheading and hanging. Beheading was reserved for high-status criminals—such as nobles guilty of treason—while the common capital offenders were subject to hanging. The colonizers of Massachusetts known as the Puritans transferred legal practice from Old England to New England, and in the total absence of nobility, hanging became the only acceptable legal means of execution.

Therefore, the pervasive myth that those found guilty of the crime of witchcraft in Puritan New England were burned at the stake is not only at odds with what really happened in Salem. It also contradicts the established legal practice in England, the country to which the Puritans remained subject. This misconception should be put to rest.

How It Became Popular

Let's examine what serves as the foundation of this erroneous belief. The capital nature of committing an act of witchcraft goes back to ancient Babylon's Code of Hammurabi in the second millennium BCE. In fact, death is prescribed as punishment for witchcraft in the first two laws of the Code of Hammurabi. Although the mode of administering capital punishment for this particular offense is not specified in the code, burning at the stake is mentioned in other sections of this ancient legal corpus. Witchcraft was regarded as a serious crime through the days of the Roman Republic and Empire and is mentioned in the Laws of the Twelve Tables, the Lex Romana, and the later Code Justinian of the Byzantine Empire. By the time of the so-called Dark and Middle Ages, virtually all of Europe and the several legal codes established by the newly arrived "barbarian" people condemned acts of malefic witchcraft, while not repressing traditional forms of "white magic." It is worth noting that the punishment of burning at the stake has always remained as a possible punishment for such crimes throughout history.

Closer to the present, the Roman Catholic Church defined witchcraft for its followers as the act of contacting Satan and invoking his spiritual powers to do harm. The ecclesiastical legal tradition regarding black magic culminated in *Malleus Maleficarum* (*Hammer of the Witches*), compiled by German monks Heirich Kramer and Jacob Sprenger. First published in Germany in 1487, this book officially declared witchcraft as a heresy and advocated that the Christian Church conduct formal inquisitions for the purpose of eliminating practitioners of witchcraft wherever discovered.

Moreover, Kramer and Sprenger provide the ecclesiastical courts with a list of procedures and punishments calculated to ferret out the guilty. Among the punishments for those found guilty of witchcraft was burning at the stake. Largely as a result of this publication and the church-sponsored emphasis on heretic hunting during the Protestant Reformation, burnings for the crime of witchcraft became increasingly common throughout continental Europe in the 1500s.

Adding further legitimacy during the 1500s, Jean Bodin (1530–1596), a French jurist and professor of law, history, and philosophy, produced yet another influential publication that greatly encouraged the treatment of suspected witches by "burning-at-the-stake." This publication was *De la Demonomanie des Sorciers* (1580), or *The Demon-Mania of the Sorcerers*. This work—which was produced in ten editions between 1580 and 1604—stressed the way a witch might become a follower of Satan by establishing a "pact" or "deal with the Devil" by agreeing to trade their immortal soul to the Devil in exchange for extraordinary supernatural powers, such as the power to create wealth, affect the weather, destroy livestock, or physically or spiritually hurt people through the supernatural power of demonic forces.

In summary, Bodin asserted that no witch could be falsely condemned if the proper procedures were adopted by the court. To Bodin, locally produced rumors concerning sorcerers and witches were almost always true. These ideas were followed in the Salem trials, as spectral and "here-say" evidence was allowed by the Court of Oyer and Terminer, and the accused were generally considered guilty if accused by their neighbors. In Bodin's France, persons guilty of the capital crime of making a bargain with Satan or confessing to having committed malefic acts of witchcraft were burned at the stake. This practice was followed in every nation on the European continent from the late Middle Ages to the late seventeenth century. One of the best-known victims of this punishment after being condemned for witchcraft is the French female military leader and religious zealot Joan of Arc in 1431.

Moving to England, public burning for witchcraft and heresy was first introduced in 1401 during the reign of King Henry IV. Both these crimes were considered by the legal authorities responsible for the law (*De Heretico Comburendo*) to be not only sacrilegious and dangerous to souls but also seditious and treasonable.

During the reign of King Henry VIII, the Act of Supremacy in 1534 separated the Church of England from the Roman Catholic Church and initially did away with the practice of burning for the crimes of witchcraft and heresy by placing punishment into the hands of the state. After the death of King Henry VIII, however, his daughter Queen Mary I—a devout Roman Catholic monarch—reinstituted the practice for the duration of her reign (1553–1558), resulting in the execution by burning of over 280 suspected heretics and dissenters.

Following Mary's death, her successor, Queen Elizabeth I, ceased the widespread practice of burning by repealing the aforementioned *De Heretico Comburendo* in 1558. From this point onward, England generally tried to avoid burning at the stake for any and all forms of heresy, including witchcraft. It might be noted that from Elizabethan times onward, the practice of burning a victim for heresy or witchcraft carried with it a distinctly Roman Catholic and Inquisition-related connotation that anti-Catholic, Reformed English Protestants would, on principle, choose to avoid.

All of those convicted of the crime of witchcraft in New England prior to 1692 were executed by hanging. In fact, all nineteen of those condemned by the Salem Court of Oyer and Terminer were executed by hanging on Gallows Hill. And only one of the victims, Giles Corey (who refused to cooperate with the court proceedings), was subjected to "pressing" or *Forte Peine et Dure*—meaning that he was gradually crushed by stones placed upon his outstretched body over a period of two days in an effort to extract a plea in order to move forward with his trial. Despite the precedent of hanging as the accepted punishment for capital crimes in New England, even those accused were well aware of burning at the stake as one of the long-standing forms of execution open to European courts when condemning individuals found guilty of witchcraft.

This popular belief is demonstrated by accused witch George Jacobs Sr., who when under interrogation of the Salem court is quoted as saying, "Well *burn me* or hang me, I will stand in the truth of Christ!" After his conviction, he was hanged on August 19, 1692, along with Martha

Carrier, John Proctor, John Willard, and Rev. George Burroughs (Essex Institute 1860, 54).

For most of the next century, the Salem trials as a subject of discussion and analysis remained largely unstudied, though the subject was raised in critiques such as Robert Calef's *More Wonders of the Invisible World*, which blames Cotton Mather, or in provincial histories such as Governor Thomas Hutchinson's three-volume *History of Massachusetts* (1767), which blames the afflicted girls. For what it is worth, Hutchinson's history of the province has an extended analysis of the Salem episode and provides a reasonably objective interpretation of the event and its impact on Massachusetts. He is very critical of the Court of Oyer and Terminer and its willingness to give credence to the testimony of the "afflicted girls." He refers to the method of execution for witchcraft victims as "death by hanging" not only for the condemned of Salem but also for other convicted witches in Massachusetts from the 1640s onward.

The primary concern of New England residents in the late seventeenth and early eighteenth centuries was in securing compensation for confiscated possessions or public exoneration for relatives and ancestors whose reputations were forever damaged by wrongful accusations. For the next two generations, these were the chief issues involving the families of the victims—restitution and exoneration—both for those executed and those imprisoned.

Discussion about the witch trials calmed down precipitously in the next few decades following the turn of the eighteenth century for several reasons. First, because it was a product of the recent past, the public's memory was still sharp. Consequently, the level of public embarrassment of the New England clergy for their involvement was still profound. But from a pragmatic perspective, apart from profound humiliation, the clerics of Massachusetts were in fear of further undermining their own religious authority with the colonial population. Consequently, little was published by Congregational ministers about the mistakes of the recent past.

This was especially true during the 1730s and 1740s with the advent of the Great Awakening movement, which would seem like an obvious place to find earlier parallels drawn between the perceived threats that might arise from the intense excitement of the revival experience and the Salem witch hunts. As historian Gretchen Adams observes, "The difficulty inherent in using Salem's witch hunt as a negative illustration while simultaneously appealing to the same Puritan past as a model for the return to faith can itself explain its absence from debates in the eighteenth century" (Adams 2008, 33) As a result, little was said about the Salem episode or, indeed, the dozens of other tragic witchcraft incidents that occurred in New England during the seventeenth century.

As time passed, the public and scholarly silence on the subject of the trials—as well as the collective memory of exactly how victims were treated and executed—faded but was not entirely forgotten. It was certainly known that lives were lost, but there developed a lack of certainty as to how many were executed and what form such executions took in the minds of subsequent generations. Added to the silence of the Great Awakening was the overwhelming dark shadow of colonial warfare that pervaded the lives and occupied the attention of American people from the 1750s through the early 1780s.

From 1755 to 1763, the worldwide conflict between France and England—known as the Seven Years' War—dominated New England life in a smaller, regional conflagration known as the French and Indian War. It was waged between British military forces and their colonial and Native American allies against the French forces and their Native American allies. The conflict was finally resolved with the Treaty of Paris in 1763, resulting in the loss of French North America and the creation of a vast English war debt requiring new sources of revenue to repay. The need to pay off this debt would become the primary motivation for the various tax legislation of the 1760s levied upon the American colonies by Parliament.

From 1765 through 1775, colonial resentment in response to tax legislation and repressive colonial policies fostered a public outcry and resentment that occupied the attention of American radical Whigs and intellectuals with more important issues than the need to analyze and reflect upon the Salem episode. The following decade was dominated by a lengthy rebellion whose end result was the termination of the dependent status of thirteen British colonies and the creation of a new nation following the ratification of the Constitution and election of George Washington as president in 1789.

Thus, throughout the almost one hundred years between the close of the seventeenth century and the dawn of the nineteenth century, American popular writers, scholars, ministers, and political leaders—with the exception of Governor Thomas Hutchinson—had very little opportunity, motivation, or interest to write about the Salem trials. It simply was not a high priority to remind succeeding generations how the trials had been conducted and, more particularly, by what means those convicted of witchcraft had tragically lost their lives. Patriots could also hang.

This cloud of general vagueness as to the exact method of execution was reinforced after independence, in the 1820s and 1830s, when American public school history textbooks were published in vast quantities to serve the needs of the nation's growing number of public school students. Of the several most popular elementary- and secondary-level textbooks distributed throughout the schools of the United States, not a single American history text published between 1820 and 1840 explained in exact detail the method of execution of the twenty Salem witch trial victims. Rather, they were all described as being either publicly or wrongfully "put to death" or "executed" as witches—leaving the precise method up to the imaginations of the schoolteacher or, worse, to the students themselves.

This vague treatment of the event, and particularly the nonspecific textbook description of the witch executions, doubtless contributed to the general ignorance of the great American public as to the exact method used to take the lives of those convicted in the Salem episode. A representative example would be this passage from one of the most popular textbooks of the period, *A History of the United States from Their Establishment as Colonies to the Close of the War with Britain in 1815*: "Many were tried and received sentences of death. A few pleaded guilty. Several were convicted upon testimony which at other times would not have induced suspicion of any other crime, and some, upon testimony retracted after conviction. Nineteen were executed, and many yet remained to be tried" (Hunt 1835, 47).

It should be noted that this text was so highly regarded that it received the top prize of $400 and a publication medal offered by the American Academy of Language and Belles Lettres of New York in 1820. It was consecutively reprinted and nationally distributed every year following as the highest-rated and most widely acclaimed American history textbook of that time. Later, popular public school textbooks used to educate students in American history follow much the same pattern as Hunt's text.

It must be noted that the subject of the Salem episode experienced a resurgence of interest and popularity from the 1830s to the 1850s because of writers such as Nathaniel Hawthorne, who almost single-handedly revitalized popular interest in early Salem, witchcraft, and the Puritans in his historical fictions and romance novels populated by evil judges, public persecutions, and colonial characters wrongfully accused of witchcraft. In fairness, despite his preoccupation with witchcraft in Puritan New England, Hawthorne never produced a short story or novel depicting a character being burned.

This growing nineteenth-century fascination with the Salem witchcraft episode finally resulted in the publication of a popular two-volume study—the first of its kind—by scholar and politician Rev. Charles W. Upham in 1867. This exhaustive analysis of the 1692 event places the blame squarely on the shoulders of the "afflicted girls" and those persons in authority who accepted the girls' testimony of "spectral evidence." However, Upham is careful to underscore that those nineteen persons convicted of witchcraft were hanged.

So, the question remains, How is it possible that a large percentage of the American population from the mid-1800s to the present persisted in making an association between the Salem trials for witchcraft and death by immolation? The answer lies in one of the dominant themes of nineteenth-century U.S. history—the influx of immigration from continental (predominantly Catholic) Europe.

Beginning with Irish refugees from the Great Potato Famine of the 1840s and 1850s, continuing with the revolutionary refugees of the German and Italian states of the 1850s and 1860s, and concluding with the many thousands of escapees from Russian and Poland in the late nineteenth and early twentieth centuries, the United States more than doubled its population size, attracting millions of immigrants from nations where burning at the stake was the only known punishment for the crime of witchcraft. If told that in the previous 150 years, individuals had been killed for witchcraft, these new arrivals would have naturally assumed that these American witchcraft victims had been burned at the stake as well. As the history books of the time refused to specify hanging but insisted on putting the witch trial victims to death by "execution," even the children and grandchildren of these millions of immigrant Americans have made the erroneous assumption that colonial witchcraft victims were burned, just like the witches "in the old country."

This widespread European witch-burning tradition, reintroduced during the Victorian era, was reinforced by such late nineteenth-century public entertainments as *The Salem Witch: An American Comic Opera in Three Acts*, which was first produced in Boston in 1883. This popular musical extravaganza concludes with the romantic heroine, Wild Spray, tied to a stake on stage surrounded by piles of firewood about to be lit by a crowd of torch-bearing Salem Puritans. The happy ending is achieved when the swashbuckling hero, Dauntless Dick, rescues her at the last moment and proves her innocence to the crowd and audience alike.

Poetically, the Salem burning-at-the-stake tradition is further entrenched by verses such as "Plymouth Rock: 1620–1870" by William Everett, Esq., presented to a large audience on the occasion of the 250th anniversary of the landing of the Pilgrims. Consider this excerpt:

We know the fun you love so well at Puritans to poke,
Your Witches and your Quakers and every threadbare joke.
Go read your history, school-boys; learn on one glorious page
The Pilgrim towers untainted above that iron age.
From stains of mightiest heroes, the Pilgrim hands are clean,
In Plymouth's free and peaceful streets *no bigot's stake was seen* [emphasis added]. (Everett 1870, 129)

Hollywood has perhaps done more than any other medium to perpetuate the myth of witch burning in Salem with a selection of feature films that all visually confirm that Puritans turned to burning at the stake whenever confronted with individuals suspected of witchcraft.

The myth was passed down to the Golden Age of Hollywood in 1937 in the Paramount Pictures film *I Married a Witch*, directed by Renee Claire and starring Veronica Lake with Frederick March. In this romantic comedy, two witches are burned in colonial Salem and their ashes buried beneath a tree to imprison their evil spirits, but a bolt of lightning frees them to mischievously work their magic once again. Similarly, in 1937, a more dramatic epic, *Maid of Salem*, starring Claudette Colbert and Fred MacMurray, accuses the innocent "maid of Salem" of witchcraft, and the townsfolk attempt to burn her. Fast-forward to 1987, and you can witness yet another comedic film, *Love at Stake*, set in colonial Salem and directed by John Moffitt, starring Patrick Cassidy and Barbara Carrera.

More recently, on November 10, 1992, on the occasion of the dedication of the Salem Witch Trial Memorial in Salem, Massachusetts, one of the wreaths placed at the site bore this inscription: "Never Again the Burnings!" Perhaps the only satisfaction that may be derived by the anonymous donor of that wreath might be that not only will the burnings never happen again but that, in Salem, they never did (Rosenthal 1993, 210).

What Really Happened

As a representative document to underscore the manner of execution followed in the Salem witch trials, and indeed all witch trial executions in seventeenth-century New England, two cojoined statements from the trials themselves are submitted. The first is Chief Magistrate William Stoughton's "Death Warrant for Bridget Bishop," and the second is High Sheriff George Corwin's official report confirming Bridget's execution by hanging:

To George Corwin gentleman High Sheriff of the County of Essex Greeting

    Whereas Bridget Bishop alias Oliver the wife of Edward Bishop of [Salem] in the County of Essex, Sawyer, at a special Court of Oyer and Terminer [held at] Salem the second day of this instant month of June for the Counties of Essex, Middlesex and Suffolk before William Stoughton, Esquire and his Associate Justices of the said court was indicted and arraigned upon five several [seal] indictments for using, practicing and exercising [on the nineteenth day of April] last, past and on diverse other days and times [before and after certain acts of] witchcraft in and upon the bodies of Abigail Williams, Anne Putnam Jun'r, Mercy Lewis, Mary Walcott, and Elizabeth Hubbard of Salem Village single-women, whereby their bodies were hurt, afflicted, pined, consumed, wasted and tormented contrary to the form of the statute in that case [made and] provided to which indictments the said Bridget Bishop pleaded [not guilty] and for trial thereof put herself upon God and her Country, whereupon she was found guilty of the felonies and witchcrafts wherein she stood indicted and sentence of death accordingly passed against her as the law directs, execution whereof yet remains to be done. These are therefore in the names of their Majesties William and Mary, now King and Queen over England and to will and command you that upon Friday next, being the tenth day of this instant month of June between the hours of eight and twelve in the afternoon of the same day, you safely conduct the said Bridget Bishop alias Oliver from their Majesties jail in Salem aforesaid to the place of execution and *there cause her to be hanged by the neck until she be dead* [emphasis added] and of your doings herein make return to the Clerk of the said Court and precept. And hereof you are not to fail at your peril. And this shall be your sufficient warrant given under my hand and seal at Boston the eighth day of June in the fourth year of the reign of our Sovereign Lord and Lady, William and Mary, now King and Queen over England. Anno Dom 1692.

    William Stoughton
    June 10, 1692

According to the within written precept I have taken the body of the within named Bridget Bishop of their Majesties jail in Salem and safely conveyed her to the place provided for her execution and caused the said *Bridget to be hanged by the neck until she was dead* [emphasis added] [and buried in the place] all which was according to the time within required and so I make return by me. George Corwin, Sheriff (Goss 2018, 96–97)

Bridget was the first person executed during the Salem episode and the only person to die alone. All of the other nineteen hanging victims were executed in groups in July, August, and September 1692. It is further important to note that although witch trial victim Giles Corey lost his life from being crushed by stones, his death was not intentional but rather the result of physical torture (pressing) that was only intended to elicit from him a statement that he would accept as "justice" the verdict of the special Court of Oyer and Terminer, submitting himself to be "tried by God and country"—something Corey simply refused to do.

More engaging is the account of the hanging of one of the more prominent victims of the Salem witch trials, a former minister of Salem Village, Rev. George Burroughs, whose hanging was immortalized by Robert Calef, a Boston merchant and scholar who was an eyewitness to the execution. Calef would record the hanging of Burroughs in his scathing critique of Rev. Cotton Mather, *More Wonders of the Invisible World*:

> Mr. Burroughs was carried in a cart with the others, through the streets of Salem to execution. When he was upon the ladder, he made a speech for the clearing of his innocence, with such solemn and serious expressions, as were to the admiration of all present; his prayer (which he concluded by repeating the Lord's Prayer) was so well worded, and uttered with such composedness, and such (at least seeming) fervency of spirit, as was very affecting, and drew tears from many, so that it seemed to some that the spectators would hinder the execution. The accuser said the black man stood (on the ladder) and dictated to him. As soon as he was turned off, Mr. Cotton Mather, being mounted upon a horse, addressed himself to the people, partly to declare that he (George Burroughs) was no ordained minister, and partly to possess the people of his guilt, saying that, the Devil has often been transformed into an "angel of light"; and this somewhat appeased the people, and the executions went on. (Burr 2002, 360–361)

What is most tragic about this myth is the fact that even in the attempt to be more humane in hanging rather than burning, the victims were all innocent of the "crime" of witchcraft, and secondarily, each hanging was attended by the local populace hoping to witness a public spectacle. In a Puritan community, public entertainment such as a play was frowned upon, but public executions were encouraged by officials to serve as a moral lesson.

Further Reading

Adams, Gretchen. 2008. *The Specter of Salem*. Chicago, IL: University of Chicago Press.

Baker, Emerson W. 2015. *A Storm of Witchcraft*. Oxford, and New York: Oxford University.

Baker, Emerson W., and John G. Reid. 1998. *The New England Knight: Sir William Phips, 1651–1695*. Toronto and Buffalo: University of Toronto Press.

Burr, George Lincoln. 2002 [1914]. *Narratives of the Witchcraft Cases: 1648–1706*. New York: Charles Scribner and Sons.

Calef, Robert. 1700. *More Wonders of the Invisible World*. London: Nathaniel Hillar.

Essex Institute. 1860. *Essex Institute Historical Collections*. Vol. 2. Salem, MA: Essex Institute.

Everett, William. 1870. "Plymouth Rock: 1620–1870." Pilgrim Society Journal, Plymouth, MA. Cambridge, MA: Press of J. Wilson and Son.

Goss, K. David. 2007. *The Salem Witch Trials: A Reference Guide*. Westport, CT: Greenwood.

Goss, K. David. 2018. *Documents of the Salem Witch Trials*. Santa Barbara, CA: ABC-CLIO.

Hoffer, Peter Charles. 1997. *The Salem Witch Trials: A Legal Primer*. Lawrence: University Press of Kansas.

Hunt, Uriah. 1835. *A History of the United States from Their Establishment as Colonies to the Close of the War with Britain in 1815*. Cooperstown, NY: H. and E. Phinney Publishers.

Mather, Cotton. 2005. *Salem Witchcraft; Comprising More Wonders of the Invisible World, Collected by Robert Calef; and Wonders of the Invisible World, by Cotton Mather; Together with Notes and Explanations by Samuel P. Fowler*. Edited by Samuel P. Fowler. Salem, MA: G. M. Whipple & A. A. Smith.

Rosenthal, Bernard. 1993. *Salem Story: Reading the Witch Trials of 1692*. Cambridge Studies in American Literature and Culture 73. Cambridge, UK, and New York: Cambridge University Press.

7

The Boston Tea Party Participants Threw Chests of Tea into the Sea to Hurt the British

What People Think Happened

The narrative of the Boston Tea Party is relatively uncomplicated, and most Americans will easily agree with the following oversimplified account. To start, one must be reminded that the British love their tea. However uncomfortable it is to admit, prior to the Revolutionary War, most of the people living in the thirteen colonies along the Eastern seaboard of the Atlantic were also British. Therefore, they consumed tea in alarming quantities. Yet, living so far away from their ancestral homeland, these Colonials also developed an independent spirit. Some even went as far as harboring thoughts about political self-governance. This had to be dealt with properly.

King George III, being a ruthless tyrant, found a clever way to show to his transoceanic subjects who was boss. He imposed a hefty tax on tea. This was unjust and burdensome. The East India Company, in cahoots with the Crown, did not even attempt to hide the tax within their price structure. This duty was an insult and an injury.

Among all the dwellers of the British colonies in North America, Bostonians were particularly fond of tea. Faced with the resulting high prices and having no other source from which to obtain their favorite drink, the citizens of Massachusetts were growing quite restless. In December 1773, three British ships arrived in the harbor carrying tea, but because the price was extraordinary, the decision was reached by Bostonians that the captains should take their vessels and their cargo back to the British Isles. However, the final authority lay with Governor Hutchinson. This king's appointee refused to let the ships go. Soon there was another problem looming. The three ships loaded with tea could not remain in the harbor indefinitely. If they did not unload and pay their dues after a certain grace period, the law required that they be unloaded forcefully, and the cargo had to be confiscated.

The Bostonians were so fed up with this issue that the very thought of expensive British tea on their soil made them ill. Thousands of people gathered to discuss the problem. Another plea was sent to the governor. Once again, he refused to let the ships go without unloading. Samuel Adams addressed the crowd that had gathered at the Old South Church in Boston, reportedly saying, "There is nothing more we can do to save the country." As if this were a signal to act as planned, the crowd dispersed and headed toward the wharf where the British ships were docked. To avoid being identified by law enforcement, and perhaps also to assert their roots in the New World, the New Englanders dressed themselves after the manner of Native Americans. Thousands of spectators then witnessed the tea-laden ships being boarded. Too much cheering and excitement, crates filled with tea were promptly thrown overboard. The matter was quickly over. Every last ounce of the tea was destroyed. America's course toward a revolution was set by this event that soon became known as the Boston Tea Party.

How It Became Popular

The Boston Tea Party was immediately perceived as a significant event by all sides of the evolving confrontation between American colonies and the king's government. Little explanation of intricate details was needed for the public when the newspapers in Boston shared the story with the rest of the world. Within a month, the news of the disturbance had reached London, where the preceding situation was already well known. A letter to the editor of the *London Evening Post*, ominously signed *Brutus*, was published on February 5, 1774. The unknown author understood exactly what was going on and did not hesitate to make some predictions:

> By all appearances we are at the eve of a civil war. Our fellow-subjects in America seem determined not to pay the tax on tea; and by every step taken at home, the government appears resolved to compel them to pay

it. Thus, for the sake of imposing a trifling tax, which would not raise more money than to pay the salaries of the collectors of it, this nation will probably lose, not only all the advantages of an immense trade and commerce with its colonies in America, but a debt of many millions of pounds sterling due from them to our merchants; and what is still worse, our hostile proceedings against them will consequently force them to throw off all obedience to, and connections with their mother country, and, in all probability, compel them to seek for protection and commerce from those very states or kingdoms, which are the natural enemies to, or rivals in trade of Great-Britain. (*London Evening Post* (London, England), February 5, 1774–February 8, 1774; Issue 8092. *17th–18th Century Burney Collection Newspapers*.)

Meanwhile, in the colonies, the retributions for the damage to the cargo in Boston Harbor affected everyone. The British government instituted a number of laws; some were specifically designed to punish Bostonians, while others asserted London's rule over the colonies. However, the most significant impact on the lives of ordinary Americans was perhaps caused by the boycott of all British goods enacted by the First Continental Congress, which went into effect on December 1, 1774. Imports from Great Britain indeed fell sharply in the following year, and this was undoubtedly felt by all colonials.

Whether the lack of British-made goods constituted a real hardship became a matter of public discourse. An example of a mock debate considering the gains and losses that could result from the boycott was printed in the February 1, 1775, issue of *Westminster Magazine or, The Pantheon of Taste* (88). Two American wives, Mrs. Hampden and Mrs. Light, debate the importance of standing up to the imperial government. Mrs. Light (London-born and used to the finest things in life) regrets that her many shopping plans (a new hooped gown, a light carriage, a new suite of lace, etc.) are "all knocked on the head by a ridiculous quarrel about a little tea, the prohibition of which is also another grievance." Her patriotically inclined friend, on the other hand, insists that "the welfare of our country" is more important, and she shockingly claims that she would rather go out without any clothes on than "submit to the unjust taxation which the M[in-istr]y would so despotically impose upon us." As far as tea, Mrs. Hampden vows that she will give it up for good, even if it is "infinitely more pleasant, rather than encourage an importation prejudicial to my country."

It was perhaps such sensibilities that linked the tea tax with despotism more strongly than the actual policies of the British government. The herbal drink was now often referred to as "detestable tea," and the actual duty required by the British government came to be known as "burdensome," "obnoxious," and "hateful." It is true there has been no enthusiastic acceptance of any tax imposed on any nation at any given point in history, but it is easy for an uninformed observer to assume that a tax on tea instituted in 1773 hit the American population quite hard.

During the first decades after the Revolutionary War, the events in Boston Harbor were known by a neutral term: "the destruction of the tea." Although the *Boston Gazette*, in its editorial story, noted that witnesses were "almost universally congratulating each other on this happy event" (*Boston Gazette*, December 20, 1773), the brute force and unexpectedness of the affair must have made some colonials uncomfortable. It took over fifty years for this momentous event to become known by the name now familiar to any student of history. The first known use of this expression in print comes from the period 1825 to 1826. News outlets of the early eighteenth century operated much in the same way as they do today. Once the fiftieth anniversary of the American Revolution was on the calendar, the interest toward the matter began to rise. As usual, there is nothing better to promote readership than a good local connection. *National Crisis and Cincinnati Emporium*, a newspaper in Ohio, had just the right story to publish. One of the participants in the destruction of the tea in Boston ended up settling in Cincinnati. The timing was right enough for numerous newspapers and journals around the country to republish the short story, which in its "syndicated" version appeared as follows:

> One of the party of "about forty unknown people dressed like Indians," who boarded the ship *Eleanor*, in Boston, in 1773, and threw overboard 114 chests of tea, now lives in Cincinnati, Ohio. He is, says the *Crisis*, a temperate, hardy old veteran, supports his family by the sweat of his brow, and often boasts of the "Boston tea party." (*Providence Patriot*, February 4, 1826)

It may seem odd that only one ship out of the three is mentioned, but this can be explained by the fact that the veteran only gave an account of his own deeds. The words "Boston tea party" are presented as a direct quote from the unnamed old man. Was he really an inventor of this apt phrase? This is not an impossible conjecture, considering that he may have been cut off from other survivors of the event. It is equally not difficult to imagine a newspaper reporter putting words into the mouth of the person being interviewed. A lengthy version of Joshua Wyeth's story (such was indeed the name of the veteran) finds no mention of the phrase.

Apart from a very long introduction (which erroneously insisted that the ships in Boston Harbor were British), the account was published nearly verbatim.

Wyeth's eyewitness account, being recorded so many years after the event, is accurate apart from some details. It is striking, however, to see how his memory amalgamated events from before and after the destruction of the tea, painting a very vivid picture of the British despotism:

> We were met together one evening, talking over the tyranny of the British government, such as the heavy duties, shutting up the port of Boston, the murdering of Mr. Gray's family, sending people to England for trial and sundry other acts of oppression. Our indignation was increased by having heard of the arrival of the tea-ships at this time. We agreed, that if the tea was landed, the people could not stand the temptation and would certainly buy it. We came to a sudden determination, to make sure work of it, by throwing it all overboard. We first talked of firing the ships, but we feared the fire would communicate to the town. We then proposed sinking them, but we dropped this project, through fear that we should alarm the town, before we could get through with it. We had observed, that very few persons remained on board the three ships, and we finally concluded, that we could take possession of them, and discharge the tea into the harbor, without danger or opposition. (Drake 1884, 71)

By "the shutting up the port of Boston," Wyeth probably refers to the Boston Port Act of 1774—one of the Intolerable Acts—a legal and administrative measure taken by the British government *after* the Boston Tea Party. "Sending people to England for trial" seems to recall another punitive law that allowed the royal governor to take a court trial to Great Britain or elsewhere within the empire, if there was a possibility that the trial was not going to be fair by the government's standards. Properly called the Administration of Justice Act, this law was also passed in 1774. It is not immediately clear what Joshua Wyeth means by "the murdering of Mr. Gray's family," but this phrase (perhaps misconstrued by the interviewer) most likely refers to Samuel Gray, the first victim of the Boston massacre, who was shot by a British private after famously yelling, "God damn you, don't fire!" on March 5, 1770.

One should also assume that the "heavy duties" that Wyeth and his friends discussed that evening are a collective notion for various taxation measures implemented by the British government. The tea ships, it seems, simply tipped the scales. It is worth noting, however, that this broad picture of British oppression (in part through heavy taxation) was even less nuanced in the eyes of Americans who grew up during the republic. Finding out that more drastic measures were considered must have also helped establish an understanding of how serious the matters became over the tax on tea in 1773.

The expression "Boston Tea Party" was quickly picked up by newsmakers and writers. It was clever enough and even added pleasant connotations to the events in Boston Harbor, in contrast to the "destruction of the tea." Just a few years after the story about the Ohio veteran, this obituary circulated in American newspapers:

> In Warren, R.I. Mr. Nicholas Cambell in the 97th year of his age. Mr. C. was born on the island of Malta, but has been a citizen of Warren, for the last 54 years. He came to the country previous to the American Revolution, and was one of the ever memorable Boston Tea Party, who committed one of the first acts of resistance to the British oppression. (Dover Gazette & Strafford Advertiser, August 11, 1829)

In 1834, a full-length memoir was published that carried the newly coined expression in its title: *A Retrospect of the Boston Tea-Party, with a Memoir of George R. T. Hewes* (1834). This book received nationwide press, and the term was now firmly fixed.

By choosing one term over another, the American colonies officially got rid of any loyalist sympathies. As if to make the sides of the conflict more clearly defined, many started to repeat the mistake made by the publisher of Joshua Wyeth's story. The three vessels that entered Boston Harbor carrying cargo tea are to this day perceived by some as British or English. This error persists even in publications, especially children's books. All three vessels were, in fact, owned by Americans. One might argue that to an eighteenth-century observer, Americans were British subjects, and so their ships were by extension also British. This may be true in theory, but contemporary documents and news dispatches often distinctly refer to Anglo-American, North American, or just American ships. When the Sons of Liberty perpetrated their daring raid, it did not happen on British-owned vessels. In their own eyes, those were American ships.

The Boston Tea Party was a spectacular event in its own right, regardless of the historic significance. It was inevitable that artists and political cartoonists would add their own vision to the story. The very first pictorial responses to the destruction of the tea were faithful to the eyewitness accounts in one important aspect. They showed the "Indians" dumping loose tea into the water out of wooden chests. This indeed made sense as a

THE BOSTON TEA PARTY PARTICIPANTS

sure way to render the "detestable herb" unusable. Loose tea is not an easy subject to draw and engrave.

As memories of the event began to fade, artists discovered that a more dramatic picture could be achieved by showing the Sons of Liberty throwing entire chests into the ocean. Cubes have always been a classic subject of drawing. The shape and size of wooden boxes could be easily represented through simple geometric projection and shading. Multiple chests floating in the water, far and wide, could also be added, giving a dramatic pictorial account of the devastation. Already at the time of the fiftieth anniversary of the American Revolution, engravings with simplified and more dramatic imagery could be seen in print. In 1846, one such illustration was produced by Sarony & Major, a well-known lithographic shop in New York. It has been copied and used for inspiration many times since then. Modern illustrators are similarly not often encouraged to make their visuals of the Boston Tea Party true to the eyewitness accounts.

This may seem like a very minor point, but the efforts of the event's participators do not receive full credit when we imagine them simply hurling some boxes overboard instead of opening the chests with hatchets (making use of the props that the "Indians" brought along). And yet this is exactly what is done during some reenactments of the Boston Tea Party; boxes are thrown into the water only to be dragged out for subsequent reuse in the same activity. If the crates containing the tea could be so easily salvaged, the entire enterprise would not have achieved its goal. As a matter of fact, Bostonians were resolved in making sure that the tea perished completely, as George R. T. Hewes recalled,

> The next morning, after we had cleared the ships of the tea, it was discovered that very considerable quantities of it was floating upon the surface of the water; and to prevent the possibility of any of its being saved for use, a number of small boats were manned by sailors and citizens, who rowed them into those parts of the harbour wherever the tea was visible, and by beating it with oars and paddles, so thoroughly drenched it, as to render its entire destruction inevitable. (Hawkes 1834, 4)

The fact that the crates containing tea were split open during the raid is in agreement with accounts that describe incidents of looting by either bystanders or participants of the event. George R. T. Hewes relates,

> Another attempt was made to save a little tea from the ruins of the cargo, by a tall aged man, who wore a large cocked hat and white wig, which was fashionable at the time. He had slightly slipped a little into his pocket,

but being detected, they seized him, together with the tea, of which they had emptied his pockets, into the water. In consideration of his advanced age, he was permitted to escape, with now and then a slight kick. (Hawkes 1834, 4)

The rough treatment of those who sought to gain a little during this essentially lawless activity may be a reason why this portion of the episode is sometimes omitted when telling the story. If kicking an old man around constituted clemency on the part of the participants, the event was less likely to be seen strictly peaceful.

The Boston Tea Party is considered to be one of the most significant unifying events leading directly to the American Revolution. However, throughout the nineteenth century, there were many references to the burning of the tea in Boston. Consider this passing reference made by an Ohio politician in 1839:

A glance at revolutionary history will show that the rubicon was passed according to tory prediction when the tea was burned in Boston; and again, when the battle was fought at Lexington, the cost was fairly calculated by Genl's. Washington and Gates at Saratoga. (*The Ohio Statesman*, September 18, 1839)

This odd notion that burning was the primary mode of destroying the tea in Boston goes back as far as 1811. The context for this reference was the burning of a French privateer ship in Norfolk. The author of an editorial for the *Raleigh Register*, while responding to the article published in the Richmond newspaper *Inquirer*, sensed that parallels were being drawn between this event and the destruction of the tea in Boston:

What have we here? The very language of an incendiary.—Far be it from me (says he) to "discourage or counteract the spirit" displayed in Norfolk. No; I admire it—it is a "manly spirit which has shewn itself in Norfolk"—it is the deed of "citizens flushed by a *revolutionary* spirit"—It is worthy of the men who burnt the tea at Boston—May it spread in every part of the Union!—And may this zeal of defence of the rights and honor of the nation afford an example which may be followed in N. York and Boston!

Are we awake? Is this dark and assassin-like achievement to be compared to the destruction of the tea at Boston? Our revolutionary spirit degenerated into the dark and sneaking spirit of an incendiary?—Forbid it, Heaven! ("The Incendiary!! From the Richmond 'Enquirer.'" *Raleigh Register, and North-Carolina Weekly Advertiser*, May 10, 1811)

Such references (of which more can be found) are very puzzling. Are we dealing with a myth that narrowly escaped spreading more and entering the public consciousness? It would be unproductive to try to understand what prompted individual authors to issue such a strange statement about the Boston Tea Party. However, one general observation can help clear things up. When the official name of this historic episode was universally changed to the "Boston Tea Party" rather than the "Destruction of the Tea," the emphasis was shifted to one single moment in a group of events (some of which took place far from Boston). The fact is that there was indeed a burning of the tea in Boston. It happened soon after the events in the harbor on December 16, 1773. John Rowe, a Boston merchant (and incidentally the owner of one of the raided ships), recorded this in his journal on December 31:

> The People of Charlestown collected what Tea they could find in The Town & burnt it in the View of a thousand Spectators. There was found in the House of One Withington of Dorchester about half a Chest of Tea—the People gathered together & took the Tea, Brought it into the Common of Boston & Burnt it this night about eleven o Clock. This is supposed to be part of the Tea that was taken out of the Ships & floated over to Dorchester. (Rowe and Pierce 1903, 259)

For Rowe, it seems that the symbolic burning of the tea in Boston's neighborhoods was a no less spectacular event than the effort to relieve three ships of their cargo. This festive bonfire (from Thomas Newell's diary, we also know that punch and wine were aplenty at this event), perhaps welcoming a new era, also did not constitute a daring criminal act. The fuel for the blaze was primarily furnished by a communal pantry cleaning, with the addition of some flotsam and jetsam in the form of utterly ruined merchandise of the East India Company.

Along the American East Coast, ships carrying tea from Britain during that period of time were either turned back or their cargo was dumped in the water or burned. A year later, in Annapolis, the brig *Peggy Stewart*, loaded with tea, was set aflame by its owners, who were severely threatened by the townsfolk. These other episodes have become largely forgotten on the national level, but the Boston Tea Party became a single representative event for the early resistance to the British governance over the colonies in North America. The episode itself was simplified, cleverly rebranded and stripped of any complications and ethically uncomfortable elements.

What Really Happened

In the 1760s, the British government decided on a series of measures designed to mitigate the heavy debt that the country had incurred during the Seven Years' War. This military conflict extended to the American continent, where it was known as the French and Indian War. Many of the costs incurred by the British troops were directly linked to their operations in North America. Unsurprisingly, the Sugar Act, put into effect in 1764, was Parliament's first attempt to tax the American colonies for the purposes of raising the empire's revenue. This act was meant to replace the Molasses Act, due to expire in 1763, which had been largely regulatory and not strictly enforced.

The importation of sugar and molasses was necessary for the making of rum, a very important industry in the colonies, and the perception of the new law in the colonies was that it negatively affected their postwar economies. Although the Sugar Act was technically short-lived (replaced by the Revenue Act in 1766), it introduced the concept of taxing the colonies when it was deemed necessary. In 1765, Parliament passed the Stamp Act, which appeared even more oppressive, as it required that all paper used for official documents, newspapers, and many other needs be marked with an embossed revenue stamp. Aside from the resulting mere inconvenience, this issue raised questions about the constitutional status of charging citizens with a tax that was not agreed to by their legislative representatives.

Despite being considered subjects to the British crown, colonial Americans did not elect members of the British Parliament. Therefore, they believed the Stamp Act violated their rights. The problem was compounded by the fact that the act targeted the industry responsible for freedom of speech and the dissemination of information. Many English-speaking colonies in North America witnessed open street protests, forging the organizational network later known as the Sons of Liberty. Parliament had to abruptly repeal the tax, but at the same time, it did not neglect to issue the so-called Declaratory Act, asserting "full power and authority to make laws and statutes of sufficient force and validity to bind the colonies and people of America, subjects of the crown of Great Britain, in all cases whatsoever" (Force 1837, 396).

After the failure of the Stamp Act to produce significant revenue, the strategy of the British government had to be adjusted. In 1767–1768, Parliament issued a series of laws proposed by Charles Townshend, the chancellor of the Exchequer. The new plan was to avoid oppressing the colonies by only charging them indirect taxes, such as duties on products that were not produced in North America and therefore had to be imported from Britain. The Townshend laws were a complex mechanism that encompassed measures to keep down the cost of importation, enforce the collection of duties, and minimize losses caused by smuggled merchandize. Tea, a very important commodity, was a unique product that did not originate in Great Britain but had to be imported there before being taken overseas. For "British" tea to compete with its smuggled Dutch counterpart, it had to be affordable. As a result, the duty on tea had to remain reasonable (the Revenue Act of 1767 set it at three pence per pound).

This carefully devised scheme did not produce the desired result. Before long, American colonists organized boycotts of certain British goods. In 1770, the Townshend Acts were partially repealed. However, the duty on tea was left intact. To some extent, this gesture was symbolic, as Parliament ostensibly maintained its position on being able to tax Americans "in all cases whatsoever."

It has been a long-standing policy that the British East India Company did not directly deliver tea to North America. Every ounce of tea legally procured in the East had to be brought to the London Tea Auction (which essentially survived until 1998), where it was acquired by entrepreneurs who then delivered it to American customers. By 1773, continuous boycotts and large-scale smuggling operations had virtually ended the British company's ability to sell tea to North American markets. Warehouses were overfilled with fine teas (considered by many superior in quality to the typical contraband product traceable to the Dutch East India Company). The tea was deteriorating, and the British East India Company that had fronted money to collect and transport it to London was on the verge of bankruptcy.

The belief that the company was "too large to fail" prompted Parliament to pass the Tea Act. This piece of legislation allowed the East India Company to sell its product directly to North America, bypassing the auctions, and without paying any duty on the way out of British ports. Such protectionist measures had a very particular goal in mind. By not paying any duties, the British East India Company could theoretically compete on the American market with the smuggled Dutch tea that was abundant in the colonies (there was hardly a tea shortage during this time). Only one tax remained included in the price structure of British tea sold in North America: the remnant of the Townshend Acts. The company would have preferred this rather insignificant tax to be removed, but Parliament was hesitant to do so because the tea duty was a token of Great Britain's declared privilege to tax the colonies.

During the summer of 1773, the British East India Company carried out a search for suitable vessels and consignees (a technical term for the recipients of transported goods) that could be trusted with the potentially troublesome cargo. In the fall of that year, the company was able to send the first ships loaded with tea to several key trading ports in North America. Four of those vessels were Boston-bound, and New York, Philadelphia, and Charleston, North Carolina, were to each receive one shipment. By that time, the news of the government's scheme to bring financial relief to the East India Company had already reached the colonies, and public opinion had already been formed. It is important to note that Americans did not object to the newly set prices on tea from Britain. If anything, the product became cheaper! The outrage was directed toward the old Townshend tax that, however insignificant, was implicitly present in the new low rate.

Contrary to what most people assume today, the tea ships heading toward Boston were not strangers to American ports. They did not belong to the British East India Company but were owned by American merchant families. The *Dartmouth* and the *Beaver* were the property of the Rotch family, whose operations were based on the island of Nantucket. The *Eleanor* was owned by the Boston merchant John Rowe. The lesser-known *William*, a tea-laden brig that shipwrecked off Provincetown before reaching Boston, was owned by the Clarke family.

Even before the "detestable herb" was in Boston Harbor, the situation had been heating up for some time. The advance knowledge about the tea's approach was used to consolidate the opposition and intimidate the consignees, whose names became public (a tactic that eventually proved effective in other North American ports). The resentment toward the merchants who agreed to import the tea started as anonymous letters and publications in the local press, described by Richard Clarke as "paper skirmishes" (Drake 1884, 282). In early November, the situation took a more official turn, as there was a demand for the consignees to publicly resign their commissions. This was done through letters, delivered in the middle of the night, that ended with a tagline popular during that tumultuous time: "Fail not at your own peril."

To the consignees' surprise, when they went out in the morning, the town was plastered with advertisements announcing that they would indeed be making a public promise to turn down the shipments and send the tea back to England. The notices invited Bostonians to witness this resignation, making it sound like a done deal. The consignees were expected to show up at Liberty Tree at noon on November 3. On that day, the bells rang for a solid hour, and the town crier called on all to be present for the occasion. However, the merchants failed to appear as summoned. The Sons of Liberty (a secret organization of patriotically minded Americans) immediately formed a committee charged with finding out the gentlemen's determination regarding the matter. It was not hard to locate the consignees, who were at the moment gathered at Richard Clarke's store. When presented with a paper that they were required to sign, the merchants refused to do so, causing much displeasure. Meetings and deliberations went on.

Although an attempt by the British East India Company to bring the tea to American ports had already been anticipated, the certain news about the four ships approaching Boston was brought by Captain Scott, who arrived in the port on November 17. John Rowe, who made a note of this news in his diary, remarked that this measure was "generally disapproved & will remain a great occasion of disagreement between England & America" (Rowe and Pierce 1903, 254). On November 18, the mob attacked the house of Richard Clarke (the *Beaver*'s owner). According to John Rowe, one of his family fired a gun from the inside, but fortunately no one was hurt. All windows in the mansion were broken, but there was "very little other damage" (254). Rowe himself received a threatening letter that was signed *Determined*. This happened on the day after the merchant had celebrated his birthday. John Rowe was so disturbed that he did not go to church that Sunday morning (255).

The arrival of the tea ships was staggered. The *Dartmouth* was the first vessel to come to Boston on November 28. John Rowe's *Eleanor* arrived on December 2. The *Beaver* approached the harbor on December 8, but it was put under official quarantine because of a supposed outbreak of smallpox on board. The *William* never made it to Boston, as she was shipwrecked. However, some of Clarke's tea was being delivered by the other ships.

The purpose of intimidating the merchants whose ships crossed the Atlantic carrying "the worst of plagues, the detestable tea," was obvious. The intent of the Sons of Liberty was that the vessels would simply be sent back without paying any duties. This would result in a considerable financial loss to the shipowners and the consignees because the vessels would have made a meaningless trip from England to Boston and back. In fact, according to John Rowe, he had already prepared the return cargo for Captain Bruce to take on board the *Eleanor* once the tea was offloaded. Nevertheless, Rowe informed the Sons of Liberty that he was sorry that his ship had tea on board; the matter caused him "much uneasiness" (256).

Rowe was apparently able to distance himself from the captain and his representatives in England, who acted autonomously, deciding which cargo to bring back from London. According to his diary, Rowe was even chosen "a committee man," against his will, as he did not dare say a word. However, a contemporary eyewitness account describes Rowe's demeanor at this meeting on November 30 as being more lively:

> Mr. Rowe being present was informed of what passed and expressed his Sorrow that any Vessel of his should be concerned in bringing any of that detestable and obnoxious Commodity, (Tea) and seeing that the Audience were pleased with what he had said, he proceeded and among other Things he asked, "Whether a little Salt Water would not do it good, or whether Salt Water would not make as good Tea as fresh." And when he had done speaking and at several other Expressions in his Speech, the people testified their Applause by Shouting Clapping etc. and some in the Circle round me boasted (but privately) that now they had brought a good Tory to their side—that Mr. Rowe had now become a good Man and they should soon make all the Rest of the Tories turn to their Side as Mr. Rowe had done. (Upton 1965, 294–295)

It is no wonder that Rowe was voted to be on the committee! As the owner of one the tea ships, he openly suggested the solution that was going to be implemented in two weeks' time. The merchant's words made such an impression that another eyewitness, writing about the events decades later, believed that Rowe's idea about mixing tea with saltwater was announced on December 16, the day of the raid. However, according to Rowe's diary, he was sick that day and not present at the meeting. Until the end of the revolution, he avoided taking sides, protecting his business from any unfortunate eventuality.

Francis Rotch, who represented the other two ships that made it to Boston Harbor, was under more pressure because the *Dartmouth* came to the port before the other ships. This meant that her grace period allowing a vessel to remain in the harbor without unloading and paying custom duties would have been the first to expire. Undeclared cargo could have been lawfully seized by the British officials, and the confiscated tea would have easily found its way to the shops of unscrupulous merchants harboring Tory sympathies. If the seized tea were to be sold at an auction (which would have likely been done), the Crown would have effectually collected the much-hated tax. The Sons of Liberty could not bear to see such an outcome. The atmosphere became so charged with potential violence that the consignees had to flee to the heavily fortified Castle William that guarded the entrance into the harbor.

It is necessary to understand that the opposition to the actions of the British ministry was not merely a strongly voiced public opinion. This was a well-organized movement democratically expressed in public meetings. A resolution passed by the mass meeting at Faneuil Hall on November 29, immediately following the *Dartmouth*'s arrival, firmly stated that "they would, to the utmost of their power, prevent the landing of the tea" ("Announcement of the Boston Tea Party, December 20, 1773"). Vigilante Bostonians were assigned to keep a close watch on the wharf. As time went on, the other two ships arrived in the harbor, more meetings were held, and the same demands were presented to the captains.

On December 16, 1773, all the elements of the crisis were in place, and the conflict begged for a resolution. The unprecedented assembly of Bostonians gathered at the Old South Meeting House wanted the tea ships to sail away. The consignees were confined to the general safety of Castle William. The cargo of the three vessels remained in a legal limbo: it had already been registered by customs (which made its reimportation to England questionable), but it could not be unloaded for fear of violence. The dues owed for the cargo on board the *Dartmouth* were supposed to be paid the next day. The owners of the ships were uneasy. John Rowe chose to stay home sick. Francis Rotch, who came to the meeting, understood very well that sending two ships—owned by his family—with the tea back to England meant financial ruin for him. However, under the increasing pressure from the Sons of Liberty, Rotch had to follow instructions to secure safe passage for his ships out of Boston Harbor. The matter seemingly lay in the hands of Governor Hutchinson, who at that moment was in his residence in Milton.

The assembly was willing to wait for Rotch to travel there for an audience with the governor, although the outcome was already clear. Apart from being a king's official whose job required him to see through the successful import of the tea by the East India Company, Hutchinson had a personal motivation in not allowing the tea to leave Boston. His own two sons were among the consignees. This conflict of interest amounted to no conflict at all; Hutchinson quickly dismissed Rotch's plea.

Rotch returned to Boston just before dark. An eyewitness account describes the immediate proceedings at the Old South Meeting House:

> He informed the People that he had applied for a Pass as directed, and that his Excellency made a Reply to this Effect viz "That he was always

disposed to oblige any Person that applied to him for a Pass when there was just Reason for one, but he could not think it his Duty in this Case and therefore should not." On which Mr. Adams said that he could think of nothing further to be done—that they had now done all they could for the Salvation of their Country and that he should go Home, set down and make himself as easy as he could. The People then voted Mr. Rotch's Conduct satisfactory to them. (Upton 1965, 297)

This remark made by Samuel Adams in response to Rotch's report (ending with advice to go home and relax) has been since interpreted as a prearranged signal by which the Sons of Liberty knew that the long-prepared plan was to be put into action. There is no factual evidence to support this claim. The meeting was not immediately dismissed, although some people did indeed start to leave. The concluding speech of the evening was by Dr. Young, who spoke about "ill effects" of tea, praising his countrymen for abstaining from this vicious drink. This address took ten to fifteen minutes and may have been a ruse to distract the authorities from what was about to happen.

Since the grace period for the *Dartmouth* was about to expire, several thousands of Bostonians headed to Griffin Wharf, where the ship was tied up. Even those unaware of the plot knew that the deadline was not going to pass uneventfully. In the meantime, the participants of the raid received their orders and proceeded to relieve the tea ships of their cargo. Although the *Eleanor* and the *Beaver* still had some time left before their cargo could be confiscated, the two ships were included in the attack.

The manner in which the raid was carried out did not leave room for speculations about its spontaneity. It was far more important to conceal the identities of those who participated in this extremely well prepared and organized act:

> It was now evening, and I immediately dressed myself in the costume of an Indian, equipped with a small hatchet, which I and my associates denominated the tomahawk, with which, and a club, after having painted my face and hands with coal dust in the shop of a blacksmith, I repaired to Griffin's wharf, where the ships lay that contained the tea. When I first appeared in the street after being thus disguised, I fell in with many who were dressed, equipped and painted as I was, and who fell in with me and marched in order to the place of our destination. (Hawkes 1834, 38)

Eyewitnesses differ from each other regarding the time that it took to empty the contents of tea chests found on board the three ships, but it likely took many hours to open up 342 cases and pour out their contents. However, the complete destruction of the tea in the harbor took several days. As already noted, some remnants of the "baneful tea" stayed on top of the water and had to be submerged by beating them down with oars. Certain quantities floated to shore and had to be destroyed later.

Despite all these efforts, it would be incorrect to say that all of the tea sent by the East India Company to Boston was destroyed during the Tea Party event. The cargo of the brig *William*, which shipwrecked on Cape Cod, was landed on American soil by the Clarke family—the ship's owners and consignees. The tea was delivered to Castle William for safekeeping. When the Sons of Liberty got their hands on this shipment, half of it was already gone. By the middle of March 1774, the last remnants of this tea had been hunted down and destroyed, but not before small amounts of it were sold and consumed, as described in this newspaper article:

Last Portion of the Tea from the *William Destroyed* in Connecticut

Lyme, March 17, 1774,

Yesterday, one William Lamson, of Martha's Vineyard, came to this town with a bag of tea (about 100 wt.), on horseback, which he was peddling about the country. It appeared that he was about business which he supposed would render him obnoxious to the people, which gave reason to suspect that he had some of the detestable tea lately landed at Cape Cod; and, upon examination, it appeared to the satisfaction of all present to be a part of that very tea (though he declared that he purchased it of two gentlemen in Newport; one of them 'tis said is a custom house officer, and the other Captain of the fort). Whereupon, a number of the Sons of Liberty assembled in the evening, kindled a fire, and committed its contents to the flames, where it was all consumed and the ashes buried on the spot, in testimony of their utter abhorrence of all tea subject to a duty for the purpose of raising a revenue in America—a laudable example for our brethren in Connecticut. —Conn. Journal March 25, 1774. (Barber 1836, 338)

The utmost determination of the Sons of Liberty in Boston certainly deserves praise, but the Boston Tea Party was also representative of events that went on in other coastal cities that were scheduled to receive tea shipments in late 1773. Notably, different scenarios played out in New York, Philadelphia, and Charleston. In Philadelphia, the captain of the *Polly* was intimidated into sailing back to England without attempting to land his cargo. In New York, the delayed ship arrived so late that the consignees did not want anything to do with the tea, and the cargo was once again sent away. The story of the tea shipped to Charleston was the most interesting.

The *London* came to the port on December 1, 1773, and caused an uproar similar to what was seen in Boston at the same time. Under pressure from the population, the consignees quickly gave up, but the captain of the ship refused to take the cargo back, citing the lack of official authorization. On December 22, fearing violence, the city decided to move the tea to the basement of the Exchange. This was not the end of troubles for the *London*, however; she was seized in New York when it was discovered that some tea remained hidden on board, and the captain was charged with smuggling, narrowly escaping death. A year later, when another ship arrived from England with a shipment of tea, the citizens of Charleston acted more boldly, dumping it in the water. As for the tea in the cellars of the Charleston Exchange, it was reputedly sold in 1776 to fund the Revolutionary War, although some earlier accounts claim that the *London*'s cargo became spoiled.

The event that later became known as the Boston Tea Party was a critical moment in the "destruction of the tea" sent over to the American colonies by the British East India Company. All four of the concerned ships were owned by local entrepreneurs. The consignees of the tea were also Americans (albeit with pro-British sympathies and connections). The destruction of the tea affected these American businesses no less than it affected the East India Company, but they were the ones who had to suffer threats of violence. The financial interests of the British government were hardly hurt because the enterprise was not necessarily meant to bring much revenue.

The rhetoric used by the Sons of Liberty over this trifle tax may seem excessive and even melodramatic (it required a very agitated state of public mind to paint the shipping of a few hundred cases of tea as an act of tyranny foreboding the potential enslavement of all free citizens). However, the symbolic significance of the Boston Tea Party was tremendous. The event set the tone by which Americans responded to all future measures of the British government in its futile attempt to retain the colonies within the realm. The Intolerable Acts, instituted to punish Boston, increased the consolidation of American patriots in the years directly going into the American War of Independence.

Further Reading

Allison, Robert J. 2015. *The American Revolution: A Very Short Introduction.* New York: Oxford University Press.

"The American Wives: A Dialogue." *Westminster Magazine: Or, the Pantheon of Taste.* February 1775. London: Richardson & Urquhart.

"Announcement of the Boston Tea Party, December 20, 1773—American Memory Timeline—Classroom Presentation: Teacher Resources." Library of Congress. Accessed May 5, 2020. http://www.loc.gov/teachers/classroommaterials/presentationsandactivities/presentations/timeline/amrev/rebelln/tea.html.

Barber, John. 1836. *Connecticut Historical Collections*. New Haven, CT: John W. Barber; Hartford, CT: A. Willard.

Beck, Derek W. 2015. *Igniting the American Revolution: 1773–1775*. Naperville, IL: Sourcebooks.

Boston Gazette, December 20, 1773, quoted in "Announcement of the Boston Tea Party, December 20, 1773: American Memory Timeline—Classroom Presentation: Teacher Resources." Library of Congress. Accessed May 5, 2020. http://www.loc.gov/teachers/classroommaterials/presentationsandactivities/presentations/timeline/amrev/rebelln/tea.html.

Carp, Benjamin L. 2010. *Defiance of the Patriots: The Boston Tea Party & the Making of America*. New Haven, CT: Yale University Press.

Cummins, Joseph. 2012. *Ten Tea Parties: Patriotic Protests That History Forgot*. Philadelphia, PA: Quirk Books.

"Died." Dover Gazette & Strafford Advertiser, August 11, 1829. Nineteenth Century U.S. Newspapers. Accessed May 5, 2020. https://link-gale-com.ezproxy.bpl.org/apps/doc/GT3012529424/NCNP?u=mlin_b_bpublic&sid=NCNP&xid=a5df1b82.

Drake, Francis Samuel. 1884. *Tea Leaves: Being a Collection of Letters and Documents*. Boston, MA: A. O. Crane.

Ellis, Markman, Richard Coulton, and Matthew Mauger. 2015. *Empire of Tea: The Asian Leaf That Conquered the World*. London: Reaktion Books.

Findling, John E., and Frank W. Thackeray, eds. 1998. *Events That Changed America in the Eighteenth Century*. The Greenwood Press "Events That Changed America" Series. Westport, CT: Greenwood Press.

Force, Peter. 1837. *American Archives: Fourth Series Containing a Documentary History of the English Colonies in North America*. Washington, DC: M. St. Clair Clarke and Peter Force.

From the Richmond "Enquirer." "The Incendiary!!" *Raleigh Register*, May 10, 1811. Nineteenth Century U.S. Newspapers. Accessed May 5, 2020. https://link-gale-com.ezproxy.bpl.org/apps/doc/GT3012656883/NCNP?u=mlin_b_bpublic&sid=NCNP&xid=fb6e7917.

Hawkes, James. 1834. *A Retrospect of the Boston Tea-Party: With a Memoir of George R. T. Hewes, a Survivor of the Little Band of Patriots Who Drowned the Tea in Boston Harbour in 1773*. New York: S. S. Bliss.

Knollenberg, Bernhard. 2003. *Growth of the American Revolution, 1766–1775*. Indianapolis, IN: Liberty Fund.

McDowell, Bart. 1972. *The Revolutionary War: America's Fight for Freedom*. 3rd ed. Print. Washington, DC: National Geographic Society.

A Member of the Late Democratic Meeting. "The Following Was Refused a Place in the Gazette, as an Evidence of Federal Attorney Liberality." *Ohio Statesman* (Columbus, OH) September 18, 1839: n.p. Nineteenth Century U.S. Newspapers. Accessed May 5, 2020. http://find.gale.com.ezproxy.bpl.org/dvnw/infomark.do?&source=gale&prodId=DVNW&userGroupName=mlin_b_bpublic&tabID=T003&docPage=article&docId=GT3010791913&type=multipage&contentSet=LTO&version=1.0.

"Multiple News Items." *Providence Patriot, Columbian Phenix* (Providence, Rhode Island) (February 4, 1826): n.p. *Nineteenth Century U.S. Newspapers*. Accessed May 5, 2020. http://find.gale.com.ezproxy.bpl.org/dvnw/infomark.do?&source=gale&prodId=DVNW&userGroupName=mlin_b_bpublic&tabID=T003&docPage=article&docId=GT3012263528&type=multipage&contentSet=LTO&version=1.0.

"News." *London Evening Post*, February 5–February 8, 1774. *Seventeenth and Eighteenth Century Burney Newspapers Collection*. Accessed May 5, 2020. https://link-gale-com.ezproxy.bpl.org/apps/doc/Z2000687848/BBCN?u=mlin_b_bpublic&sid=BBCN&xid=86dd78a4.

Puls, Mark. 2006. *Samuel Adams: Father of the American Revolution*. 1st ed. New York: Palgrave Macmillan.

Rowe, John, Edward Lillie Pierce, and Edward Lillie. 1903. *Letters and Diary of John Rowe: Boston Merchant, 1759–1762, 1764–1779*. Boston, MA: W. D. Clarke Company.

Unger, Harlow G. 2011. *American Tempest: How the Boston Tea Party Sparked a Revolution*. 1st Da Capo Press ed. Cambridge, MA: Da Capo Press.

Upton, L. F. S. 1965. "Proceedings of Ye Body Respecting the Tea." *The William and Mary Quarterly* 22, no. 2 (April): 287–300.

Volo, James M. 2012. *The Boston Tea Party: The Foundations of Revolution*. Santa Barbara, CA: ABC-CLIO.

Young, Alfred Fabian. 1999. *The Shoemaker and the Tea Party: Memory and the American Revolution*. Boston, MA: Beacon Press.

8

The American Revolution Was Fought by United Patriots against an Evil Oppressor

What People Think Happened

Perhaps no one has done a better job at clearly distilling the great myths of the American Revolution than the noted historian and scholar Dr. Carol Berkin, in three sentences, when she states,

> For most Americans, young and old, the history of the American Revolution can be summed up something like this: In 1776, all the colonists rose up in unison to rebel against a tyrannical king and the horrible burden of unfair taxes the British had imposed upon them for over a hundred years. During the long war that followed, citizen soldiers shivered in the cold, shared the hardships together, admired George Washington, and won the war single-handedly against the most powerful army in the world. Then they created a democracy and everyone lived happily ever after. (Berkin 2009)

Berkin packed a good number of misconceptions into this succinct passage, and some of them would require a dedicated treatment. However, the most important myth about the American Revolution lies in the perception of this great event's moral nature, easily reducible to the struggle between good and evil.

The relatively short span of American history (when compared to histories of most other nations) is rich with events that are not easy to digest. Many old wounds in this country's past are still healing.

People like to believe that there was a time when the entire population of the country's founding colonies were predominantly of English descent and showed a remarkable union in thought and action. These colonists fought bravely against their uniformly tyrannical common enemy, the British Empire, led by an equally repressive royal tyrant, King George III. This then becomes a two-sided myth that first implies that British colonists were fighting against a hostile mother country committed to depriving the colonies of their rights.

In the minds of most Americans, this constitutional monarchy, so remote and disconnected from the lives of its colonial subjects, overstepped the boundaries of what was to be tolerated from a government they did not elect.

Most Americans are taught that, by the 1760s, the Crown and Parliament had treated the American colonies so unfairly that a popular uprising was almost inevitable. In actuality, the rebellion took so long to happen only because Americans had enjoyed the salutary neglect of the mother country for so long. Until the last moment, the colonists cherished the hope that sanity would prevail in the heads of their British overlords, who would then turn to a more conciliatory and just treatment of all their subjects, no matter where they lived. The leaders of the British ministry, however, continued to oppress instead of cooperate. Therefore, it is no surprise that the population of American colonies was so uniformly opposed to the king's rule.

As always, there were a few individuals who, in their obstinacy, ignorance, and simplemindedness, contradicted the unanimous voice of the people. Their presence was hardly noticeable. Generally being rather well-to-do, these so-called loyalists stayed in their mansions, sipping tea and waiting for the redcoats to suppress the revolutionary crowds so that they could reap the rewards for remaining obedient. As the situation got serious, these miscreants became more fearful, despite the fact that their patriotic countrymen would never harass them for simply having a different opinion.

During the active military stage of the American Revolution, the patriots fought bravely because they all adhered to a just and common cause. There was certainly no difficulty at all for George Washington to raise his army of American-born soldiers. After a few short campaigns, they drove off the mercenary horde of British infantrymen, and the loyalists fled the country, virtually unnoticed.

How It Became Popular

The two-pronged myth about the abhorrent oppression of the American colonies and the resulting unanimous appeal of the revolutionary cause among the colonists has long been understood as the quintessential struggle between good and evil. The current generation of Americans is hardly familiar with any other interpretation of history. It is commonplace to see Great Britain painted as a repressive mother country that ruthlessly exploited its colonies and overseas subjects, while the American colonial population as a whole is seen as largely supportive of a war for independence, endorsing the idea of separation from the British Empire. In recent times, this view has been encouraged by a variety of sources, including films such as Disney's *Johnny Tremain* and Mel Gibson's *The Patriot* as well as countless popular publications and federally supported interpretive programs, such as those experienced by the public at U.S. National Park Service sites. However, the origin of this good-versus-evil narrative has its early (and very prominent) beginnings during the time when the great events of the American Revolution took place.

The British colonies in the New World were well fairly well equipped with all the means of communication typical for the middle of the eighteenth century. Many cities had more than one newspaper, and contemporary editorial policies demanded that important pieces of information were to be republished by independent periodicals without any copyright scruples. Broadsides came off the press just hours after important events. Magazines allowed for analytical observations on a virtually unrestrained number of subjects.

News traveled fast, but opinions and ideas traveled just as fast. It is notable that when the Stamp Act created a perceived tax on the printed word, American intellectuals saw this as an attack on their freedom of expression; in the years preceding the revolution, this freedom was exercised at its fullest, never lacking in strong words and incendiary images. There was much artistic and literary talent ready to do their best as soon as events in the colonies called for a memorable reaction. Poetry was frequently employed for added emphasis, as was the case during the Boston Massacre crisis of 1770. Consider the effect produced on colonial citizens by these lines published alongside Paul Revere's famous engraving of the massacre:

Unhappy Boston! see thy Sons deplore,
Thy hallow'd walks besmear'd with guiltless Gore:
While faithless PRESTON, and his savage Bands,

> With murd'rous Rancour stretch their bloody Hands;
> Like fierce Barbarians grinning o'er their Prey,
> Approve the Carnage and enjoy the Day.
> (Waller 2009, 134)

The watershed between the forces of good and evil is clearly drawn in this poem. Colonial readers of the time may have been surprised by the mention of the "hallow'd walks" of Boston, a city that had not yet celebrated its 150th birthday at the time of the poem's creation. However, the shedding of innocent blood certainly called for this trope as well as the strongest possible words to describe His Majesty's soldiers, who were likened to ungodly barbarians.

Even when the current affairs did not amount to violence and hostile acts against the colonists, it was customary to raise the profile of events, thus suggesting that they were more important than it might seem. In 1773, the American Whig press played a crucial role in escalating what could have been an insignificant moment in the history of maritime trade. The British tea sent by the East India Company to American consignee merchants was labeled "obnoxious," "baneful," "detestable," and so on. One of these tea consignees, Abraham Lott, admitted there could be "no such thing as selling it, as the people would rather buy so much poison, than the tea with the duty thereon, calculated (they say) to enslave them and their posterity, and therefore are determined not to take what they call the nauseous draft" (Roberts 1899, 117). Needless to say, this New York merchant did not think that a few shipments of tea should have been seen as an act of enslavement (surely the worst thing that one nation can do to another, outside of complete obliteration), but he was powerless against the well-orchestrated rhetoric that was not going to pull any punches.

It may be summed up that the efforts of American patriots were well justified, but, more importantly, their use of propaganda was exceptional. Nevertheless, not all Americans were convinced about the need to actively oppose the mother country by all available means in an effort to gain political rights and possibly claim the status of an independent nation. Later in this chapter, we will discuss how prevalent this dissenting attitude was in colonial America, but for now, the question that needs to be addressed is how it happened that these people have been largely forgotten. Lorenzo Sabine, the author of the first comprehensive biographical study of American loyalists, provides a simple but powerful answer to this question:

> Men who, like the Loyalists, separate themselves from their friends and kindred, who are driven from their homes, who surrender the hopes and expectations of life, and who become outlaws, wanderers, and exiles,—such men, leave few memorials behind them. Their papers are scattered and lost, and their very names pass from human recollection. (Sabine 1847, iii)

It is well known that those of the loyalists who did not wish to conform to the new situation in the colonies had to abandon their properties and escape the country. Many went to England, and large groups of them settled in Nova Scotia and New Brunswick. Their voices indeed ceased to be heard in the land where they had lived. Perhaps, more importantly, everything they used to represent became irrelevant.

This ultimate disconnect is well illustrated in Washington Irving's short story "Rip Van Winkle." The protagonist is a Dutch American villager who, under mysterious circumstances, falls asleep in the Catskill Mountains just before the beginning of the American Revolution. After a slumber that lasted twenty years, Rip finally wakes up and makes his way back to the village. He is unable to recognize anyone. Even the sign at the local tavern is now different (George Washington's image has replaced that of King George III). As it turns out, this unwilling time traveler arrived at a momentous time. His countrymen have just expressed their political sentiments concerning a recent democratic election, prompting them to inquire of the stranger how he voted. These odd questions cause Rip's confusion to boil over, as he exclaims, "I am a poor, quiet man, a native of the place, and a loyal subject of the King, God bless him!" Much commotion follows, and Rip Van Winkle is fortunate in remaining unscathed as a result of his loyalist declaration.

This image of an old man in antique clothing, out of touch with reality, unable to make sense of the modern world, and struggling to attach himself to anything familiar or anyone recognizable in his hometown is the popular perception of loyalists in America after the revolution. The loyalists' problem was not that they had simply picked the wrong side; they were also hopelessly outmoded to the point of not being taken seriously by their fellow countrymen.

In postrevolution America, there was no place for crown sympathizers. The fictional Rip Van Winkle could not have cast his vote in the elections as a loyalist. The only options available to him were Federalist or Democratic-Republican. Indeed, in real life, to be a loyalist automatically meant to be considered a traitor, a spy, or a banished refugee. Following the mass exodus of those American "Tories" who were outwardly unhappy with the results of the revolution, there were many who remained for whom there was now no reason not to be supportive of the patriot cause.

Those who stayed in the colonies were very likely to have vivid memories of the British occupation and oppression. They could now safely reminisce about the narrowly avoided taxation enslavement to which they had seemed almost doomed. The "winners' vision" of the revolution could now be perpetuated without restraint.

After the American War of Independence, there were no incentives to mitigate the effects of the anti-British sentiment that helped mobilize the Americans in their fight against Great Britain. During the years following the conflict, the two nations went through many episodes of open hostility and territorial disputes. These would include the War of 1812, the Oregon Dispute of the 1830s, and the American Civil War.

Only after one hundred years of gradual diplomatic improvements would Britain and the United States finally achieve the status of close allies. Fortunately, the British Empire of the late 1800s was very different in most respects from the Georgian monarchy lampooned in American newspapers during the 1770s, so no adjustment was necessary in the good-versus-evil dichotomy remnant from that period in time. However, many Americans remained sympathetic to democratically expressed aspirations of British territories to gain sovereignty. The Irish American support for Ireland's fight for independence being the prime example of this tendency.

PRIMARY DOCUMENT

WASHINGTON IRVING'S SHORT STORY "RIP VAN WINKLE" (EXCERPT)

The good-versus-evil comparison is evident in the dramatic before-and-after image of the transformed American social landscape reflected in the whimsical prose of Washington Irving (1783–1859) in his classic tale "Rip van Winkle." It recounts the effects of the American Revolution on Rip's rural New York village following his return from a twenty-year slumber in the Catskills. Having slept through the entire revolution, the protagonist Rip van Winkle wanders back to his hometown to discover his old neighbors and good friends gone and his world entirely transformed—the public sentiment now virulently against all things British.

He now hurried forth, and hastened to his old resort, the village inn—but it too was gone. A large rickety wooden building stood in its place, with great gaping windows, some of them broken, and mended with old hats and petticoats, and over the door was painted, "The Union Hotel, by Jonathan Doolittle." Instead of the great tree that used to shelter the quiet little Dutch inn of yore, there now was reared a tall naked pole, with something on the top that looked like a red nightcap, and from it was fluttering a flag, on which was a singular assemblage of stars and stripes—all this was strange and incomprehensible. He recognized on the sign, however, the ruby face of King George, under which he had smoked so many a peaceful pipe, but even this was singularly metamorphosed. The red coat was changed for one of blue and buff, a sword was held in the hand instead of a sceptre, the head was decorated with a cocked hat, and underneath was painted in large characters, "GENERAL WASHINGTON."

There was, as usual, a crowd of folk about the door, but none that Rip recollected. The very character of the people seemed changed. There was a busy, bustling, disputatious tone about it, instead of the accustomed phlegm and drowsy tranquility. He looked in vain for the sage Nicholas Vedder, with his broad face, double chin, and fair long pipe, uttering clouds of tobacco-smoke, instead of idle speeches; or Van Bummel, the schoolmaster, doling forth the contents of an ancient newspaper. In place of these, a lean, bilious-looking fellow, with his pockets full of handbills, was haranguing, vehemently about rights of citizens-elections—members of Congress—liberty—Bunker's hill—heroes of seventy-six-and other words, which were a perfect Babylonish jargon to the bewildered Van Winkle.

The appearance of Rip, with his long, grizzled beard, his rusty fowling-piece, his uncouth dress, and the army of women and children at his heels, soon attracted the attention of the tavern politicians. They crowded round him, eying him from head to foot, with great curiosity. The orator bustled up to him, and, drawing him partly aside, inquired, "on which side he voted?" Rip stared in vacant stupidity. Another short but busy little fellow pulled him by the arm, and rising on tiptoe, inquired in his ear, "whether he was Federal or Democrat." Rip was equally at a loss to comprehend the question; when a knowing, self-important old gentleman, in a sharp cocked hat, made his way through the crowd, putting them to the right and left with his elbows as he passed, and planting himself before Van Winkle, with one arm akimbo, the other resting on his cane, his keen eyes and sharp hat penetrating, as it were, into his very soul, demanded in an austere tone, "What brought him to the election with a gun on his shoulder, and a mob at his heels; and whether he meant to breed a riot in the village?"

"Alas! gentlemen," cried Rip, somewhat dismayed, "I am a poor, quiet man, a native of the place, and a loyal subject of the King, God bless him!"

Here a general shout burst from the bystanders—"a tory! a tory! a spy! a refugee! hustle him! away with him!" It was with great difficulty that the self-important man in the cocked hat restored order; and having assumed a tenfold austerity of brow, demanded again of the unknown culprit, what he came there for, and whom he was seeking. The poor man humbly assured him that he meant no harm, but merely came there in search of some of his neighbors, who used to keep about the tavern.

Source: Irving, Washington. 1893. *Rip Van Winkle and the Legend of Sleepy Hollow.* London and New York: Macmillan and Company.

What Really Happened

The prevailing and popular idea that the English administration of the American colonies was economically repressive and harmful to the Anglo-American population during the 150-plus years prior to the outbreak of the revolution actually stands in sharp contrast to the facts of history. Unlike its Spanish, Portuguese, and French counterparts, England remained largely uninvolved and quite lenient in the administrative activities of her American colonies. Indeed, the colonies enjoyed a surprising amount of freedom in self-government, electing their own provincial assemblies, levying and spending their own taxes, waging their own wars, defending themselves with their own militias, and generally acting in a semiautonomous fashion until the end of the Seven Years' War in 1763. Following the signing of the Treaty of Paris in 1763, the administration of King George III became more assertive in its efforts to influence and control colonial activities—especially in limiting the popular business practice of smuggling—and discovering new ways to generate sources of colonial revenue. Both were deeply resented by the merchants of the semiautonomous colonies.

There remains a question as to why the British government was accustomed to treating the American colonies in a generous and liberal fashion.

This happened because each colony had been commissioned and chartered into existence for private spiritual or economic reasons. These included the sponsorship and economic support of special interest groups such as the Calvinist Puritans of New England, the merchant adventurers of the London Company of Virginia Colony, the dissenting Society of Friends with Sir William Penn in Pennsylvania, the Roman Catholic Calvert Family and the English Catholics in Maryland Colony, and many others.

Each American colony was privately funded and willing to recruit its colonists and transport them without government expense or sponsorship. The major advantage for England was the overseas expansion of the British Empire—that might prove economically profitable to the empire but at someone else's expense. In other words, England was willing to trade political autonomy to English colonists in the hope of building a colonial empire without the usual—as in the case of France and Spain—investment of royal or state funds.

Thus, it was that the process of Anglo-American colonization was made relatively easy and cheap for England with the hope and expectation that the potential profitability of the American colonies would enhance the coffers of the British Empire through maritime trade and the influx of raw materials such as lumber and fish. The maritime trade certainly developed, the raw materials were shipped back to England, and American vessels sailed the Atlantic trade routes carrying and selling cargoes of lumber, salt-codfish, sugar, rum, and molasses—and sometimes slaves. Sadly for England, the economic profits hoped for were never realized, and the American colonies grew to become commercial rivals not supporters of the mother country.

Far from gaining profits for England, the colonial merchants and shipowners of the American colonies managed to earn huge profits for themselves in avoiding every attempt—such as the four Navigation Acts, the Molasses Act of 1733, and the Sugar Act of 1764—by England to garner an American shilling. In fact, among the colonial maritime community, smuggling became a common practice, even after Parliament established custom houses in most major seaports along the Eastern seaboard of North America.

This administrative leniency—sometimes referred to as salutary neglect—by England concerning the management of American trade continued unabated down to the outbreak of revolutionary hostilities, with little being done to seriously enforce colonial compliance except the transference of prospective smuggling cases from more sympathetic civilian courts of common plea to British Admiralty Courts. Thus, it seems that England heavily leaned on the side of restraint and mercy when it came to handling the rebellious American maritime community. Of those contemporary European powers engaged in the ruthless activity of creating and sustaining colonial empires, England's more benign policies actually compare favorably. Most Anglo-American colonists knew they lived under a very beneficial system.

Another common misunderstanding concerns the role of England as an unreasonable, tyrannical government and the presence of British military forces in North America during the Seven Years' War. From the late seventeenth century through the mid-eighteenth century, colonial America had been a battleground in an ongoing conflict between the French Empire and British Empire, involving not only each nation's respective military forces but also large numbers of native peoples allied to both sides as well as French and English colonial civilian militia. In some respects, the final stage of this conflict known as the Seven Years' War could have been called the "First World War," as it was ultimately waged on several oceans and in lands across the globe, from the West Indies and Canada to Northern Europe and India.

In North America, American colonists had suffered for many years from the threat of attacks from the French and their Native American allies, resisting with homegrown and equipped militia companies sent out by independent colonial governments to protect their respective frontiers. The war was renewed in 1754 as frontier settlements and farms in the upstate New York colony and western Pennsylvania came under French and Indian attack.

After over a year of this independent and bloody struggle, England's Parliament finally responded to calls for assistance and dispatched a fleet of British naval vessels and a large number of British troops to lead the assault on French Canada. Over the next six years of fighting, the British military, assisted by American militia, seized the French naval base of Louisburg and, by 1761, the strategically important cities of Quebec and Montreal, thus eliminating the long-term threat of attack on Anglo-American colonies. The war's end was negotiated by the Treaty of Paris in February 1763, which granted all of French Canada, the French portions of India, and islands of the West Indies to England.

The good news for North American colonists was that the potential for a surprise attack was ended, but there was a negative aspect to the war's end. For the government of the British Empire, the Seven Years' War was very costly in both military lives and equipment. New British ships had to be built and outfitted, and older vessels needed to be refitted and equipped in the costly shipyards of England to carry on the war effort. Additionally, more British troops needed to be recruited, trained, outfitted, and dispatched to North America. The overall cost was indeed staggering.

Current scholars estimate that the total expense of the Seven Years' War was greater than all other British conflicts until World War I. Parliament reasoned that some of the war cost—especially that part related to North America's share—should be shouldered by the American colonies, who greatly benefited from the elimination of the French and Native American threat. In this way, the creation of the Stamp Act in 1765 was merely an indirect attempt by Parliament to help raise much-needed funds to diminish the heavy national war debt.

England had never previously asserted itself over its American colonies or enforced a colony-wide policy of taxation—unlike Spain, France, and Portugal; consequently, this action was viewed by the colonists as a form of *tyranny*. From a parliamentary perspective, as it was purely optional and *not* mandatory, only being applied to paper goods such as official legal documents, newspapers, playing cards, and wallpapers, the Stamp Act was viewed by Parliament as an optional tax that would only be paid by those who made common use of those taxable paper-based products.

Another common misconception related to this revolutionary myth is that *all* the British North American colonies were involved in the political confrontations between colonial legislatures, the Continental Congress, and Parliament. In actuality, only thirteen of eighteen colonies chose to become directly involved in the struggle for independence. The rebellious thirteen were Connecticut, Delaware, Georgia, Maryland, Massachusetts, New Hampshire, New Jersey, New York, North Carolina, Pennsylvania, Rhode Island, South Carolina, and Virginia. The North American colonies who remained loyal to England were Nova Scotia (including present-day New Brunswick), (East and West) Florida, Prince Edward Island (or St. John's Island), Quebec (including present-day Ontario), and Newfoundland.

The Stamp Act Congress held in New York City in October 1765 was a first attempt by nine of the eighteen British American colonies of North America to seek redress for the Stamp Act and resulted in the creation of a Declaration of Rights and Grievances claiming that Parliament cannot legally tax British colonies that are not represented in Parliament. Also, domestically, the Stamp Act Congress enacted a colony-wide boycott of British imports calculated to hurt British trade with the colonies and minimize the number of stamps sold. The boycott was successful in achieving its goals.

However, what undoubtedly had the greatest effect on Parliament in 1766 was the reasonable testimony of Benjamin Franklin before the House of Commons concerning the American character and attitude and how best to deal with them. In Parliament's efforts to understand the resistance of American colonists to the Stamp Act, the famous American printer and inventor—who then lived in London—was invited to answer questions concerning the American colonies and the future of the Stamp Act.

Franklin's sympathetic and candid testimony before Parliament was instrumental in bringing about the quick repeal of the Stamp Act in late 1766. This response, while surprising, cannot be overlooked or dismissed and should hardly be regarded as the act of a tyrannical and unreasonable government. More accurately, Parliament might be better described as a body of detached and uninformed political observers seeking to solve major economic issues with a population of subjects that they did not properly understand. Had Franklin remained in England to advise, who knows the possible result? The sincere concern of Parliament for the sentiments of Britain's American colonies is clearly reflected in the rather naïve questions posed by Parliament to Benjamin Franklin. It is clear that the members of the House of Commons are honestly seeking to better understand the reasons for colonial protests (author notes in italics):

Q. What is your name and place of abode?
A. Franklin of Philadelphia.

Q. Do the Americans pay any considerable taxes among themselves?
[The fact that this question needed to be asked at all clearly indicates that the members of Parliament were profoundly uninformed on the subject of the economic disposition of American taxpayers. Uninformed though they were, they still press Franklin to come to a correct understanding of the nuances of American domestic taxation.]
A. Certainly, many, and very heavy taxes.

Q. For what purposes are those taxes laid?
A. For the support of the civil and military establishments of the country, and to discharge the heavy debt contracted in the last [Seven Years'] war . . .

Q. Are not all the people very able to pay those taxes?
A. No. The frontier counties, all along the continent, have been frequently ravaged by the enemy and greatly impoverished, are able to pay very little tax . . .

Q. Are not the colonies, from their circumstances, very able to pay the stamp duty?
A. In my opinion there is not gold or silver enough in the colonies to pay the stamp duty for one year.

Q. Don't you know that the money arising from the stamps was all to be laid out in America?
[Here Parliament expresses complete frustration that the American colonists do not seem to understand or appreciate that stamp tax revenue raised in the American colonies was only intended to reduce the debts generated by the American phase of the Seven Years' War.]
A. I know it is appropriated by the act to the American service; but it will be spent in the conquered colonies, where the soldiers are, not in the colonies that pay it . . .

Q. Do you think it right that America should be protected by this country and pay no part of the expense?
[Finally, Parliament touches on the key issue, fair payment for military services rendered by Great Britain on behalf of the American colonies. For England, the Stamp Act was a means by which the American colonies might, through an optional tax, help alleviate the war costs generated by a conflict fought by the British military on the colonies' behalf.]
A. That is not the case. The colonies raised, clothed and paid during the last war, near 25,000 men, and spent many millions.

Q. Do you think the people of America would submit to pay the stamp duty, if it were moderated *[lessened]*?
A. No, never, unless compelled by force of arms.

Q. What is your opinion of a future tax, imposed on the same principle with that of the Stamp Act? How would the Americans receive it?
A. Just as they do this. They would not pay it.

Q. Can anything less than a military force carry the Stamp Act into execution?
A. I don't see how a military force can be applied to that purpose.

Q. Why may it not?
A. Suppose a military is force sent into America; they will find nobody in arms; what are they then to do? They cannot force a man

to buy stamps who chooses to do without them. They will not find a rebellion; they may indeed make one.

Q. If the act is not repealed, what do you think will be the consequences?
A. A total loss of respect and affection the people of America bear to this country, and of all the commerce that depends on that respect and affection.

Q. If the Stamp Act should be repealed, would it induce the Assemblies of America to acknowledge the right of Parliament to tax them, and would they erase their resolutions *[against the Stamp Act]*?
A. No. Never.

Q. Is there no means of obliging them to erase those resolutions?
A. None that I know of; they will never do it, unless compelled by force of arms.

Q. Is there a power on earth that can force them to erase them?
A. No power, how great-so-ever, can force men to change their opinions . . .

Q. What used to be the pride of the Americans?
A. To indulge in the fashions and manufacturers of Great Britain.

Q. What is now their pride?
A. To wear their old clothes over again, till they can make new ones.
[These final observations were intended to impress upon the minds of those delegates in attendance that something valuable was lost by Parliament forcing an unwanted tax upon the American colonies—their "pride" in being British subjects. This point seems to have profoundly affected the members, who would soon vote in sympathy with the American cause by rescinding the hated act.] (Franklin quoted in Cobbett 1813, 137–138)

The end result of this discussion was Parliament's final decision to rescind the Stamp Act but to simultaneously issue the Declaratory Act announcing that Parliament was, and should be regarded as, the supreme political authority within the British Empire, retaining for itself the absolute right to tax Britain's possessions and colonies "in all cases whatsoever."

Thus, Parliament does not conform to the stereotypical myth of a sinister and tyrannical government but is rather an executive legislature frustrated by the legacy of many years of benign neglect resulting in a colonial population that simply refuses to acknowledge parliamentary authority. Instead of tyranny, we have a frustrated parliamentary legislature that chose to, as Dr. Berkin observes, "ignore petitions, refuse to engage in negotiations or discussions and to generally display a bewilderment at the colonists' failure to understand how an empire worked" (Berkin 2009).

Another facet of the great Revolutionary War myth revolves around the idea that the movement toward independence was a uniformly popular idea supported by the great majority of American colonists. This position has been argued and supported by those historians who point to the impressive initial troop recruitment following the successful April 19, 1775, Battles of Lexington and Concord, where nearly sixteen thousand militiamen, or citizen soldiers, gathered from every corner of New England, laying siege to Boston during the summer of 1775 (Ferling 2010).

While there is no doubt that many colonists positively responded to the initial victories of the conflict, many modern scholars seriously doubt that the American War for Independence had universal support or even the support of the majority of colonists. Many contemporary historians point at the exchange between President Adams and Thomas McKean in which they came to agree that "about a third of the people of the Colonies were against the Revolution" (Adams and Adams 1856, 87). Most likely, while "Radical-Whigs" and loyalists constituted two distinct extreme political factions, there were others less committed. These semicommitted patriots would take the position of "Conservative-Whigs" before risking their lives and fortunes. And, finally, there were many who would simply "ride the fence" to wait and see in what direction the political and military winds might blow before showing their true colors. This diversity of political opinions is distinctly at odds with the prevailing myth of universal colonial patriotism.

It would be a grave error to assume that the third of American colonists who, according to John Adams, opposed the idea of independence were content with observing the raging conflict from the sidelines. On the contrary, American loyalists volunteered to serve in locally raised regiments. The British commanders often assigned these troops to secondary and auxiliary roles, partially because there already was a heavy military presence of regular troops, properly trained and equipped. But it was also well understood that the blood feuds that could have resulted from open confrontations between different colonial factions did not bode well for the future. Nevertheless, such regiments as Butler's Rangers, De Lancey's Brigade ("the Cowboys"), and the New Jersey Volunteers ("the Skinners") participated in raids and campaigns. However, the discipline in loyalist troops was lacking, and they were known for occasional marauding and lawless behavior, including interfighting, as in the case of the Cowboys and the Skinners. The harsh treatment of loyalist households by the patriots contributed to the resolve that the American supporters of the British crown demonstrated.

Under these circumstances, the American Revolution begins to look more like a civil war in which a foreign power supported one of the sides. This would have had an effect on the raising of American troops for General Washington's army. Indeed, while recruitment for the Continental Army in 1775 was certainly impressive, the "summer soldiers"—described by political pamphleteer Thomas Paine—quickly discovered how arduous and dangerous military life could be by 1776. Continental ranks were soon depleted as New England volunteer militia soldiers left the ranks for home to farm and earn a living for their families. They were replaced by those who, without farms, were enticed by cash recruitment bounties, free blankets, free uniforms, and free food.

In other words, the myth of patriotic citizen soldiers staunchly suffering hardship purely for the sake of liberty is largely unfounded. Patriotism for the American cause quickly waned, and even General Washington himself bitterly complained that it would not be possible to continue the war effort with a voluntary army: "Those who were willing to serve from a belief in the 'goodness of the cause' would amount to little more than 'a drop in the Ocean'" (*George Washington to Congress*, quoted in Ferling 2010). This difficulty in finding committed and able soldiers resulted in a Continental Army that was different from what most people would envision today. The American revolutionary forces were not primarily comprised of recruits of Anglo or English descent and local lineage. Instead, the patriotic armies were composed of a more diverse mix, including several other major ethnic groups: Scots-Irish, French, Dutch, German, and even a significant number of African American troops.

Of the abovementioned, the Scots-Irish were by far the most numerous ethnic group in the American Continental forces, especially after 1776. This was largely because the new recruits raised to replace the "citizen militia" of New England, those that gradually returned to their farms after the White Plains and New York disasters, largely came from Pennsylvania, Virginia, and North and South Carolina—all colonies with high concentrations of Scots-Irish settlers. And in these colonies, as historian John G.

Leyburn observes, "The Scots-Irish were enthusiastic supporters of the American Revolution," and their willingness to fight for independence from England was "practically unanimous" (Leyburn 1962, xi).

The Continental troops became increasingly Scots-Irish from 1778 until 1781 as the main focus of the war moved into Virginia and the Carolinas, a region heavily populated with the first- and second-generation Scots-Irish settlers. Racial-military historian Ashanti White in his article, "Irish-Americans—1775–1860" makes a strong case for the predominance of the Revolutionary Scots-Irish drawing upon the post-war testimony of a British major before the House of Commons stating that "half the rebel Continental army were from Ireland." Recent demographic evidence indicates that this testimony was probably an exaggeration, but that troops of Scots-Irish descent "comprised about 40% of American forces . . . " (White 2013, 326).

As if more evidence were needed, a perceptive and discouraged Hessian officer from America simply wrote, "Call this was by whatever name you may, dear friend, only call it not an American rebellion; it is nothing more or less than an Irish-Scotch, Presbyterian rebellion" (Heinrichs 1898, 137).

Transforming the image of the revolution as a distinctly English American affair, the Germans, such as the abovementioned Captain Heinrichs, constituted the largest non-English-speaking group involved in the American Revolution—as a surprisingly large number of German-speaking people fought on *both* sides of the conflict. King George III was actually of German ancestry and hereditarily ruled the German principality of Hanover (or the Electorate of Brunswick-Luneburg); it was natural for him to recruit German mercenaries to assist the British military effort to subdue the American colonies. So, far from fighting English troops alone, a sizable number of German troops were transported from Europe to the colonies. Some returned home at the war's end, some died in combat or from sickness, and a surprisingly large number chose to remain after the conflict was concluded.

Statistically, the number of Germans involved in the American Revolution is somewhat more significant than most people expect. Current demographic analysis places the British-German contribution at an estimated grand total of 28,883 German troops from a variety of territories and principalities: Hessen-Kassel (16,000), Hessen-Hanau (2,422), Brunswick-Wolfenbuttel (5,723), Ansbach-Bayreuth (2,353), Waldeck (1,225), and Anhalt-Zerbst (1,160). In addition, five battalions of German troops were raised and dispatched from Brunswick-Luneburg to

Gibraltar "to relieve the British garrison stationed there, allowing them to transfer to the American colonies" (Eelking and Rosengarten 1987, 257–263).

On the patriotic side, there were also a significant number of German-speaking troops. Germans had been traveling to the New World since the mid-seventeenth century and had become well established as farmers in the mid-Atlantic colonies of New York, Pennsylvania, Maryland, and New Jersey. As a result, Germans were recruited from these colonies, formed into companies and later regiments, and given German-speaking officers. Two of the best-known German regiments were Pennsylvania's Marechausee Corps. and the Eighth Maryland Infantry, or the "German Regiment," which served steadily from its formation in 1776 until it was disbanded in 1781. Besides including four infantry companies from Maryland, the German Regiment also contained five German-speaking companies from Pennsylvania. It distinguished itself at the Battles of Trenton and Princeton, and was ably commanded by Lieutenant Colonel Nicholas Haussegger, a German American officer formally attached to the staff of General "Mad" Anthony Wayne.

Concerning African American soldiers in the American colonial army, at first, only New England recruited this specific ethnic minority because they had been involved in the struggle for liberty from the very beginning. Nearly everyone is aware of Crispus Attucks, a member of the Sons of Liberty who was one of the five victims killed by British troops in 1770 during the Boston Massacre. By the outbreak of war in 1775, many militia companies in New England included free blacks as riflemen, the best known being Salem Poor, who distinguished himself at the Battle of Bunker Hill and was commended by his militia company's commanding officer as "a brave and gallant soldier" under fire who deserved official recognition for his service. Another anonymous black patriot is vividly described in the journal of eighteen-year-old fifer John Greenwood as he neared the battlefield on the morning of June 17, 1775:

> I went toward the battle to find the company [Captain Bliss's Company] I belonged to. . . . Never having beheld such a sight before, I felt very much frightened, and would have given the world if I had not enlisted as a soldier; I could positively feel my hair stand on end. Just as I came near the place a negro man, wounded in the back of his neck, passed me and, his collar being open and he not having anything on except his shirt and trousers, I saw the wound quite plainly and the blood running down his back. I asked him if it hurt him much, as he did not seem to mind it. He

said, "No," and that he "was only going to get a plaster (bandage) put on it, and meant to return. You cannot conceive what encouragement this immediately gave me. I began to feel brave and like a soldier from that very moment, and fear never troubled me afterward during the whole war." (Greenwood 1922, 28–29)

But such service by black soldiers was not limited to the occasional individual; in reality, a fairly large number of African Americans served as regulars during the revolution. Recent estimates place the total number of black patriot soldiers at approximately five thousand—amounting to 5 percent of the total number of men who served in the Continental Army. As to their reputation in military service, the well-known Continental Army officer and journalist Baron Ludwig von Closen, after observation of black troops in combat, noted in 1781 that, in his opinion, the "best regiment under arms in the Continental Army" was one where three-quarters of the unit consisted of free black soldiers.

Lest one think that African Americans only fought on the side of American independence and freedom, it should be noted that a very large number of former slaves were recruited into the British army and navy. Early in the American War of Independence, British commanders were instructed to offer personal freedom to any slaves who escaped from their rebellious masters and offered their services to the British military service.

The risk these "black loyalists" took was that, if recaptured, they would be severely beaten, re-enslaved, and returned to their masters, if possible, by American patriot forces. But the possibility of freedom was tempting enough to encourage large numbers to attempt to join the British. Under British military protection, between 1776 and 1785, approximately thirty-five hundred loyalist African Americans were safely transported to Canada and given their freedom as British citizens. These "fugitives from these states," as Thomas Jefferson would refer to them, formed only a small part of the total of thirty-four thousand loyalists who would flee to safety in Canada before the end of the revolution in 1783.

Other black loyalists chose to remain in the rebellious colonies and formed loyalist military units of their own. These distinguished black loyalist regiments included the Black Pioneers, the Ethiopian Regiment, the Jersey Shore Volunteers, the Jamaica Rangers, the Mosquito Shore Volunteers, and the Black Dragoons of the South Carolina Royalists. Perhaps the most famous of all black loyalist military units was organized by Virginia's royal governor, Lord Dunmore, who recruited and outfitted a regiment of eight hundred former slaves into a regular British army infantry unit, promising each recruit his freedom. This was accomplished with a document called "Lord Dunmore's Proclamation," which was issued in November 1775. It resulted in the recruitment of over eight hundred former slaves and the creation of America's first all-black military unit, the Ethiopian Regiment.

Participation in the military campaigns of the American Revolution actually involved huge numbers of combatants on both sides. They represented a wide variety of ethnic groups, whose members were motivated to action for many reasons beyond the idea of "taxation without representation." Such present-day misconceptions of those diverse people who were actively involved in the American Revolution often leave the many stories of soldiers and everyday civilians untold and misunderstood while distorting the dynamics of England's management policies concerning its American colonies.

It therefore appears that the myth of an American Revolution fought between freedom-loving English colonists and English soldiers of the tyrannical and repressive mother country is somewhat at odds with the reality of the American struggle for freedom and individual liberty. The concept of a necessary war of independence also seems misleading because political differences with England were not perceived as reasonable grounds for a military confrontation by many—perhaps a majority of citizens in the colonies. In fact, large contingents of native-born loyalists fought on the side of the British. People of the same upbringing and the same social status took different sides in the conflict. Who you were at that time did not by necessity make you support the Crown or believe that the British Empire was bringing nothing but oppression to the colonial America of the mid–eighteenth century. The American Revolution was not clearly defined by the colonists as a conflict between good and evil.

PRIMAWRY DOCUMENT

LORD DUNMORE'S PROCLAMATION, NOVEMBER 7, 1775

The following proclamation is an excellent example of precisely how the royal governor of Virginia perceived the situation that faced him and those loyal to the Crown in late 1775. Violent and lawless ruffians who thoughtlessly endangered the lives and safety of His Majesty's subjects clearly needed to be dealt with in a direct and uncompromising manner. Here, Governor Dunmore offers his insight and outlines a course of action against an army of armed "traitors," which from the loyalist perspective seems quite reasonable, justified, and even patriotic.

By His Excellency the Right Honorable JOHN Earl of DUNMORE, His Majesty's Lieutenant and Governor General of the Colony and Dominion of Virginia, and Vice Admiral of the same.
A PROCLAMATION.
AS I have ever entertained Hopes, that an Accommodation might have taken Place between Great-Britain and this Colony, without being compelled by my Duty to this most disagreeable but now absolutely necessary Step, rendered so by a Body of armed Men unlawfully assembled, firing on His Majesty's Tenders, and the formation of an Army, and that Army now on their March to attack His Majesty's Troops and destroy the well-disposed Subjects of this Colony. To defeat such reasonable Purposes, and that all such Traitors, and their Abettors, may be brought to Justice, and that the Peace, and good Order of this Colony may be again restored, which the ordinary Course of the Civil Law is unable to effect; I have thought fit to issue this my Proclamation, hereby declaring, that until the aforesaid good Purposes can be obtained, I do in Virtue of the Power and Authority to ME given, by His Majesty, determine to execute Martial Law, and cause the same to be executed throughout this Colony: and to that the Peace and good Order may the sooner be restored, I do require every Person capable of bearing Arms, to resort to His Majesty's STANDARD, or be looked upon as Traitors to His Majesty's Crown and Government, and thereby become liable to the Penalty the Law inflicts upon such Offences; such as forfeiture of Life, confiscation of Lands, &c. &c. And I do hereby further declare all indented Servants, Negroes, or others, (appertaining to Rebels,) free that are able and willing to bear Arms, they joining His Majesty's Troops as soon as may be, for the more speedily reducing this Colony to a proper Sense of their Duty, to His Majesty's Crown and Dignity. I do further order, and require, all His Majesty's Leige Subjects, to retain their Quitrents, or any other Taxes due or that may become due, in their own Custody, till such Time as Peace may be again restored to this at present most unhappy Country, or demanded of them for their former salutary Purposes, by Officers properly authorized to receive the same.

GIVEN under my Hand on board the Ship WILLIAM, off Norfolk, the 7th Day of November, in the SIXTEENTH Year of His Majesty's Reign.
DUNMORE.
(GOD save the KING.)

Source: "Lord Dunmore's Proclamation" (Virginia. (1775) *By His Excellency the Right Honourable John Earl of Dunmore, His Majesty's Lieutenant and Governour-General of the Colony and Dominion of Virginia, and Vice-Admiral of the Same. a Proclamation Declaring Martial Law and to Cause the Same to Be*. Norfolk. [Pdf] Retrieved from the Library of Congress https://www.loc.gov/item/rbpe.17801800).

Further Reading

Adams, John, and Charles Francis Adams. 1856. *The Works of John Adams, Second President of the United States*. Vol. 10. Boston, MA: Little, Brown & Co.

Berkin, Carol. 2009. "Teaching the American Revolution." Gilder Lehman Institute of American History. Accessed July 3, 2020. https://www.gilderlehrman.org/history-now/essays/teaching-revolution.

Cobbett, William. 1813. *The Parliamentary History of England from the Earliest Times to the Year 1803*. London: T.C. Hansard Printer.

Dunmore, Lord John. 1775. "By His Excellency the Right Honourable John Earl of Dunmore, His Majesty's Lieutenant and Governour-General of the Colony and Dominion of Virginia, and Vice-admiral of the same. A Proclamation. [Declaring Martial Law and to Cause the Same to Be.]" Web. Accessed June 8, 2020. https://www.loc.gov/item/rbpe.17801800.

Eelking, Max von, and J. G Rosengarten. 1987. *The German Allied Troops in the North American War of Independence, 1776–1783*. Bowie, MD: Heritage Books.

Ferling, John. 2010. "Myths of the American Revolution." *Smithsonian Magazine* (January). Web. Accessed June 8, 2020. https://www.smithsonianmag.com/history/myths-of-the-american-revolution-10941835.

Greenwood, John. 1922. *The Revolutionary Services of John Greenwood of Boston and New York, 1773–1783, Edited with Notes from the Original by His Grandson, Isaac A. Greenwood*. New York: Joseph R. Greenwood.

Heinrichs, Johann. 1898. "Extracts from the Letter Books of Captain Johann Heinrichs of the Hessian Jaeger Corps, 1778–1780." *Pennsylvania Magazine of History and Biography* 22 (2): 137–170.

Leyburn, James G. 1962. *The Scotch-Irish: A Social History*. Chapel Hill: University of North Carolina Press.

Roberts, Richard A. 1899. *Calendar of Home Office Records of the Reign of George III, 1773–1775*. London: Royal Printing Office.

Sabine, Lorenzo. 1847. *The American Loyalists, or Biographical Sketches of Adherents to the British Crown in the War of the Revolution*. Boston, MA: C. C. Little and J. Brown.

Waller, J. Michael. 2009. *Founding Political Warfare Documents of the United States*. Washington, DC: Crossbow Press.

White, Ashanti. 2013. "Irish-Americans—1775–1860." In *Ethnic and Racial Minorities in the U.S. Military: An Encyclopedia*. Vol. 1, 325–327. Santa Barbara, CA: ABC-CLIO.

9

Paul Revere Completed His Famous Ride Alone

What People Think Happened

For most Americans, the story of Boston's patriot messenger Paul Revere remains an iconic image indelibly etched in the national subconscious, at once both mysterious and dark. To many Americans, Revere is a lonely and brave figure whose simple task was to bring warning and alarm to every Middlesex village and farm in an effort to protect hidden supplies of munitions and resist by force of arms the imminent threat of a British army soon to descend upon the quiet outlying communities of Lexington and Concord.

Paul Revere was an all-American man who was gifted in many ways and had succeeded in every occupation that he ever tried. He was a silversmith, an engraver, a dental surgeon, and even an artist. He was also a well-known champion of the noble cause of American independence well before it became popular.

On April 18, 1775, the redcoats were planning a raid designed specifically to capture weapons and munitions stored by the rebels in the countryside in preparation for a future military confrontation. Once the patriots learned about the British regulars' plans, they had to act quickly on this intelligence. Time was of the essence, and so Paul Revere left Boston in the middle of the night. This was quite a daring act in an era when darkness covered the landscape from dusk to dawn. Before leaving, Revere received a signal about the mode of the British advance. Two lanterns briefly shone from the steeple of the Old North Church. This prearranged coded message was deciphered using the now famous mantra "one if by land, two if by sea." Paul Revere now knew that the British troops were planning to row across the harbor as they left their stations in Boston. He mounted his noble steed and headed into the night. The dauntless hero rode all the way to Concord, shouting to everyone he met, "The British are coming! The British are coming!" In the excitement of the moment, Paul must have forgotten that he himself was a British subject. Nevertheless, his mission was a complete success.

Little did Paul Revere know that his midnight ride would jump-start the American Revolution. He and his ride have come to symbolically represent the duty expected of every loyal American citizen to risk life and personal comfort for the sake of the public good and the well-being of the nation as a whole. It is a praise-worthy image, and it placed Paul Revere in the pantheon of the demigods of the American Revolution, a place in American history always assured.

And yet, this image is, in fact, badly distorted. In actuality, the "myth" bears little resemblance to the "reality" as reflected in the event known to have actually occurred. What follows is a narrative that will explore the origin of this myth, who may be responsible for its invention and dissemination, and how the myth contrasts sharply with the reality of "Paul Revere's ride"—as reflected in the primary source documents that shed light upon this important historical event.

How It Became Popular

What has contributed to the creation of the Revere myth? Without doubt, the primary contributing factor rests with the epic poem "Paul Revere's Ride," which was written in 1860–1861 by renowned American poet and educator Henry Wadsworth Longfellow (1807–1882). The poem was first published in the January 1861 issue of the *Atlantic Monthly* magazine.

The poem would later be immortalized as one of the tales found in Longfellow's best-selling anthology of poems *Tales of a Wayside Inn*, first published in 1863. In the republished version, Longfellow changed the title of the poem to "The Landlord's Tale," in some respects making it similar to the literary format of Chaucer's *Canterbury Tales*.

The alleged inspiration for the poem, according to the author, was a visit paid by him to the Old North Church in 1860, which resulted in a climbing of the church tower. He began composition of the poem on April 6, 1860 (Triber 1998, 1).

Like Chaucer, Longfellow was primarily a good storyteller who saw the opportunity to tell a tale with a good moral lesson. For Longfellow, the immediate danger in 1861 was the possible collapse of the United States, and the lesson was that every patriotic American should respond like a "Paul Revere" to the looming crisis and the impending "hour of darkness." Secondarily, as a good friend of the antislavery intellectual circle of Massachusetts, he also wanted to raise an alarm against the moral danger posed by slavery.

It is therefore worthwhile to examine the mythical version of Longfellow's account of Paul Revere's ride and discover how and in what respects it differs from the reality. Did Longfellow know what really happened on the night of April 18, 1775? Perhaps, and most importantly, why did Longfellow's poem have a greater impact on public opinion than all the history books in all the American history classrooms from 1861 to the present?

The truth is that the myth of Paul Revere owes more to Longfellow's poem than the work of any scholar or journalist. It was the poem's incredible popularity and Longfellow's use of dramatic license in making Revere the sole participant that created the fictitious image of the ride that has come to be regarded by Americans as the unvarnished truth.

Paul Revere's Ride
by Henry Wadsworth Longfellow (1807–1882)

Listen, my children, and you shall hear
Of the midnight ride of Paul Revere,
On the eighteenth of April, in Seventy-Five:
Hardly a man is now alive
Who remembers that famous day and year.

He said to his friend,—"If the British march
By land or sea from the town to-night,
Hang a lantern aloft in the belfry-arch
Of the North-Church-tower, as a signal-light,—
One if by land, and two if by sea;
And I on the opposite shore will be,
Ready to ride and spread the alarm
Through every Middlesex village and farm,
For the country-folk to be up and to arm."

Then he said good-night, and with muffled oar
Silently rowed to the Charlestown shore,

Just as the moon rose over the bay,
Where swinging wide at her moorings lay
The Somersett, British man-of-war:
A phantom ship, with each mast and spar
Across the moon, like a prison-bar,
And a huge, black hulk, that was magnified
By its own reflection in the tide.

Meanwhile, his friend, through alley and street
Wanders and watches with eager ears,
Till in the silence around him he hears
The muster of men at the barrack-door,
The sound of arms, and the tramp of feet,
And the measured tread of the grenadiers
Marching down to their boats on the shore.

Then he climbed to the tower of the church,
Up the wooden stairs, with stealthy tread,
To the belfry-chamber overhead,
And startled the pigeons from their perch
On the sombre rafters, that round him made
Masses and moving shapes of shade,—
Up the light ladder, slender and tall,
To the highest window in the wall,
Where he paused to listen and look down
A moment on the roofs of the town,
And the moonlight flowing over all.

Beneath, in the churchyard, lay the dead
In their night-encampment on the hill,
Wrapped in silence so deep and still,
That he could hear, like a sentinel's tread,
The watchful night-wind, as it went
Creeping along from tent to tent,
And seeming to whisper, "All is well!"
A moment only he feels the spell
Of the place and the hour, the secret dread
Of the lonely belfry and the dead;
For suddenly all his thoughts are bent
On a shadowy something far away,
Where the river widens to meet the bay,—

A line of black, that bends and floats
On the rising tide, like a bridge of boats.

Meanwhile, impatient to mount and ride,
Booted and spurred, with a heavy stride,
On the opposite shore walked Paul Revere
Now he patted his horse's side,
Now gazed on the landscape far and near,
Then impetuous stamped the earth,
And turned and tightened his saddle-girth;
But mostly he watched with eager search
The belfry-tower of the old North Church,
As it rose above the graves on the hill,
Lonely, and spectral, and sombre, and still.

And lo! as he looks, on the belfry's height,
A glimmer, and then a gleam of light!
He springs to the saddle, the bridle he turns,
But lingers and gazes, till full on his sight
A second lamp in the belfry burns!

A hurry of hoofs in a village-street,
A shape in the moonlight, a bulk in the dark,
And beneath from the pebbles, in passing, a spark
Struck out by a steed that flies fearless and fleet:
That was all! And yet, through the gloom and the light,
The fate of a nation was riding that night;
And the spark struck out by that steed, in his flight,
Kindled the land into flame with its heat.

It was twelve by the village-clock,
When he crossed the bridge into Medford town.
He heard the crowing of the cock,
And the barking of the farmer's dog,
And felt the damp of the river-fog,
That rises when the sun goes down.

It was one by the village-clock,
When he rode into Lexington.
He saw the gilded weathercock
Swim in the moonlight as he passed,

And the meeting-house windows, blank and bare,
Gaze at him with a spectral glare,
As if they already stood aghast
At the bloody work they would look upon.

It was two by the village-clock,
When he came to the bridge in Concord town.
He heard the bleating of the flock,
And the twitter of birds among the trees,
And felt the breath of the morning-breeze
Blowing over the meadows brown.
And one was safe and asleep in his bed
Who at the bridge would be first to fall,
Who that day would be lying dead,
Pierced by a British musket-ball.

You know the rest. In the books you have read
How the British regulars fired and fled,—
How the farmers gave them ball for ball,
From behind each fence and farmyard-wall,
Chasing the red-coats down the lane,
Then crossing the fields to emerge again
Under the trees at the turn of the road,
And only pausing to fire and load.

So through the night rode Paul Revere;
And so through the night went his cry of alarm
To every Middlesex village and farm,—
A cry of defiance, and not of fear,—
A voice in the darkness, a knock at the door,
And a word that shall echo forevermore!
For, borne on the night-wind of the Past,
Through all our history, to the last,
In the hour of darkness and peril and need,
The people will waken and listen to hear
The hurrying hoof-beat of that steed,
And the midnight-message of Paul Revere.
(Longfellow 1867, 290–292)

To what degree was Longfellow aware of the historical inaccuracies of his poem? We know that Longfellow had access to primary source materials providing firsthand accounts of the actual ride in Paul Revere's own words. One of these was a relatively brief deposition written by Revere and submitted to the Continental Congress in 1775, and the second was a letter addressed to Boston merchant Jeremy Belknap, the then corresponding secretary of the Massachusetts Historical Society, dated in 1798. This last and most detailed account of the ride in Revere's own words was published at least twice. The first printing was in the *Collections of the Massachusetts Historical Society for the year 1798* (1835). The second printing of this original Revere account appeared in the *New England Journal* in 1832, in a volume containing one of Longfellow's early essays, "The School Master," excerpted from his later published work *Outre-Mer*. Thus, it is reasonably certain that Longfellow was aware of the facts of the Paul Revere ride, and he deliberately chose to change many details to serve his literary objective.

Interestingly, despite the moral lessons of "Paul Revere's Ride" and the general popularity of *Tales of the Wayside Inn*, Longfellow's poem did not have an enormous impact on the American consciousness until 1875— immediately prior to the national centennial celebration in 1876. In 1875, the Old North Church instituted a new "tradition" derived directly from the poem known as "The Lantern Ceremony" (Fischer 1995, 334). In the years that followed the national centennial, an ever-increasing authenticity was attached to Longfellow's poetic tale, transforming it from a mere poetic tale encouraging patriotism and "courageous moral action" to being considered an historically accurate account of the ride itself—a role that Longfellow had never intended.

For example, several popular textbooks used in American classrooms were responsible for popularizing Longfellow's version of the event. These included *A Drill Book in the Elements of the English Language* by Edward Conant and *The Complete English Grammar* published by the Indiana Schoolbook Company in 1891. By the end of the nineteenth century, every school pupil in the United States knew about Paul Revere's heroism through the lens offered by Henry Wadsworth Longfellow.

What Really Happened

To best understand the difference between myth and reality, it will be important to look at those places where Longfellow deliberately altered the facts as they are known by comparing Longfellow's tale with Revere's most detailed published account.

To begin, Revere's actual account begins with his clandestine 10:00 p.m. meeting with Dr. Joseph Warren, who assigned him the task of the midnight ride, whereas the poem implies that the ride was Revere's idea alone.

This solitary theme is consistent throughout the Longfellow tale, but, in reality, the midnight activities of April 17–18 were clearly a team effort on the part of the Boston chapter of the Sons of Liberty.

For example, regarding the famous hanging of the signal lanterns, although both accounts agree that the signal code would be "one if by land and two if by sea," according to Revere, the idea was arrived at by a committee consisting of Revere, "Col. Conant & some other Gentlemen" that "if the British went out by Water, we would shew two Lanthorns in the North Church Steeple & if by Land, one as a Signal" (Massachusetts Historical Society 1835, 107).

Another discrepancy noticed by many is the purpose of the signal. In Longfellow's version, Revere is the intended recipient waiting "on the opposite shore" to *learn* whether the British are crossing "by sea" or marching "by land." In short, Longfellow has the steeple signal directed toward Revere, but according to Revere's account, he personally directed the signals to be placed while he was in Boston specifically to pass the message of troop movements to the waiting Sons of Liberty in Charlestown—just in case he was intercepted by the British prior to reaching the Charlestown shoreline. As Revere recalls, "We were apprehensive it would be difficult to Cross the Charles River, or get [sic] over Boston Neck" (Massachusetts Historical Society 1835, 107).

In the original account, Revere paints a more complex picture: "I left Dr. Warrens', called upon a friend, and desired him to make the Signals. I then went Home, took my Boots, and my Surtout (Overcoat), and went to the North part of the Town where I kept a Boat; (and) two friends rowed me across the Charles River." This image of Revere in his boat being rowed by his two friends is in contrast to the poem, in which a lonely Revere is depicted as he, "with muffled oar, silently rowed to the Charlestown shore" (Massachusetts Historical Society 1835, 107).

The next comparative phase involves the ride itself, which both versions agree begins in Charlestown. Longfellow has Revere already standing in the dark with his saddled steed restlessly waiting for the North Church lantern signal, "impatient to mount and ride" and ready to embark upon his midnight adventure. Conversely, Revere vividly recalls landing in Charlestown, stepping from the boat, and then he "went to git me a Horse"—a quest which thankfully proved successful, as he triumphantly claims that he "got a Horse of Deacon Larkin." Like Longfellow's legendary mount, the real steed proved to be better than average by Revere's estimation; he recalled that he "set off on a very good Horse" (Massachusetts Historical Society 1835, 107).

Interestingly, while the poetic midnight ride "through every Middlesex village and farm" is entirely free of life-threatening danger, the reality was quite different. Paul Revere claims that on at least two occasions he actually faced danger from armed British soldiers. The first confrontation took place in Charlestown shortly after the start of the action. Revere recalls that he "saw two men on Horseback, under a Tree." And when he "got near them," he "discovered they were British officers" who then "tried to get a-head of me," forcing him to turn his horse "very quick, & Galloped towards Charlestown neck" and then "for the Medford Road." Fortunately for Revere—despite one of the mounted soldiers "endeavoring to cut me off"—the patriot managed to outrace the British horseman and finally "got clear of him" (Massachusetts Historical Society 1835, 108).

Which brings us to one of the greatest discrepancies of the mythic version of the ride, Revere's lonely isolation on that fateful night. According to the poem and the present-day popular image, Paul Revere undertook the effort to warn the countryside *alone*. In Revere's account, however, he was informed in Boston by his dispatcher, Dr. Joseph Warren, that at least one additional rider had already been sent. Or, according to Revere, "When I got to Dr. Warren's House, I found he had sent an express by land to Lexington" (Massachusetts Historical Society 1835, 107).

Indeed, when Revere finally reaches Lexington, he "found both Messrs. (John) Hancock & (Samuel) Adams at the home of Reverend Mr. Clark" and inquired as to the whereabouts of "Mr. Daws," being told that "he had not been there[,] . . . but after about a half an Hour, Mr. Daws came. . . . We refreshed ourselves and set off for Concord to secure the Stores, etc., there." Shortly after departing Rev. Clark's House, the pair of riders—Dawes and Revere—"were overtaken by a young Doctor Prescot," bringing the total number of midnight riders en route to Concord to a count of three (Massachusetts Historical Society 1835, 108).

At this juncture, the greatest life-threatening danger of the evening yet faced by the group of riders presented itself. Revere recalled that "Mr. Dawes and the Doctor stoped [*sic*] to alarm the people of a House . . . when I saw two men in nearly the same situation as those officers were near Charlestown. I called for the Doctor & Daws to come up[,] . . . and in an instant we were surrounded by four. The Doctor being foremost, he came up, and we tried to git past them: but they being armed with pistols & swords, they forced us into a pasture" (Massachusetts Historical Society 1835, 108).

This dramatic turn of events is jarringly missing from Longfellow's poem, as it resulted in the unhorsing of Revere and the dramatic escape of Dawes and Prescott from British custody. Revere concluded that "the Doctor jumped his horse over a low stone wall, and got to Concord" to spread the alarm and continued on to warn the towns of Bedford and Lincoln (Massachusetts Historical Society 1835, 108).

William Dawes rode in an opposite direction followed by two mounted British troopers, who ceased to follow him when he turned into a darkened farmyard while crying out that he had lured two British officers into an ambush. Sadly, Dawes, though free from his pursuers, was quickly thrown from his horse and forced to walk back to the town of Lexington.

As for Paul Revere's ride, it ended abruptly with his capture. He never reached his final destination of Concord, but he did succeed in raising the alarm among the several communities between Boston and Lexington. This stands in sharp contrast to Longfellow's conclusion; Revere is depicted as not only reaching the town but at a specific time:

> It was two by the village clock,
> When he came to the bridge in Concord town.

Somewhat ironically, the greatest danger of Revere's ride—never mentioned by Longfellow—occurred to him after his capture. He later recalled that one of the mounted officers

> ordered me to dismount, one of them, who appeared to have command, examined me, Where I came from? & What my name was? I told him. He asked me if I was an express? I answered in the affirmative. He demanded what time I left Boston? I told him, and added that their troops had catched aground in passing the (Charles) River, and that there would be five hundred Americans there in a short time, for I had alarmed the Country all the way up. (Massachusetts Historical Society 1835, 109)

The interrogation of Revere proceeded, and the intensity of the confrontation increased as more mounted British soldiers arrived "upon a full gallop; one of them, whom I afterwards found to be Major Mitchel, of the 5th Regiment, clapped his pistol to my head, and called me by name, & told me he was going to ask me some questions, & if I did not give him true answers, he would blow my brains out" (Massachusetts Historical Society 1835, 109).

The final major discrepancy involves Revere's activities for the remainder of the night of the ride. In Longfellow's version, in the last passage, we are told,

So through the night rode Paul Revere;
And so through the night went his cry of alarm
To every Middlesex village and farm,
A cry of defiance, and not of fear,
A voice in the darkness, a knock at the door,
And a word that shall echo for evermore!
For, borne on the night wind of the Past,
Through all our history, to the last,
In the hour of darkness, peril and need,
The people will waken and listen to hear
The hurrying hoof-beats of that steed,
And the midnight message of Paul Revere.

The reality is that Paul Revere walked his final steps without his steed that night because it was given to replace a tired horse worn out by a mounted British trooper.

The final chapter of the midnight ride is best expressed in Revere's own words: "The Major inquired of me how far it was to Cambridge, and if there were any other Road? After some consultation, the Major Rode up to the Sargent, & asked if his horse was tired? He answered him, 'He was'—(He was a Sargent of Grenadiers, and had a small Horse)—then, said he, take that man's Horse. I dismounted, and the Sargent mounted my Horse, when they all rode toward the Lexington Meeting House." Revere walked across the Lexington "Burying Ground, & some pastures, & came to the Reverend Mr. Clark's House" where he "found Messrs. Hancock and Adams" and warned them to remove themselves to a safer location, which they did. This stands in sharp contrast to the rendition of the event described by Longfellow in his poem. And yet, in many respects, the poem remains the definitive source of historical information on the "midnight ride" (Massachusetts Historical Society 1835, 109).

Henry Wadsworth Longfellow was not the only poet to immortalize Paul Revere's ride. In 1795, Ebenezer Stiles attempted to include the story of Revere's patriotic adventure in his unpublished poem "The Story of the Battle of Concord and Lexington and Ride Twenty Years Ago." In his own way, Stiles, like Longfellow, tried to focus public attention on Paul Revere alone, to the exclusion of the other riders who may have also been the subjects of such an epic poem. In fact, had Stiles produced a poem of the quality of Longfellow's work, the myth of the midnight ride might have been attributed to him instead. But only a portion of Stiles's poem was published in the nineteenth century by the Massachusetts Historical Society in its *Proceedings of 1878*. Consider the opening stanzas:

> He spared neither horse, nor whip nor spur,
> As he galloped through mud and mire,
> He thought of naught but "Liberty,"
> And the lanterns that hung from the spire.
> He raced his steed through field and wood,
> Nor turned to ford the river.
> But faced his horse to the foaming flood,
> They swam across together.
>
> He madly dashed o'er mountain and moor
> Never slacked spur nor rein.
> Until with shout he stood by the door
> Of the church by Concord green.
> "They come, they come," he loudly cried
> "They are marching their legions this way
> Prepare to meet them ye true and tried
> They'll be here by Break of day."
> (quoted in Forbes 1999, 446)

The similarities between Stiles's and Longfellow's approaches in making Revere the sole hero of the midnight ride and the deliverer of the prophetic warning may infer that there was already, as early as the 1790s, a tradition that Revere was the primary actor in this heroic adventure. Neither of these writers sought to provide an accurate historical narrative; rather, each sought to inspire and move his readers to action by careful modification of the facts. Only Longfellow would have been surprised to discover that his artistic license would eventually overshadow the historical event.

In Longfellow's poem, we see the shifting of emphasis from a team effort of the Sons of Liberty to the patriotic action of an independent hero, the intensity of commitment to spread the word of warning to every Middlesex village, and the indomitable spirit to accomplish his task of reaching Lexington and Concord. These changes that Longfellow made were necessary for the creation of a moral tale to achieve the inspirational goals of the author: the reader must respond to the midnight warnings delivered on the eve of what would become, for America, a second American Revolution.

PRIMARY DOCUMENT

A LETTER FROM COL. PAUL REVERE TO THE CORRESPONDING SECRETARY

[JEREMY BELKNAP]. (TRANSCRIPT OF THE ORIGINAL MANUSCRIPT.)

In Revere's own words, nearly forty years later, Jeremy Belknap and the members of the Massachusetts Historical Society were treated to an in-depth, personal recollection of the events of April 18, 1775. In the following letter, the elderly patriot recounts numerous details and actions that, in their complexity and exactitude, have the ring of truth. Clearly, Revere, near the end of his life, wished to tell the tale with precise clarity so that future generations would know, without question, exactly how the nation began.

Dear Sir,—Having a little leisure, I wish to fulfil my promise of giving you some facts and anecdotes prior to the battle of Lexington, which I do not remember to have seen in any History of the American Revolution.

In the year 1773, I was employed by the Selectmen of the town of Boston to carry the account of the Destruction of the Tea to New York; and afterwards, 1774, to carry their despatches to New York and Philadelphia for calling a Congress; and afterwards to Congress several times.

In the fall of 1774, and winter of 1775, I was one of upwards of thirty, chiefly mechanics, who formed ourselves into a committee for the purpose of watching the movements of the British soldiers, and gaining every intelligence of the movements of the Tories.

We held our meetings at the Green Dragon Tavern. We were so careful that our meetings should be kept secret, that every time we met, every person swore upon the Bible that they would not discover any of our transactions but to Messrs. Hancock, Adams, Doctors Warren, Church, and one or two more. About November, when things began to grow serious, a gentleman who had connections with the Tory party, but was a Whig at heart, acquainted me, that our meetings were discovered, and mentioned the identical words that were spoken among us the night before. We did not then distrust Dr. Church, but supposed it must be some one among us. We removed to another place, which we thought was more secure;

but here we found that all our transactions were communicated to Governor Gage. (This came to me through the then Secretary Flucker; he told it to the gentlemen mentioned above.) It was then a common opinion, that there was a traitor in the Provincial Congress, and that Gage was possessed of all their secrets. (Church was a member of that Congress for Boston.) In the winter, towards the spring, we frequently took turns, two and two, to watch the soldiers, by patrolling the streets all night. The Saturday night preceding the 19th of April, about twelve o'clock at night, the boats belonging to the transports were all launched, and carried under the sterns of the men-of-war. (They had been previously hauled up and repaired.) We likewise found that the grenadiers and light infantry were all taken off duty.

From these movements, we expected something serious was to be transacted. On Tuesday evening, the 18th, it was observed that a number of soldiers were marching towards the bottom of the Common. About ten o'clock, Dr. Warren sent in great haste for me, and begged that I would immediately set off for Lexington, where Messrs. Hancock and Adams were, and acquaint them of the movement, and that it was thought they were the objects. When I got to Dr. Warren's house, I found he had sent an express by land to Lexington,—a Mr. William Dawes. The Sunday before, by desire of Dr. Warren, I had been to Lexington, to Messrs. Hancock and Adams, who were at the Rev. Mr. Clark's. I returned at night through Charlestown; there I agreed with a Colonel Conant and some other gentlemen, that if the British went out by water, we would show two lanthorns in the North Church steeple; and if by land, one as a signal; for we were apprehensive it would be difficult to cross the Charles River, or get over Boston Neck. I left Dr. Warren, called upon a friend, and desired him to make the signals. I then went home, took my boots and surtout, went to the north part of the town, where I kept a boat; two friends rowed me across Charles River a little to the eastward where the Somerset Man of War lay. It was then young flood, the ship was winding, and the moon was rising. They landed me on the Charlestown side. When I got into town, I met Colonel Conant and several others; they said they had seen our signals. I told them what was acting, and went to get me a horse; I got a horse of Deacon Larkin. While the horse was preparing, Richard Devens, Esq., who was one of the Committee of Safety, came to me, and told me that he came down the road from Lexington, after sundown, that evening;

that he met ten British officers, all well mounted and armed, going up the road.

I set off upon a very good horse; it was then about eleven o'clock, and very pleasant. After I had passed Charlestown Neck, and got nearly opposite where Mark was hung in chains, I saw two men on horseback, under a tree. When I got near them, I discovered they were British officers. One tried to get ahead of me, and the other to take me. I turned my horse very quick, and galloped towards Charlestown Neck, and then pushed for the Medford road. The one who chased me, endeavoring to cut me off, got into a clay pond, near where the new tavern is now built. I got clear of him, and went thru Medford, over the bridge, and up to Menotomy. In Medford, I awaked the Captain of the minute men; and after that, I alarmed almost every House, till I got to Lexington. I found Messrs. Hancock and Adams at the Rev. Mr. Clark's; I told them my errand, and enquired for Mr. Dawes; they said he had not been there; I related the story of the two officers, and supposed that he must have been stopped, as he ought to have been there before me. After I had been there about half an hour, Mr. Dawes came; we refreshed ourselves, and set off for Concord, to secure the stores, &c., there. We were overtaken by a young Dr. Prescott, whom we found to be a high Son of Liberty. I told them of the ten officers that Mr. Devens met, and that it was probable we might be stopped before we got to Concord; for I supposed that after night, they divided themselves, and that two of them had fixed themselves in such passages as were most likely to stop any intelligence going to Concord. I likewise mentioned that we had better alarm all the inhabitants till we got to Concord; the young Doctor much approved of it, and said he would stop with either of us, for the people between that and Concord knew him, and would give the more credit to what we said. We had got nearly half way; Mr. Dawes and the Doctor stopped to alarm the people of a house; I was about one hundred rods ahead, when I saw two men, in nearly the same situation as those officers were, near Charlestown. I called for the Doctor and Mr. Dawes to come up; in an instant I was surrounded by four;—they had placed themselves in a straight road, that inclined each way; they had taken down a pair of bars on the north side of the road, and two of them were under a tree in the pasture. The Doctor being foremost, he came up; and we tried to get past them; but they being armed with pistols and swords, they forced us into the pasture; the Doctor jumped his horse over a low stone wall, and got to Concord. I observed a wood at a small distance, and made for that. When I got there, out started six officers, on horseback, and ordered me to dismount;—one of them, who appeared to have the command, examined me, where I came from, and what my name was? I told him. He asked me if I was an express? I answered in the affirmative. He demanded what time I left Boston? I told him; and added, that their troops had catched aground in passing the river, and that there would be five hundred Americans there in a short time, for I had alarmed the country all the way up. He immediately rode towards those who stopped us, when all five of them came down upon a full gallop; one of them, whom I afterwards found to be a Major Mitchel, of the 5th Regiment, clapped his pistol to my head, called me by name, and told me he was going to ask me some questions, and if I did not give him true answers he would blow my brains out. He then asked me similar questions to those above. He then ordered me to mount my horse, after searching me for arms. He then ordered them to advance and to lead me in front. When we got to the road, they turned down towards Lexington. When we had got about one mile, the Major rode up to the officer that was leading me and told him to give me to the Sergeant. As soon as he took me, the Major ordered him, if I attempted to run, or anybody insulted them, to blow my brains out. We rode till we got near Lexington meeting-house, when the militia fired a volley of guns, which appeared to alarm them very much. The Major inquired of me how far it was to Cambridge, and if there were any other road. After some consultation, the Major rode up to the Sergeant, and asked if his horse was tired. He answered him he was—he was a Sergeant of Grenadiers, and had a small horse—then, said he, take that man's horse. I dismounted, and the sergeant mounted my horse, when they all rode towards Lexington meeting-house. I went across the burying-ground, and some pastures, and came to the Rev. Mr. Clark's house, where I found Messrs. Hancock and Adams. I told them of my treatment, and they concluded to go from that house towards Woburn. I went with them, and a Mr. Lowell, who was a clerk to Mr. Hancock. When we got to the house where they intended to stop, Mr. Lowell and myself returned to Mr. Clark's to find what was going on. When we got there, an elderly man came in; he said he had just come from the tavern, that a man had come from Boston, who said there were no British troops coming. Mr. Lowell and myself went towards the tavern, when we met a man on a full gallop, who told us the troops were coming up the rocks. We afterwards met another, who said they were close by. Mr. Lowell asked me to go to the tavern with him, to get a trunk of papers belonging to Mr. Hancock. We went up chamber, and while we were getting the trunk, we saw the British very near, upon a full march. We hurried towards Mr. Clark's house. In our way, we passed through the militia. There were about fifty. When we had got about one hundred yards from the meeting-house, the British troops appeared on both sides of the meeting-house. In their front was an officer on horseback. They made a short halt; when I saw and heard a gun fired, which appeared to be a pistol. Then I could distinguish two guns, and then a continual roar of musketry; when we made off with the trunk.

As I have mentioned Dr. Church, perhaps it might not be disagreeable to mention some matters of my own knowledge respecting him. He appeared to be a high Son of Liberty. He frequented all the places where they met, was encouraged by all the leaders of the Sons of Liberty, and it appeared he was respected by them, though I knew that Dr. Warren had not the greatest affection for him. He was esteemed a very capable writer, especially in verse, and as the Whig party needed every strength, they feared as well as courted him. Though it was known that some of the liberty songs which he composed were parodized by him in favor of the British, yet none dare charge him with it. I was a constant and critical observer of him, and I must say that I never thought him a man of principle; and I doubted much in my own mind whether he was a real Whig. I knew that he kept company with a Captain Price, a half-pay British officer, and that he frequently dined with him and Robinson, one of the Commissioners. I knew that one of his intimate acquaintances asked him why he was so often with Robinson and Price. His answer was, that he kept company with them on purpose to find out their plans. The day after the battle of Lexington, I met him in Cambridge, when he shew me some blood on his stocking, which he said spirted on him from a man who was killed near him, as he was urging the militia on. I well remember, that I argued with myself, if a man will risk his life in a cause, he must be a friend to that cause; and I never suspected him after, till he was charged with being a traitor.

The same day I met Dr. Warren. He was President of the Committee of Safety. He engaged me as a messenger, to do the outdoors business for that committee: which gave me an opportunity of being frequently with them. The Friday evening after, about sunset, I was sitting with some, or near all that committee, in their room, which was at Mr. Hastings' house in Cambridge. Dr. Church, all at once, started up—Dr. Warren, said he, I am determined to go into Boston to-morrow (it set them all a-staring). Dr. Warren replied, Are you serious, Dr. Church? they will hang you if they catch you in Boston. He replied, I am serious, and am determined to go at all adventures. After a considerable conversation, Dr. Warren said, If you are determined, let us make some business for you. They agreed that he should go to get medicine for their and our wounded officers. He went next morning; and I think he came back on Sunday evening. After he had told the committee how things were, I took him aside and inquired particularly how they treated him. He said, that as soon as he got to their lines, on Boston Neck, they made him a prisoner, and carried him to General Gage, where he was examined, and then he was sent to Gould's barracks, and was not suffered to go home but once. After he was taken up, for holding a correspondence with the British, I came across Deacon Caleb Davis;—we entered into conversation about him;—he told me, that the morning Church went into Boston, he (Davis) received a billet for General Gage—(he then did not know that Church was in town)—when he got to the General's house, he was told, the General could not be spoke with, that he was in private with a gentleman; that he waited near half an hour, when General Gage and Dr. Church came out of a room, discoursing together, like persons who had been long acquainted. He appeared to be quite surprised at seeing Deacon Davis there; that he (Church) went where he pleased, while in Boston, only a Major Caine, one of Gage's aids, went with him. I was told by another person, whom I could depend upon, that he saw Church go into General Gage's house, at the above time; that he got out of the chaise and went up the steps more like a man that was acquainted than a prisoner.

Some time after, perhaps a year or two, I fell in company with a gentleman who studied with Church; in discoursing about him, I related what I have mentioned above; he said, he did not doubt that he was in the interest of the British; and that it was he who informed General Gage; that he knew for certain, that a short time before the battle of Lexington (for he then lived with him, and took care of his business and books), he had no money by him, and was much drove for money; that all at once, he had several hundred new British guineas; and that he thought at the time, where they came from.

Thus, Sir, I have endeavored to give you a short detail of some matters, of which perhaps no person but myself has documents or knowledge. I have mentioned some names which you are acquainted with; I wish you would ask them, if they can remember the circumstances I allude to.

I am, Sir, with every sentiment of esteem, your humble servant,
Paul Revere.

Source: Goss, Elbridge Henry. 1891. *The Life of Colonel Paul Revere*. Vol. 1. Boston, MA: Joseph George Cupples, 180–212.

Further Reading

Arvin, Newton. 1977. *Longfellow, His Life and Work*. Westport, CT: Greenwood Press.
Boston National Historical Park and United States, eds. 1998. *Boston and the American Revolution*. Handbook 146. Washington, DC: The Service.
Brooks, Victor. 1999. *The Boston Campaign: April 1775–March 1776*. Great Campaigns. Conshohocken, PA: Combined Pub.
Carp, Benjamin L. 2010. *Defiance of the Patriots: The Boston Tea Party & the Making of America*. New Haven, CT: Yale University Press.
Curtis, Edward E. 2005. *The Organization of the British Army in the American Revolution*. Cranbury, NJ: Scholars Bookshelf.
Fales, Martha Gandy. 1961. "Paul Revere's Three Accounts of His Famous Ride: A Massachusetts Historical Society Picture Book." *New England Quarterly* 34 (4): 556.
Fischer, David Hackett. 1995. *Paul Revere's Ride*. Oxford Paperbacks: History. New York: Oxford University Press.
Forbes, Esther. 1999. *Paul Revere and the World He Lived In*. Boston, MA: Houghton Mifflin.
Irmscher, Christoph. 2009. *Public Poet, Private Man: Henry Wadsworth Longfellow at 200*. Amherst: University of Massachusetts Press; Published in cooperation with the Houghton Library, Harvard University.
Knollenberg, Bernhard. 2003. *Growth of the American Revolution, 1766–1775*. Indianapolis, IN: Liberty Fund.
Longfellow, Henry Wadsworth. 1867. *The Poetical Works of H. W. Longfellow. Complete Edition*. Boston, MA: Ticknor & Fields.
Massachusetts Historical Society. 1835. *Collections of the Massachusetts Historical Society for the year 1798*. Boston, MA: John E. Eastburn.

McDowell, Bart. 1972. *The Revolutionary War: America's Fight for Freedom.* Washington, DC: National Geographic Society.

Miller, Joel. 2010. *The Revolutionary Paul Revere.* Nashville, TN: Thomas Nelson.

Revere, Paul. 1798. "Letter to Jeremy Belknap." Paul Revere Heritage Project. Accessed June 8, 2020. www.paul-revere-heritage.com/one-if-by-land-two-if-by-sea.html.

Triber, Jayne E. 1998. *A True Republican: The Life of Paul Revere.* Amherst: University of Massachusetts Press.

Warren, Mercy Otis, and Lester H. Cohen. 1988. *History of the Rise, Progress, and Termination of the American Revolution: Interspersed with Biographical, Political, and Moral Observations.* Indianapolis, IN: Liberty Classics.

10

George Washington Had Wooden Teeth

What People Think Happened

The story of George Washington's wooden teeth is as widely known as the "cannot tell a lie" myth of the cut down cherry tree. But unlike the fables originating in Parson Weems's worshipful and often fictional biography of the first president, this presumed tidbit of history does not elevate Washington to the status of a demigod. It simply purports to convey the harsh living conditions of the late eighteenth century, when even the rich and mighty did not have access to the mere necessities that are granted to all properly insured individuals in the United States today. As such, this story does not immediately sound false or implausible, and the power of this myth is such that we even have an incredible eyewitness account of Washington's wooden dentures:

> The set was indeed an awesome sight. The teeth were made of wood, two rounded slabs bristling with separate pegs. They might have been anything from a wall for a toy fortress to an intricate nutcracker, but teeth they were, according to the inscription lying beside them. Furthermore, and most important, the Father of our Country had worn them. They were of a magnificent mahogany or rosewood color, and it's a legend as old as the cherry tree that this patina was caused by the quantities of Madeira consumed by eighteenth-century gentlemen. They were a prime example of Yankee ingenuity and an extraordinary thing to see along with teacups, swords, fans, and Bibles. (Gibbs 1959, 36)

This description places Washington's wooden teeth in the venerable surroundings of the general's estate at Mount Vernon, preserved as a museum since the mid-1800s (the reader should be forewarned that this account published in *The Reporter* magazine in 1959 has no bearing on the veracity of the myth).

As often happens, curious details have been attached to the fictitious story, despite making it rather nonsensical. It is sometimes claimed that the president's teeth were lovingly crafted for him by none other than Paul Revere. The irony is, of course, that this historic figure was primarily known in his lifetime as a silversmith. How could wood have been his material of choice?

Another assumption so easily made by modern people is that Washington himself was solely responsible for the poor condition of his teeth. We live in an age when one is constantly reminded about proper oral hygiene through TV ads about toothbrushes, toothpaste brands, and the latest rinsing solutions. Washington was obviously not doing something right if his teeth ended up in such a peril.

There has also been speculation about the net weight of Washington's dentures, wooden or not. It is sometimes stated that they weighed three pounds. Although quite improbable, this conjecture adds to the impression of extreme discomfort experienced by George Washington while wearing his dentures. The pain endured by the Father of the Nation and the day-to-day bravery with which he stood up to dental frailty undoubtedly make him more approachable, although still quite heroic. Making a definite reference to the cherry tree story, a nineteenth-century author noted that Washington had only one false thing about him—his false teeth.

How It Became Popular

The myth of George Washington's wooden teeth does not seem to have a clear point of origin. A fairly correct understanding of the president's dental problems and accounts of the professionally implemented solutions actually predated the spreading of the wooden teeth theory. The first introduction of the general public to the topic of presidential dentures happened as late as 1843, when the *Boston Daily Bee* printed a brief note suggesting that "it is probably new to most of our readers, that Gen. Washington wore an entire set (upper and under) of artificial teeth." The *Bee* indicated that the teeth were made of hippopotamus ivory and identified Dr. John Greenwood as the maker of this set. This exact set of false teeth could also be seen on display at various times during the nineteenth century. On one occasion, these dentures were even exhibited as a curiosity at the Tiffany store in New York, alongside more of Washington's relics, such as the sword that he wore during the inauguration, a brooch containing a lock of his hair, original letters, and so on. Wood, as a material used for this set's construction, was only mentioned in its descriptions because some of the pegs holding the teeth together were wooden. Perhaps this detail caused some initial speculation about the main material from which the dentures were made. It appears, however, that this belief took some time before fully becoming engraved in the public's mind.

To trace the earliest mention of the wooden teeth myth, we have to turn our attention to the already cited publication in *The Reporter*. On March 5, 1959, the magazine published an article by Margaret Gibbs entitled "What Happened to Washington's Teeth?" The two-page piece related the contributor's fond memories of visiting Mount Vernon with her little daughter. Every time the trip was announced to her, the little girl used to light up because she once again anticipated seeing the object that interested her above all else: "Those teeth!"

> Her eccentricity was shared by others. We were often accompanied on these jaunts by small cousins and friends. They were all in the know. At the entrance gate, an air of excitement flared up among them. They pushed and hauled their adults up to and through the mansion. We could not stop to gaze at the Palladian Window, for the game of catch was on the minute we entered the door. We were forced to chase our darlings past the West Parlor, the Music Room, the Library. Upstairs, one of them might point out the funny bed that was so high a pair of steps had to be used to get into it, but they all hopped from foot to foot while the grownups insisted on admiring the view from the East Piazza. Then we were whizzed through the vegetable gardens, the rose garden. The outbuildings were completely ignored as they made a final sprint for the museum. When we caught up with them, the children were already glued in front of the glass case that displayed George Washington's false teeth at their eye level. There they would stay as long as our patience could bear it, uttering no sound other than an occasional "Gee!" of incredulity. (Gibbs 1959, 36)

Young Miss Gibbs's fascination with the oddity faded away soon after she turned twelve. The next visit only came about when she accompanied her mother as a "young matron, delicately interested in antiques and historic monuments of all sorts." They entered the museum with a very nostalgic feeling, expecting to see the much-revered curiosity as an old friend. To the pair's great disappointment, the teeth were missing. When they inquired of the present attendant about the teeth's whereabouts, the answer was that the museum had not had Washington's teeth on display in the last forty years. Mrs. Gibbs and her daughter went home confused.

The matter would have likely been left alone if it were not for the memories of seeing Washington's teeth at Mount Vernon that came pouring in from friends and relatives. *The Reporter*'s contributor finally decided to share her confusion with the museum's executive staff in writing. The response from the assistant director confirmed that Washington's teeth had not been on display at Mount Vernon for at least twenty-five years (the exact time that the highly ranked museum employee had worked there and could vouchsafe for). While the museum had recently acquired a set of false teeth from Martha Washington's descendants, such an item was considered too indelicate to be exhibited. In her article, Gibbs admitted that such an answer could not be refuted without causing one to suppose that "any number of people are suffering from a mass mirage of national dimensions." Yet, she pleaded for anyone who could shed more light on the situation to come forward.

The article generated a great deal of interest. In a few months, *The Reporter* published some of the received correspondence. The earliest memories of seeing Washington's dentures at Mount Vernon came from one Dorothy Ingram. She visited the museum between 1910 and 1913, when "the sight of the wooden teeth" assumed a permanent place in her memory. Another reader recalled seeing the teeth in 1932 during the Washington bicentenary. Others remained incredulous or facetious. The most important response, however, came from the museum itself. Charles C. Wall, the resident director, noted that "the article on General Washington's teeth highlighted a phenomenon which has long puzzled" the staff of the museum. Wall informed the editor of *The Reporter* that "no set of General Washington's false teeth has ever been displayed in the Mount Vernon museum." He continued to say that the museum acquired a set of the general's dentures in 1949, but he expressed the belief that "public display outside the confines of a medical museum would constitute an impropriety" (Wall 1959).

So, it seems that in the late 1950s, many people of different ages and upbringing had unsubstantiated belief about the existence of wooden teeth at Mount Vernon. One could probably discard their recollections as untrustworthy or even ascribe them to the so-called Mandela effect (a poorly conceived theory that capitalizes on unreliable collective memories, claiming that they prove the existence of alternate realities). However, a real twist in this story is that Joseph Ellis, a Pulitzer Prize–winning historian and the author of one of the recent biographies of George Washington, also shared his own childhood memories about seeing the general's teeth at the Mount Vernon museum in the later 1940s (Ellis 2011, ix). The main difference is that the historian recalls that the myth of Washington's wooden teeth was dispelled by the staff in the actual presence of the hallowed relic (Washington's teeth that *were not* wooden). Ellis is very much aware of the alluded phenomenon, admitting that the museum's current employees have no explanation for his memories. Considering this testimony from a professional historian, it is best to leave this entire episode under the category of unexplained phenomena (although some have speculated that the museum simply removed the sensitive object from the exhibit, instructing the staff never to acknowledge that it has ever been there).

For our purposes, it suffices to know that as early as the beginning of the twentieth century there were individuals who were convinced that George Washington's false teeth were made out of wood and even claimed to have seen them. This myth became widely known and believed in the following decades and perhaps became one of the few facts that immediately come to one's mind when Washington's name is mentioned. Sometimes this bit of false historical knowledge was used with humorous effect. In a school play entitled *Little Red Riding Hood*, a character facetiously notes that Washington was afraid of termites because he had wooden teeth. More than once, educators have resorted to this myth as a way to encourage better dental hygiene. Such jokes and levity indicate that the myth is universally known, although it seemed to have no definite origin. At the same time, this false belief is also very easily debunked because Washington's dentures actually survive. As a result, this myth is among the ones most commonly confronted in popular books. And yet, the authors of these numerous attempts to put an end to this strange misconception have to admit that they do not have a way of explaining where the myth came from. There is only one notable exception.

In 1990, a York Rite Masons' magazine, the *Knight Templar*, published an article by Sir Knight William A. Brown entitled "Washington's Teeth." The author shared a memory of an excursion to the Medical Museum in Washington, DC, during which a curator implored the visiting historians and curators to spread the news about the outrageous falsehood of the wooden teeth myth. As a way of disproving it, the unnamed museum professional produced images of the set of teeth then on display at the museum and also gave his account of how this myth came about.

According to him, the story began in 1841 when a certain dentist produced a paper describing his successes in treating patients under anesthesia. George Washington's name was used passingly to indicate the time when "some poor people had to wear teeth of wood" (Brown 1990, 25). The paper contained no information about the general's actual dental predicaments. Unfortunately, the use of belladonna, laudanum, and cocaine was supposedly frowned upon by people of various religious convictions. This caused the paper's rejection by the publisher. Twenty years later, the Civil War broke out, and doctors had to deal with severely injured soldiers who required long and complicated operations that were simply impossible without general anesthesia. They had no choice but to bypass what William A. Brown believes to have been "a religious ban" and use heavy painkillers. To justify their actions, many doctors felt the need to publicize their successes while also pointing out those cases when unmitigated pain caused suffering and the eventual deaths of patients.

If the article in the *Knight Templar* is to be believed, there came a point when any doctor who did not write papers about his advanced methods could be considered unsuccessful by people in the community. In 1871, an unnamed doctor having to write his own white paper simply reworked the rejected article penned by his predecessor, making changes as he pleased:

> At that time a dentist who had a copy of his predecessor's paper, which was now over twenty years old, decided it was worth repeating, so he rewrote the paper, following the same continuity but changing a word here and there. When he got to the place where his predecessor had written, "During Washington's time, some poor people had to wear teeth of wood," he changed it to say, "Even Washington, in his time, wore teeth of wood." (Brown 1990, 26)

This outrageous false piece of knowledge supposedly "spread like wildfire," even though the truth about Washington's teeth was documented in pictures, documents, and medical records. According to Brown, this was the exact point from which the myth originated.

This comprehensive explanation, lacking names and citations, does not sound completely unreasonable (with the possible exception of the power that religious authorities exercised over medical practices; this may have been an exaggeration). However, our search for a news story about Washington's teeth around 1871 failed to discover anything of significance, especially keeping in mind that the piece of news in question "spread like wildfire." It is safe to say that such a story did not exist. To demonstrate how a news story could indeed receive a wide circulation, one can point out an article called "A Toothless People" that was indeed picked up by many newspapers and journals in the continental United States during the 1870s. It is a humorous account of a dentist arriving in Warrenton, Virginia, and offering substantial discounts on artificial teeth. After two solid weeks of pulling teeth, the man absconded with the money and the hotel owner's wife. All the town's butchers closed their businesses because most of Warrenton's denizens could eat nothing but soup and farina (milled wheat cereal). One toothless man became so desperate that he whittled out a set of wooden teeth for himself, but when he took a sip of local whiskey, it set the flammable dentures ablaze. The man's funeral was held the next day.

If this ridiculous anecdote became so widely disseminated, surely a story about the first president's wooden teeth would have gotten some attention. But this did not happen. It appears that even if William A. Brown's account contains some grains of truth, it does not hold together as a whole. The only available explanation for the myth of George Washington's wooden teeth is itself just another myth.

We are left to conclude, like many other debunkers of the myth, that its origin is unknown. With relative certainty, it can be established that the myth already circulated in the early twentieth century. It has been thus far impossible to locate any mention of this false assumption in the 1800s—neither in the form of a statement nor in the form of debunking a false story. The *American Journal of Dental Science* found it important enough to reprint the obviously facetious story about the toothless people of Warrenton (1875, v. 8, p. 472) while commenting that the only dentists residing in that locale and known to the editors were actually very fine practitioners of their trade. It is unfathomable that no contemporary dentistry publication would have left unnoticed any printed story about the wooden teeth of the first president. At the same time, there has never been a shortage of professionals discussing the actual dentures worn by George Washington.

The myth probably originated among those who did not have any interest in scientific details while, at the same time, not having access to any forms of publicizing their observations (which may have come from seeing the real dentures on display). Given the well-known adolescent interest in all things macabre (correctly highlighted in Margaret Gibbs's account), American schoolyards could have been a breeding ground for this myth, acting as a counterweight to the overplayed cherry tree story. Impressionable young audiences remain well served today, as references to George Washington's wooden teeth can be found in modern cartoons and comics. The lack of adult intervention continuously allows one to grow up while taking this myth at face value. Instead of citing examples from modern pop culture, media and politics, a fitting quote comes from the book *Our American Presidents* by (Bumann et al. 1997, 6): "Washington did have wooden teeth. He also had teeth made of whale bone and deer antlers. But he never chopped down a cherry tree in his life." If the myth about Washington's teeth is even brought up by those who are trying to debunk other myths about the first president, is there any hope for the rest of us?

PRIMARY DOCUMENTS
PAUL REVERE'S NEWSPAPER ADS

Newspapers played a crucial role in dissemination of information in the eighteenth century. Commercial activities of all sorts relied on them as the main form of advertisement. Ads taken out by Paul Revere could be seen as a reason for believing that the Boston silversmith was responsible for the fabrication of one set of Washington's false teeth.

"ARTIFICIAL TEETH."
PAUL REVERE
Whereas many persons are so unfortunate as to lose their fore teeth by accident and otherwise, to their great detriment, not only in looks but speaking both in public and private: This is to inform all such that they may have them replaced with artificial ones that look as well as the natural, and answers the end of speaking to all intents, by Paul Revere, Goldsmith. Near the head of Dr. Clark's Warf. All persons who have had false teeth fixt by Mr. John Baker, Surgeon Dentist, and they have got loose (as they will in time) may have them fastened by the above who learnt the method of fixing them from Mr. Baker.

Source: *Boston Gazette and Country Journal,* September 1, 1768.

"ARTIFICIAL TEETH."
PAUL REVERE
Takes this method of returning his most sincere thanks to the gentlemen and ladies who have employed him in the care of their teeth. He would now inform them and all others who are so unfortunate as to lose their teeth by accident or otherwise, that he still continues business of a dentist and flatters himself that from the experience he has had these two years (in which time he has fixt some hundreds of teeth) that he can fix them as well as any surgeon dentist who ever came from London. He fixes them in such a manner that they are not only an ornament but also a real use in speaking and eating. He cleanses the teeth and will wait on any gentlemen.

Source: *Boston Gazette and Country Journal*, July 30, 1770.

LETTERS TO THE EDITOR OF *THE REPORTER* MAGAZINE

The Reporter was an influential publication of the 1950s–1960s. The article that was published by Margaret Gibbs in 1959 stirred a lot of interest in Washington's teeth, but it left many people confused and puzzled.

WASHINGTON'S TEETH: TRUE OR FALSE?
To the Editors: I chuckled with the pleasure of a shared recollection when I read Margaret Gibbs's tale ("What Happened to Washington's Teeth?," The Reporter, March 5) till shock set in at the discovery that the dentures had disappeared. After leaving college, I lived in Washington from 1911 to 1913, during which time I visited Mount Vernon, where the sight of the wooden teeth found a permanent place in my memory. In the intervening years, had anyone ever asked me what I recalled most vividly about the contents of Mount Vernon, I should have answered without hesitation, "Washington's wooden teeth."
    DOROTHY C. INGRAM
    Asheville, North Carolina

Source: Ingram, Dorothy C. 1959. Letter to the editor. *The Reporter*, March 5, 1959: 8.

To the Editors: Although I am not good at figures and have a poor memory for dates, it seems to me that it was during the Washington Bicentenary in 1932 that I first saw George Washington's teeth at

Mount Vernon. My home was in Richmond then and I took several out of state or foreign visitors to Washington and, of course, Mount Vernon, and continued to see the dentures from time to time. In 1951, when I returned to live in the Washington area from overseas, our home was within a mile of Mount Vernon, on former Mount Vernon land, and we took a considerable interest, naturally, in visiting it. The dentures were noticeably not there and we remarked on it at once. After two or three visits we asked a guard and then a curator or minor official of some sort to whom we were directed and were told that they were not and had never been on display. The information was given in a tone which was a mixture of nauteur and belligerent defensiveness. It was my opinion then and is now that the removal of the dentures from the display was a bit of Nice-Nellyism.
AUSTIN W. MORRILL
Alexandria, Virginia

Source: Morrill, Austin W. 1959. Letter to the editor. *The Reporter*, March 5, 1959: 8.

What Really Happened

George Washington was born in 1732. It is generally assumed that his strong constitution and stature indicated good health; however, such was not the case. Throughout his life, the first president suffered from bouts of different illnesses, including malaria, which is known to have an adverse effect on oral health. The lack of preventative measures available at the time also contributed to early problems with Washington's teeth. The future president's dental bills were constantly increasing, and at least on one occasion he apparently tried (out of modesty?) to conceal payments made to his dentist. However, it would be unfair to accuse Washington of neglecting his teeth. Records exist of his purchasing dental care products both before and after he had to fully switch to using artificial teeth. These products included toothbrushes, powders, scrapers, pincers, and files. Over time, he developed an appreciation for dental science and was actively involved in the work that went into relieving his own pain.

When Washington was forty years old, a serious medical intervention was unavoidable. Dr. John Baker, an English-born professional dentist, extracted several of George's teeth, bringing some relief from the pain. Baker also introduced Washington to additional elements of dental hygiene, although, in its most primitive form, it was not enough to prevent further tooth decay.

It is very likely that Dr. Baker was inadvertently responsible for the genesis of the myth crediting Paul Revere with the fabrication of Washington's dentures. After all, he was the very same Mr. Baker whom Revere mentioned in his newspaper ads and who apparently taught the Boston patriot his own "method" of "fixing" loose teeth. However, no record exists showing that Revere participated in any work performed on George Washington's teeth, let alone that the silversmith took on the future president as his own client. Besides, dentistry was never Paul Revere's main occupation. According to his own notes, he stopped practicing dentistry in 1774 (Wynbrandt 2000, 125).

Washington availed of Dr. Baker's services just before the Revolutionary War. There are records of this doctor receiving payment in 1772–1773 for making partial ivory dentures that were wired to his patient's remaining teeth. At that time, Washington also became acquainted with Charles Willson Peale (1741–1827), an officer serving in the Continental Army. Having received proper education in fine arts, Peale produced portraits of many key figures of the Revolutionary War, including almost sixty of George Washington. Similarly, to Washington, he suffered from severe tooth decay, and, being scientifically inclined, he designed his own dentures. At one point, he offered to make false teeth for his commander, and this offer was accepted, resulting in dentures made out of lead alloy and steel springs with teeth crafted out of ivory as well as cattle and human teeth.

In 1783, another prominent practitioner of dentistry got a chance to work on the general's teeth. Washington charged Lieutenant Colonel Smith with the task of verifying the skills of a certain French doctor. To add another level of secretiveness, he did not even include the Frenchman's name in the letter, simply adding that Samuel Fraunces, a notable tavern owner in New York, would be able to point him out. Washington's sensitivity about the issue was summarized by his stated concern "that this matter should be made a parade of." The doctor's credentials were verified to Washington's satisfaction, and he extended his invitation to Jean-Pierre Le Mayeur. It is worth noting that the rigorous vetting process this new dentist had to go through (even if unbeknownst to him) might not have allowed Paul Revere to step into the same position because Revere was less experienced.

Jean-Pierre Le Mayeur came to America three years prior and built a reputation for his excellent skills. Particularly good at extracting teeth, Le Mayeur placed ads in American newspapers that invited individuals to sell their healthy teeth to him for subsequent transplantation. As one of his ads states, "Any person that will dispose of their Front Teeth (slaves excepted) may receive Two Guineas for each." No matter how insufficient the price of two large golden coins (each equaling twenty-one shillings) may sound, the real interest for us lies in the fact that Le Mayeur did not want enslaved persons to take advantage of this offer.

However, Le Mayeur's stay at Mount Vernon coincides with a record made in the plantation's records (Ledger B, now at the Library of Congress) in which the sum of six pounds two shillings was disbursed to nine slaves. It is unclear how many teeth were extracted, but the amount offered appears to be much less generous than what Le Mayeur paid to other donors. It is unclear whether those teeth were used by the French dentist in attending to the dental health of Washington and his family. There is a possibility that he kept them for subsequent patients.

The extent of Le Mayeur's work on Washington's teeth in particular is also unknown. However, during his visits to Mount Vernon, he became well appreciated by the family. A letter survives in which the dentist talks about presenting "little master George" (George Washington Parke Custis, the general's stepson) with a red horse as a way of thanking him for frequently loaning a blue horse.

By the time of Washington's inauguration, he had only one of his natural teeth left in place. This sole remaining premolar was used by Dr. John Greenwood (1760–1819) of New York as an anchor for the set of dentures designed in 1789. The anchoring tooth was submitted to much pressure. It soon became loose and fell out. Designing dentures for the president was now even more challenging. Greenwood's next set of false teeth was fastened to a golden piece that fit the palate of Washington's mouth. Curiously, half a dozen wooden pegs, each a few millimeters in diameter, were employed to hold the teeth together. As far as we know, this is the only plausible kernel of truth behind the claim that Washington's teeth were wooden. Hippopotamus and elephant ivory were used for the actual teeth in those dentures.

Washington was very pleased with the work that Greenwood performed for him. The New York dentist remained the president's main purveyor of dental services for the rest of his life, despite the inconvenience of living far away. This doctor-patient relationship often had to be carried out through mail exchanges that now provide us with many valuable clues into the difficulties of caring for dentures in the late eighteenth century. In one of his letters, George Washington provides feedback regarding what needs to be done to his dentures. Apart from lack of comfort while wearing them, he is concerned that they give his lips "the pouting and swelling appearance" (Fitzpatrick 1939, 29). Washington even filed the dentures down in an apparent attempt to improve his looks (he was responsible for the routine maintenance of his false teeth).

Greenwood's advice for his patient includes suggestions on how to clean the dentures and how to give them a desired color. He also admonishes the president to remove his false teeth while consuming port wine because it is highly acidic: "Acid is Used in Couloring every kind of Ivory, therefore it is very perncious to the teeth" (Fitzpatrick 1939, 29. Greenwood's spelling is preserved). It is difficult to judge how much friendly jest is present in these comments, but they provide clear evidence for materials used to create Washington's teeth.

John Greenwood was the last of George Washington's dentists. In an uncharacteristic departure from the usual rather secretive way in which the president's dental affairs were carried out, Greenwood actually used this acquaintance with the general to his own advantage. He used his illustrious patient's name in various newspaper advertisements, correctly identifying himself as "Dentist to His Excellency, George Washington," but this was more than just mere name-dropping. John Greenwood had a profound admiration for the first president, to the point of sentimentality. We know for a fact that the very last of Washington's teeth had been preserved by the dentist and passed down in his family as a precious heirloom.

Throughout his life, George Washington owned several sets of false teeth. The materials used for them varied, depending on the maker's choice and availability. These dentures have been an object of morbid curiosity and legitimate historic interest among the general public. Members of the dental community have always expressed genuine professional interest toward these examples of eighteenth-century medical science. One such presidential relic even received some undesired attention from the criminal world in 1981 when it was determined to be missing from a locked room at the Smithsonian's National Museum of American History. Eventually, the lower denture was recovered on the museum's premises (perhaps indicating an inside job), but the upper part is still missing. Sadly, the possibility of an unscrupulous private collector ending up in possession of this artifact represents the best possible and also unlikely scenario. It is feared that the dentures, containing a good amount of gold, were promptly melted down for the sake of this precious metal component. In fact, it is believed that these particular dentures are the very same that were made by John Greenwood in 1795 using gold springs and a solid golden plate fitted to the roof of Washington's mouth.

The thieves certainly did not have any false presumptions about Washington's teeth. One might surmise that they used the recent research by a man who knew in depth not only those particular dentures but every other existing relic of Washington's dental history. Reider Sognnaes, one of the most prominent historians of dentistry, spent a lifetime studying everything that could be learned about this subject. A highly trained dentist with an interest in forensics, Sognnaes even attempted to create replicas of all known sets of Washington's teeth. His research was publicized in the 1970s by many media outlets, including the Smithsonian's own magazine. On numerous occasions, the historian of dentistry confirmed that Washington's teeth were not wooden, listing the materials that he found in the dentures that he had a chance to observe: hippopotamus and elephant ivory, walrus tusks, cattle teeth, and, of course, gold. Did the thieves become intrigued by these publications? Fortunately, when the Smithsonian turned to Sognnaes to fabricate a replica of the missing dentures, he was able to perform the task using his research records.

As far as the sometimes heard claim that George Washington's dentures weighed a total of three pounds, it suffices to consider the set that was apparently made by Charles Wilson Peale. This contraption included a lead alloy base and steel springs, but its entire weight is just under four ounces (Grizzard 2002, 105).

The information gathered from primary sources as well as the research done by Reider Sognnaes and others demonstrate that there is absolutely no reason to believe that George Washington's dentures were wooden. In fact, wood was not seen as a good material for false teeth even in the eighteenth century. It is true that the wearer of these early devices experienced much discomfort, but they were still worth having as long as improvements were being made and a proper maintenance schedule followed.

We still do not know the entire story of Washington's dental problems. The president's misgivings about making his dental predicaments public likely contributed to speculations. It is unfortunate that George Washington did not use his status and fame to promote dental science, but popular culture should finally resist portraying him as someone who had to "brush daily and see his carpenter twice a year" (Larsen 1982).

PRIMARY DOCUMENTS

GEORGE WASHINGTON'S LETTERS

Washington's correspondence is an invaluable source of information about his dental troubles. One of his letters to Dr. Baker was even intercepted by the British, who ended up mocking Washington for requesting supplies, such as pincers and wires, for holding his dentures in place. The original spelling used in these documents has been preserved.

To Lieutenant Colonel William Stephens Smith
Newburgh, May 15, 1783.
Dear Sir: Sometime in the Winter, or early this Spring, a Frenchman in New York applied after representing the manner of his getting to that place for leave to come out. Being a stranger of whom I had no knowledge and only his own word to support his narrative, I informed him that his application would go with more propriety to the Minister of France at Phila, than it came to me, and referred him there accordingly. The other day at Orange Town Mr. Fraunces informed me, that, this applicant was the Dentist of whose skill much has been said; and that he was very uneasy at not being able to get out. Having some Teeth which are very troublesome to me at times, and of wch. I wish to be eased, provided I could substitute others (not by transplantation, for of this I have no idea, even with young people, and sure I am it cannot succeed with old,) and Gums which might be relieved by a Man of skill, I would thank you for making a private Investigation of this Mans Character and knowledge in his profession and if you find them such as I can derive any benefit from encourage him to come out, and to take this in his way to whatever post, or place he may be bound. At any rate, if he really is skilful, I should be glad to see him with his Apparatus. I would not wish that this matter should be made a parade of, and therefore give you the trouble of arranging it. I cannot (having forgot it) give you this Mans name, but Mr. Frauncis can point you to him. I think he told me he lodged at a Mr. Lispenards where he had exhibited some proofs of his skill.

Source: Fitzpatrick, John C. 1931. *The Writings of George Washington from the Original Manuscript Sources 1745–1799*. Vol. 26. Washington, DC: Government Printing Office, 434.

To John Greenwood
Philadelphia, December 7, 1798.

Sir: What you sent me last, answer exceedingly well; and I send the first to be altered and made like them, if you can.

Your recollection of these, with the directions and observations contained in my two last letters, the latter especially, supercedes the necessity of being particular in this.

I will however just remark that the great error in those (now returned to you) is, that the upper teeth and bars do not fall back enough thus [\] but stand more upright, so [|] by which means the bar at (a) shoots beyond the gums and not only forces the lip out just under the nose but by not having its proper place to rest upon frets, and makes that part very sore.

I shall add no more than to request you will be so good as to let me have them as soon as you conveniently can; altered or not altered. Direct for me at this place, or at Mount Vernon, as it is not likely I shall be here more than two or three days longer.

I thank you very much for your obliging attention to my requests, and am Sir

With esteem and regard, etc.

P. S. I am willing and ready to pay whatever you may charge me.

Source: Fitzpatrick, John C. 1939. *The Writings of George Washington from the Original Manuscript Sources 1745–1799*. Vol. 37. Washington, DC: Government Printing Office, 27.

To John Greenwood
Philadelphia, December 12, 1798.

Sir: Your letter of the 8th. came Safe. And as I am hurrying, in order to leave this City tomorrow, I must be short.

The principal thing you will have to attend to, in the alteration you are about to make, is to let the upper bar fall back from the lower one thus [\] ; whether the teeth are quite straight, or incling a little in thus, [] or a little rounding outwards thus [] is immaterial, for I find it is the bars alone, both above and below that gives the lips the pouting and swelling appearance; of consequence, if this can be remedied, all will be well.

I Send you the old bars, which you returned to me with the new set, because you have desired. But they may be destroyed, or any thing else done with them you please, for you will find that I have been obliged to file them away so much above, to remedy the evil I have been complaining of as to render them useless perhaps to receive new teeth. But of this you are better able to judge than I am. If you can fix the teeth (now on the new bars which you have) on the old bars which you will receive with this letter I should prefer it, because the latter are easy in the mouth. and you will perceive moreover that when the edges of the upper and lower teeth are put together that the upper falls back into the mouth, which they ought to do, or it will have the effect of forcing the lip out just under the nose.

I shall only repeat again, that I feel much obliged by your extreme willingness, and readiness to accomodate me and that I am, etc.

Source: Fitzpatrick, John C. 1939. *The Writings of George Washington from the Original Manuscript Sources 1745–1799*. Vol. 37. Washington, DC: Government Printing Office, 28.

Greenwood to Washington
December 28

I send you inclosed two setts of teeth, one fixed on the Old Barrs in part and the rest you sent me from Philadelphia which when I Received was very black. Ocationed either by your soaking them in port wine, or by your drinking it. Port Wine being sower takes of all the polish and All Acids has a tendency to soften every kind of teeth and bone. Acid is Used in Coulouring every kind of Ivory, therefore it is very pernicious to the teeth. I Advice you to Either take them out After dinner and put them in clean water, and put in another seett, or Cleaen them with a brush and som Chalk scraped fine, it will Absorbe the Acid which Collects from the mouth, and preserve them longer. I have found another and better way of useing the sealing wax, when holes is eaten in the teeth by acid &ca. first Observe and dry the teeth, then take a peice of Wax and Cut it into As small peices as you think will fill up the hole, then take a large nail or any other peice of Iron and heat it hot. into the fier, then put your peice of wax into the hole. and melt it by meanes of introduceing the point of the Nail to it. . . . If your teeth Grows black take some chalk and a pine or Cedar stick, it will rub it of. If you whant your teeth more yellower soake them in Broath or pot liquer, but not in tea or Acid. Porter is a Good thing to Coulor them and will not hurt but preserve them but it must not be in the least pricked. You will find I have Altered the upper teeth, you sent me from Philadelphia leaveing the enamel on the teeth dont, preserve them any longer then if it was of, it only holds the Color better, but to preserve them they must be very Often Changed and Cleaned for whatever Atacks them, must, be repelled, as Often or it will gain Ground and destroy the works, the two setts I repaired is done on a different plan then when they are done when made intirely new, for the teeth are screwed on the barrs, insted of haveing the barrs Cast red hot on them, which is the reason I believe the destroy or desolve so soone, near to the barrs.

Source: Fitzpatrick, John C. 1939. *The Writings of George Washington from the Original Manuscript Sources 1745–1799.* Vol. 37. Washington, DC: Government Printing Office, 29–30.

Further Reading

Axelrod, Alan. 2009. *The Real History of the American Revolution: A New Look at the Past.* New York: Sterling.

Brown, William A. 1990. "Washington's Teeth." *Knight Templar*, February 1990, 25–27.

Bumann, Joan, John Patterson, and Doug Byrum. 1997. *Our American Presidents.* St. Petersburg, FL: Worthington Press.

Cunliffe, Marcus, Gordon S. Wood, and Mount Vernon Ladies' Association of the Union. 1998. *George Washington: Man and Monument.* Mount Vernon, VA: Mount Vernon Ladies' Association.

Editorial, etc. 1875. "A Toothless People." *American Journal of Dental Science* 8 (10): Baltimore: Snowden & Cowman.

Ellis, Joseph J. 2011. *His Excellency: George Washington.* New York: Alfred A. Knopf.

Fitzpatrick, John C. 1931. *The Writings of George Washington from the Original Manuscript Sources 1745–1799.* Vol. 26. Washington, DC: Government Printing Office.

Fitzpatrick, John C. 1939. *The Writings of George Washington from the Original Manuscript Sources 1745–1799.* Vol. 37. Washington, DC: Government Printing Office.

Furstenberg, François. 2011. "Atlantic Slavery, Atlantic Freedom: George Washington, Slavery, and Transatlantic Abolitionist Networks." *The William and Mary Quarterly* 68 (2): 247.

Gibbs, Margaret. 1959. "What Happened to Washington's Teeth?" *The Reporter*, March 5, 1959, 36–37.

Grizzard, Frank E. 2002. *George Washington: A Biographical Companion.* Santa Barbara, CA: (Biographical Companion). ABC-CLIO.

Hoffmann-Axthelm, Walter. 1981. *History of Dentistry.* Quintessence Books. Chicago, IL: Quintessence Pub. Co.

Ingram, Dorothy C., letter to the editor, 1959. Letter to the editor. *The Reporter*, March 5, 1959, 8.

Larsen, Dave. 1982. "Little Could Ease Washington's Dental Misery." *Boston Globe*, February 15, 1982.

Levy, Philip. 2013. *Where the Cherry Tree Grew: The Story of Ferry Farm, George Washington's Boyhood Home*. 1st ed. New York: St. Martin's Press.

Morrill, Austin W., letter to the editor, 1959. Letter to the editor. *The Reporter*, March 5, 1959, 8.

Parry, Jay A., Andrew M. Allison, W. Cleon Skousen, and George Washington. 1991. *The Real George Washington*. American Classic Series, Vol. 3. Washington, DC: National Center for Constitutional Studies.

Schwarz, Philip J., and Jean B. Lee, eds. 2001. *Slavery at the Home of George Washington*. Mount Vernon, VA: Mount Vernon Ladies' Assoc.

Sognnaes, R. F. 1973. "America's Most Famous Teeth." *Smithsonian* 3 (11): 47–51.

Sognnaes, R. F. 1976. "George Washington's Bite." *Journal of the California Dental Association* 4 (6): 36–40.

Wall, Charles C., letter to the editor, 1959. Letter to the editor. *The Reporter*, March 5, 1959, 8.

Washington, George. *George Washington Papers, Series 5, Financial Papers: General Ledger* B, -1793. /1793, 1772. Manuscript/Mixed Material. Accessed January 5, 2020. https://www.loc.gov/item/mgw500002.

Wynbrandt, James. 2000. *The Excruciating History of Dentistry: Toothsome Tales & Oral Oddities from Babylon to Braces*. New York: St. Martins Griffin.

Bibliography

Adam of Bremen. 1978. *Beskrivelse af øerne i Nordern [Description of the Islands in the North]*. Copenhagen: Wormianum.
Adams, Gretchen. 2008. *The Specter of Salem*. Chicago, IL: University of Chicago Press.
Allison, Robert J. 2015. *The American Revolution: A Very Short Introduction*. New York: Oxford University Press.
Anbinder, Tyler. 2016. *City of Dreams: The 400-Year Epic History of Immigrant New York*. Boston, MA: Houghton Mifflin Harcourt.
Arvin, Newton. 1977. *Longfellow, His Life and Work*. Westport, CT: Greenwood Press.
Ashton, John. 1883. *The Adventures and Discourses of Captain John Smith*. Oxford: Cassell.
Axelrod, Alan. 2009. *The Real History of the American Revolution: A New Look at the Past*. New York: Sterling.
Baker, Emerson W. 2015. *A Storm of Witchcraft: The Salem Trials and the American Experience*. New York: Oxford University.
Baker, Emerson W., and John G. Reid. 1998. *The New England Knight: Sir William Phips, 1651–1695*. Toronto and Buffalo: University of Toronto Press.
Bangs, Jeremy Dupertuis, and New England Historic Genealogical Society. 2004. *Pilgrim Edward Winslow: New England's First International Diplomat: A Documentary Biography*. Boston, MA: New England Historic Genealogical Society.
Barbour, Philip L. 1971. *Pocahontas and Her World: A Chronicle of America's First Settlement in Which Is Related the Story of the Indians and*

the Englishmen, Particularly Captain John Smith, Captain Samuel Argall, and Master John Rolfe. London: Robert Hale.

Beck, Derek W. 2015. *Igniting the American Revolution: 1773–1775.* Naperville, IL: Sourcebooks.

Boston National Historical Park and United States, eds. 1998. *Boston and the American Revolution.* Handbook 146. Washington, DC: The Service.

Boyer, Paul, and Stephen Nissenbaum. 1974. *Salem Possessed: The Social Origins of Witchcraft.* Cambridge, MA: Harvard University Press.

Bradford, William. 1967. *Of Plimoth Plantation.* Edited by Samuel Eliot Morison. New York: Random House.

Bradford, William. 1967. *Of Plymouth Plantation with Introduction by S. E. Morison.* New York: Modern Library Edition.

Bremer, Francis J. 1994. *Shaping New England: Puritan Clergymen in Seventeenth-Century England and New England.* Twayne's United States Authors Series, TUSAS 631. New York: Twayne.

Bremer, Francis J. 1995. *The Puritan Experiment: New England Society from Bradford to Edwards.* Hanover, NH: University Press of New England.

Brittain, Alfred. 1903. *The History of North America.* Philadelphia, PA: Barrie.

Brodhead, John Romeyn. 1853. *History of the State of New York.* Vol. 1. New York: Harper & Brothers.

Brodhead, John Romeyn, comp. 1853–1858. *Documents Relative to the Colonial History of the State of New-York.* 10 vols. Translated and edited by E. B. O'Callaghan. Albany, NY: Weed, Parsons and Company, 1853.

Brooks, Victor. 1999. *The Boston Campaign: April 1775–March 1776.* Great Campaigns. Conshohocken, PA: Combined Pub.

Bumann, Joan, John Patterson, and Doug Byrum. 1997. *Our American Presidents.* St. Petersburg, FL: Worthington Press.

Bunker, Nick, 2010. *Making Haste from Babylon: The Mayflower Pilgrims and Their World.* New York: Vintage Books.

Burr, George Lincoln. 2002 [1914]. *Narratives of the Witchcraft Cases: 1648–1706.* New York: Charles Scribner and Sons.

Burrows, Edwin G., and Mike Wallace. 2000. *Gotham: A History of New York City to 1898.* Oxford: Oxford University Press.

Calef, Robert. 1700. *More Wonders of the Invisible World.* London: Nathaniel Hillar.

Carp, Benjamin L. 2010. *Defiance of the Patriots: The Boston Tea Party and the Making of America.* New Haven, CT: Yale University Press.

Castiglioni, Luigi, Antonio Pace, and Joseph Ewan. 1983. *Luigi Castiglioni's Viaggio*. Syracuse, NY: Syracuse University Press.

Clark, Joseph Silvester. 1831. *The History of the Pilgrims*. Boston, MA: J. R. Marvin.

Cobbett, William. 1813. *The Parliamentary History of England from the Earliest Times to the Year 1803*. London: T.C. Hansard Printer.

Coffey, John, and Paul Chang-Ha Lim, eds. 2008. *The Cambridge Companion to Puritanism*. Cambridge Companions to Religion. Cambridge, UK, and New York: Cambridge University Press.

Columbus, Christopher, Diego Alvarez Chanca, Giuliano Dati, Richard Henry Major, Diego Méndez de Segura, and Luis de Santángel. 1870. *Select Letters of Christopher Columbus*. London: Printed for the Hakluyt Society.

Cronon, William. 2003. *Changes in the Land: Indians, Colonists, and the Ecology of New England*. Rev. ed. New York: Hill and Wang.

Cummins, Joseph. 2012. *Ten Tea Parties: Patriotic Protests That History Forgot*. Philadelphia, PA: Quirk Books.

Cunliffe, Marcus, Gordon S. Wood, and Mount Vernon Ladies' Association of the Union. 1998. *George Washington: Man and Monument*. Mount Vernon, VA: Mount Vernon Ladies' Association.

Curtis, Edward E. 2005. *The Organization of the British Army in the American Revolution*. Cranbury, NJ: Scholars Bookshelf.

Custalow, Linwood, and Angela L. Daniel. 2007. *The True Story of Pocahontas: The Other Side of History: From the Sacred History of the Mattaponi Reservation People*. Golden, CO: Fulcrum Pub.

Dent, J. M. 1920. *Chronicles of the Pilgrim Fathers*. New York: E. P. Dutton & Co.

Desai, Christina M. 2014. "The Columbus Myth: Power and Ideology in Picture Books about Christopher Columbus." *Children's Literature in Education* 45 (3): 179–196.

Dexter, Henry Martyn, ed. 1865. *Mourt's Relation or Journal of the Plantation at Plymouth*. Boston, MA: J. K. Wiggin.

Drake, Francis Samuel. 1884. *Tea Leaves: Being a Collection of Letters and Documents*. Boston, MA: A. O. Crane.

Eelking, Max von, and J. G. Rosengarten. 1987. *The German Allied Troops in the North American War of Independence, 1776–1783*. Bowie, MD: Heritage Books.

Ellis, Joseph J. 2011. *His Excellency: George Washington*. New York: Alfred A. Knopf.

Ellis, Markman, Richard Coulton, and Matthew Mauger. 2015. *Empire of Tea: The Asian Leaf That Conquered the World*. London: Reaktion Books.

Endicott, Charles M. 1847. *Memoir of John Endicott*. Salem, MA: Observer Office.

Essex Institute. 1860. *Essex Institute Historical Collections*. Vol. 2. Salem, MA: Essex Institute.

Everett, William. 1870. "Plymouth Rock: 1620–1870." Pilgrim Society Journal, Plymouth, MA. Cambridge, MA: Press of J. Wilson and son.

Ferguson, Robert. 2014. *The Vikings*. New York: Penguin Books.

Ferling, John. 2010. "Myths of the American Revolution." *Smithsonian Magazine* (January). Accessed July 3, 2020. https://www.smithsonianmag.com/history/myths-of-the-american-revolution-10941835.

Findling, John E., and Frank W. Thackeray, eds. 1998. *Events That Changed America in the Eighteenth Century*. Events That Changed America series. Westport, CT: Greenwood Press.

Fischer, David Hackett. 1995. *Paul Revere's Ride*. Oxford Paperbacks: History. New York: Oxford University Press.

Fitzhugh, William W., Elisabeth I. Ward, and National Museum of Natural History (U.S.), eds. 2000. *Vikings: The North Atlantic Saga*. Washington, DC: Smithsonian Institution Press in association with the National Museum of Natural History.

Forbes, Esther. 1999. *Paul Revere and the World He Lived In*. Boston, MA: Houghton Mifflin.

Force, Peter. 1837. *American Archives: Fourth Series Containing a Documentary History of the English Colonies in North America*. Washington, DC: M. St. Clair Clarke and Peter Force.

Fraser, Rebecca. 2017. *The Mayflower: The Families, the Voyage, and the Founding of America*. New York: St. Martin's Press.

Furstenberg, François. 2011. "Atlantic Slavery, Atlantic Freedom: George Washington, Slavery, and Transatlantic Abolitionist Networks." *William and Mary Quarterly* 68 (2): 247.

Gleach, Frederic W. 1997. *Powhatan's World and Colonial Virginia: A Conflict of Cultures*. Studies in the Anthropology of North American Indians. Lincoln: University of Nebraska Press.

Goss, K. David. 2007. *The Salem Witch Trials: A Reference Guide*. Westport, CT: Greenwood.

Goss, K. David. 2012. *Daily Life during the Salem Witch Trials*. Santa Barbara, CA: Greenwood.

Goss, K. David. 2018. *Documents of the Salem Witch Trials*. Santa Barbara, CA: ABC-CLIO.

Greenwood, John. 1922. *The Revolutionary Services of John Greenwood of Boston and New York, 1773–1783, Edited with Notes from the Original by His Grandson, Isaac A. Greenwood*. New York: Joseph R. Greenwood.

Greer, Allan. 2012. "Commons and Enclosure in the Colonization of North America." *American Historical Review* 117 (2): 365–386.

Grizzard, Frank E. 2002. *George Washington: A Biographical Companion.* Santa Barbara, CA: ABC-CLIO.

Hanson, John. 1782. "Congressional Thanksgiving Day Proclamation." October 11, 1782. Exeter, NH.

Hawthorne, Nathaniel. 1870. *Works of Nathaniel Hawthorne.* Boston, MA: Houghton, Mifflin and Company.

Heckewelder, John. 1876. *History, Manners, and Customs of the Indian Nations Who Once Inhabited Pennsylvania and the Neighbouring States.* Philadelphia, PA: Historical Society of Pennsylvania.

Heinrichs, Johann. 1898. "Extracts from the Letter Books of Captain Johann Heinrichs of the Hessian Jaeger Corps, 1778–1780." *Pennsylvania Magazine of History and Biography* 22 (2): 137–170.

Hillard, George Stillman. 1902. *Captain John Smith.* New York and London: Harper & Brothers.

Hoffer, Peter Charles. 1997. *The Salem Witch Trials: A Legal Primer.* Lawrence: University Press of Kansas.

Hoffmann-Axthelm, Walter. 1981. *History of Dentistry.* Chicago, IL: Quintessence Pub. Co.

Hoobler, Dorothy, and Thomas Hoobler. 2007. *Captain John Smith: Jamestown and the Birth of the American Dream.* Hoboken, NJ: John Wiley & Sons.

Hunt, Uriah. 1835. *A History of the United States from Their Establishment as Colonies to the Close of the War with Britain in 1815.* Cooperstown, NY: H. and E. Phinney Publishers.

Hutchinson, Thomas. 1769. "A Proclamation from the Governor Declaring a Day of Thanksgiving." October 23, 1769. Boston, MA: Richard Draper.

Ingram, Dorothy C. 1959. Letter to the editor. *The Reporter*, March 5, 1959, 8.

Ingstad, Anne Stine. 1977. *The Discovery of a Norse Settlement in America.* Oslo: Universitetsforlaget.

Irmscher, Christoph. 2009. *Public Poet, Private Man: Henry Wadsworth Longfellow at 200.* Amherst: University of Massachusetts Press; Published in cooperation with the Houghton Library, Harvard University.

Jackson, Kenneth T., and New York Historical Society, eds. 2010. *The Encyclopedia of New York City.* 2nd ed. New Haven, CT: Yale University Press.

Jacobs, Jaap. 2005. *New Netherland: A Dutch Colony in Seventeenth-Century America.* Vol. 3 of *The Atlantic World.* Leiden, Netherlands: Brill.

Jones, Gwyn. 1986. *The Norse Atlantic Saga: Being the Norse Voyages of Discovery and Settlement to Iceland, Greenland, and North America*. Oxford, and New York: Oxford University Press.

Knollenberg, Bernhard. 2003. *Growth of the American Revolution, 1766–1775*. Indianapolis, IN: Liberty Fund.

Koning, Hans. 1991. *Columbus: His Enterprise: Exploding the Myth*. New York: Monthly Review Press.

Kunz, Keneva, ed. 2008. *The Vinland Sagas: The Icelandic Sagas about the First Documented Voyages across the North Atlantic; the Saga of the Greenlanders and Eirik the Red's Saga*. Penguin Classics. London: Penguin Books.

Langdon, George D. 1966. *Pilgrim Colony: A History of New Plymouth, 1620–1691*. New Haven, CT: Yale University Press.

Levy, Philip. 2013. *Where the Cherry Tree Grew: The Story of Ferry Farm, George Washington's Boyhood Home*. New York: St. Martin's Press.

Leyburn, James G. 1962. *The Scotch-Irish: A Social History*. Chapel Hill: University of North Carolina Press.

Loewen, James W. 2007. *Lies across America: What Our Historic Sites Get Wrong*. New York: Simon & Schuster.

Love, Ronald S. 2006. *Maritime Exploration in the Age of Discovery, 1415–1800*. Westport, CT: Greenwood Press.

Mather, Cotton. 2005. *Salem Witchcraft; Comprising More Wonders of the Invisible World, Collected by Robert Calef; and Wonders of the Invisible World, by Cotton Mather; Together with Notes and Explanations by Samuel P. Fowler*. Edited by Samuel P. Fowler. Salem, MA: G. M. Whipple & A. A. Smith.

McDowell, Bart. 1972. *The Revolutionary War: America's Fight for Freedom*. Washington, DC: National Geographic Society.

Melyn, Cornelius. 1914. "Melyn Papers 1640–1699." Collections of the New-York Historical Society for the Year 1913. New York: Printed for the Society.

Miller, Joel. 2010. *The Revolutionary Paul Revere*. Nashville, TN: Thomas Nelson.

Miller, Perry. 1956. *The American Puritans*. Garden City, NY: Doubleday-Anchor Books.

Milton, Giles. 2000. *Big Chief Elizabeth: The Adventures and Fate of the First English Colonists in America*. 1st American ed. New York: Farrar, Straus and Giroux.

Morgan, Edmund S. 2007. *The Puritan Dilemma: The Story of John Winthrop*. 3rd ed. The Library of American Biography. New York: Pearson Longman.

Morison, Samuel Eliot. 1994. *The Oxford History of the American People*. New York: New American Library.
Morone, James A. 2003. *Hellfire Nation: The Politics of Sin in American History*. New Haven, CT: Yale University Press.
Morrill, Austin W. 1959. Letter to the editor. *The Reporter*, March 5, 1959, 8.
Norton, Mary Beth. 2002. *In the Devil's Snare*. New York: Random House.
Noyes, J. O. 1858. "The Dutch in New Amsterdam." *National Magazine* 12 (May).
O'Callaghan, E. B. 1846. *History of New Netherland; or, New York under the Dutch*. New York: D. Appleton & Company.
Ogilby, John. 1671. *America Being the Latest and Most Accurate Description of the New World*. London: Printed by the author.
Oldboy, Felix. 1890. *The Island of Manhattan, a Bit of Earth*. New York: n.p.
O'Shaughnessy, Andrew Jackson. 2013. *The Men Who Lost America: British Leadership, the American Revolution, and the Fate of the Empire*. Lewis Walpole Series in Eighteenth-Century Culture and History. New Haven, CT: Yale University Press.
Parry, Jay A., Andrew M. Allison, W. Cleon Skousen, and George Washington. 1991. *The Real George Washington*. American Classic Series, Vol. 3. Washington, DC: National Center for Constitutional Studies.
Price, David A. 2003. *Love and Hate in Jamestown: John Smith, Pocahontas, and the Heart of a New Nation*. New York: Knopf.
Puglionesi, Alicia. April 4, 2019. History News. "How a Romanticized Take on Pocahontas Became a Touchstone of American Culture." Last Modified April 4, 2019. https://www.history.com/news/how-early-american-stage-dramas-turned-pocahontas-into-fake-news.
Puls, Mark. 2006. *Samuel Adams: Father of the American Revolution*. New York: Palgrave Macmillan.
Reeves, Arthur Middleton, and William Dudley Foulke. 1895. *The Finding of Wineland the Good*. London: Frowde.
Reich, Jerome R. 2011. *Colonial America*. New York: Routledge Press.
Reitano, Joanne R. 2010. *The Restless City: A Short History of New York from Colonial Times to the Present*. 2nd ed. New York: Routledge.
Richardson, James Daniel, comp. 1896. *A Compilation of the Messages and Papers of the Presidents, 1789–1897*. Vol. 1, *1789–1817*. Washington, DC: Government Printing Office.
Rosenthal, Bernard. 1993. *Salem Story: Reading the Witch Trials of 1692*. Cambridge Studies in American Literature and Culture 73. Cambridge, UK, and New York: Cambridge University Press.

Rountree, Helen C. 1990. *Pocahontas's People: The Powhatan Indians of Virginia through Four Centuries*. The Civilization of the American Indian Series, Vol. 196. Norman: University of Oklahoma Press.

Rowe, Elizabeth Ashman. 2005. *The Development of Flateyjarbók*. Odense: University Press of Southern Denmark.

Rowe, John, and Edward Lillie Pierce. 1903. *Letters and Diary of John Rowe: Boston Merchant, 1759–1762, 1764–1779*. Boston, MA: W. D. Clarke Company.

Ryken, Leland. 1990. *Worldly Saints: The Puritans as They Really Were*. Grand Rapids, MI: Academie Books.

Sabine, Lorenzo. 1847. *The American Loyalists, or Biographical Sketches of Adherents to the British Crown in the War of the Revolution*. Boston, MA: C. C. Little and J. Brown.

Saunders, Frederick. 1893. *Addresses, Historical and Patriotic*. New York: E. B. Treat.

Schilling, Vincent. 2014. "The True Story of Pocahontas: Historical Myth versus Sad Reality." *Indian Country Today*, April 5, 2014.

Schmidt, Gary D. 1999. *William Bradford: Plymouth's Faithful Pilgrim*. Grand Rapids, MI: Eerdmans Books for Young Readers.

Schwarz, Philip J., and Jean B. Lee, eds. 2001. *Slavery at the Home of George Washington*. Mount Vernon, VA: Mount Vernon Ladies' Assoc.

Scobey, David M. 2003. *Empire City: The Making and Meaning of the New York City Landscape*. Philadelphia, PA: Temple University Press.

Sephton, John. 1880. *The Greenlanders' Saga and Erik the Red's Saga: A Translation*. Liverpool: D. Marples & Co.

Shorto, Russell. 2005. *The Island at the Center of the World: The Epic Story of Dutch Manhattan and the Forgotten Colony That Shaped America*. New York: Vintage.

Smith, John. 1866. *A True Relation of Virginia*. Cambridge, MA: John Wilson and Sons.

Smith, John. 1908. *The True Travels, Adventures and Observations*. Cambridge, UK: Cambridge University.

Smith, John, Richard Potts, et al. 1612. *The Proceedings of the English Colonie in Virginia*. Oxford: Joseph Barnes.

Sognnaes, R. F. 1973. "America's Most Famous Teeth." *Smithsonian* 3 (11): 47–51.

Sognnaes, R. F. 1976. "George Washington's Bite." *California Dental Association Journal* June: 36–40.

Stedman, Edmund Clarence. 1900. *An American Anthology, 1787–1900*. Boston, MA: Houghton-Mifflin and Co.

Stedman, Edmund Clarence, and Ellen MacKay Hutchinson, eds. 1892. *A Library of American Literature: Early Colonial Literature, 1607–1675.* New York: Charles L. Webster and Company.

Thackeray, William Makepeace. 1889. *The Complete Works of William Makepeace Thackeray: Christmas Stories; Ballads, and Other Poems; Tales.* Boston, MA and New York: Houghton, Mifflin.

Thorpe, Francis Newton. 1909. *The Federal and State Constitutions, Colonial Charters, and Other Organic Laws of the State, Territories, and Colonies Now or Heretofore Forming the United States of America.* Washington, DC: Government Printing Office.

Townsend, Camilla. 2005. *Pocahontas and the Powhatan Dilemma: An American Portrait.* New York: Hill and Wang.

Triber, Jayne E. 1998. *A True Republican: The Life of Paul Revere.* Amherst: University of Massachusetts Press.

Tyler, John W. 1986. *Smugglers & Patriots: Boston Merchants and the Advent of the American Revolution.* Boston, MA: Northeastern University Press.

Ulrich, Laurel Thatcher. 1991. *Good Wives: Image and Reality in the Lives of Women in Northern New England, 1650–1750.* New York: Random House.

Unger, Harlow G. 2011. *American Tempest: How the Boston Tea Party Sparked a Revolution.* 1st Da Capo Press ed. Cambridge, MA: Da Capo Press.

Upton, L. F. S. 1965. "Proceedings of Ye Body Respecting the Tea." *William and Mary Quarterly* 22 (2) (April): 287–300.

Verney, Jack. 1994. *O'Callaghan: The Making and Unmaking of a Rebel.* Carleton Library Series 179. Ottawa: Carleton University Press.

Vespucci, Amerigo, Luciano Formisano, and David Jacobson. 1992. *Letters from a New World: Amerigo Vespucci's Discovery of America.* Marsilio Classics. New York: Marsilio.

Volo, James M. 2012. *The Boston Tea Party: The Foundations of Revolution.* Santa Barbara, CA: ABC-CLIO.

Wall, Charles C. 1959. Letter to the editor. *The Reporter*, March 5, 1959, 8.

Waller, J. Michael. 2009. *Founding Political Warfare Documents of the United States.* Washington, DC: Crossbow Press.

Warren, Mercy Otis, and Lester H. Cohen. 1988. *History of the Rise, Progress, and Termination of the American Revolution: Interspersed with Biographical, Political, and Moral Observations.* Indianapolis, IN: Liberty Classics.

Weisman, Richard. 1984. *Witchcraft, Magic, and Religion in 17th Century Massachusetts.* Amherst: University of Massachusetts Press.

Weslager, C. A., and Kalmar Nyckel Foundation. 1990. *A Man and His Ship: Peter Minuit and the Kalmar Nyckel.* Wilmington, DE: Kalmar Nyckel Foundation.

White, Ashanti. 2013. "Irish-Americans—1775–1860." In *Ethnic and Racial Minorities in the U.S. Military: An Encyclopedia.* Vol. 1, 325–327. Santa Barbara, CA: ABC-CLIO.

Winroth, Anders. 2014. *The Age of the Vikings.* Princeton, NJ: Princeton University Press.

Winship, Michael P. 2018. *Hot Protestants: A History of Puritanism in England and America.* New Haven, CT: Yale University Press.

Winslow, Edward. 1622. *Mourt's Relation.* London: G. Mourt.

Woolley, Benjamin. 2008. *Savage Kingdom: The True Story of Jamestown, 1607, and the Settlement of America.* First Harper Perennial edition. New York: Harper Perennial.

Wynbrandt, James. 2000. *The Excruciating History of Dentistry: Toothsome Tales & Oral Oddities from Babylon to Braces.* New York: St. Martins Griffin.

Young, Alfred Fabian. 1999. *The Shoemaker and the Tea Party: Memory and the American Revolution.* Boston, MA: Beacon Press.

Index

Adam of Bremen, 12
Adams, John, President, 80–81, 163
Adams, Samuel, 130, 144
Aeneid, 112
African Americans, 164, 167
Albany, 99
America, xiii, 2, 7, 58, 130, 138, 153, 161, 165, 184; discovery of, 6, 10, 18
American colonies, 108, 130, 134, 138, 146, 150–151, 156–157, 159–162, 165–166, 168
American Revolution, 32, 78, 153, 164–165, 174, 185
Amsterdam, 57
Anglican Church, 58
Anne of England, Queen, 29, 45, 47
Arabella, 60–61, 65
Aragon, 1
Atlantic Monthly, 174
Attucks, Crispus, 166

Baffin Island, 18, 21
Baptism of Pocahontas, The, 32
Baptists, 64, 75
Barker, James Nelson, 33
Battle of Saratoga, The, 77

Beaver, 140–141, 144
Bible, The, 68, 73, 117, 185, 193
Bishop, Bridget, 125–126
Bishop, Edward, 126
Black Dragoons, 167
Black Pioneers, 167
Bodin, Jean, 119
Boston Harbor, 131–134, 140, 142–143
Boston Massacre, 76, 133, 151, 166
Boston Port Act, 133
Boston Tea Party, 129, 132, 143, 146
Bradford, William, 53–55, 57–58, 65–68, 71–72, 74, 81–88, 101
Brattahlid, 15, 17, 20
Bray, John, 33
British Empire, 150, 162
Brodhead, John R., 99, 102, 107
Brown, William A., 197–199
Burroughs, George, 121, 127

Calef, Robert, 121, 127
Calvin, John, 51, 57, 59, 66
Calvinism, 51, 55, 58, 64, 66, 75
Cambell, Nicholas, 134
Canada, 23, 158, 167

INDEX

Cape Ann, 57
Cape Cod, 66–67, 145
Castiglioni, Luigi, *Viaggio: Travels in the United States of North America, 1785–1787*, 32
Castile, 1, 4
Castle William, 143, 145
Catskill Mountains, 153–154
Cave, Edward, 7
Chagollan, Steve, 35–36
Chapman, John Gadsby, 32
Charlemagne, Emperor, 6
Charles I, King, 54, 59–60, 65
Charleston, 137, 140, 145–146, 180–181, 186–187
Charter of Massachusetts Bay, xii, 55, 60, 65
Christian faith, 3, 6, 11, 32, 66
Christianity, 15–17, 37, 46, 48
Christians, non-Separatist, 72
Church of England, 51–52, 54, 56–60, 64, 67, 120
Civil War, English, 59
Claire, Renee, 125
Clark, Joseph Sylvester, 83
Clarke, Richard, 140–141
Clarke family, 140, 145
Columbia, mythical goddess of North America, 6–7
Columbia, South Carolina, 7
Columbia College, 7
Columbian Exchange, 3
Columbian Exposition, 8
"Columbus," 8–10
Columbus, Christopher, 1–8, 10–12, 15, 22–23; descendants, 4; epitaph, 4; legend, 3, 5, 7–8, 10; poem, 8; tomb, 5
Columbus Day, 10–11
Committee of Safety, 186, 189
Conant, Edward, 179–180
Concord, xv, 85, 163, 173, 178, 181–182, 187

Congregational church, 52, 59–60, 121
Congress, of the United States, 11, 77, 155, 164, 185, 204
Connecticut, 145, 159
Connecticut Courant, 89
Conservative-Whigs, 163
Continental Army, 164–165, 167, 203
Continental Congress, 159, 179
Corey, Giles, 120, 127
Corwin, George, 126
Cotton, John, 68
Court of Oyer and Terminer, xii, 119–121, 126–127
Craddock, Matthew, 53
Custalow, Dr. Linwood, 38

Dartmouth, 140–144
Davis, John, 33
Davis Strait, 18
Dawes, William, 182, 186
De Bry, Theodor, 6
De Heretico Comburendo, 120
Descriptio Insularum Aquilonis, 22
Devil, 42, 119, 127
Dominican Republic, 5
Duty, 132–133, 139, 141–142, 152; on tea, 129, 140, 145

East India Company, 129, 137, 139–140, 143, 145–146, 152; Dutch, 139
Ecclesiastical courts, 118–119
Eirik. *See* Erik the Red
Elizabeth I, Queen, 73, 81, 118, 120
Enclosures, 110
Endicott, John, 53–55, 65
England, 46–48, 51–52, 55–60, 62, 64–65, 67, 73, 75, 77, 118, 120, 126, 133, 141–143, 156–160
Erikson, Leif, 15–22
Erik the Red, 12–17, 20–21, 23

Erik the Red's Saga, 12, 15–16, 20, 21, 23
Ethiopian Regiment, 167–168
Europa, goddess, 6
Everett, William, 124
Execution: beheading, 59, 118; burning at the stake, 118, 124, 127; by hanging, 121; method of, 121, 123; public, 127

Faroes, 11
Ferdinand, King, 3–4
First Anglo-Powhatan War, 28
Fort Casimir, 107
Francis, Lady (Duchess of Richmond), 44
Franklin, Benjamin, 160, 162
Fuller, Dr. Samuel, 54–55

Gage, Thomas, 186, 190
Generall Historie of Virginia, 27, 33, 42, 48
Gentleman's Magazine, The, 7
George III, King, 129, 150, 153, 155, 156, 165
Gibbs, Margaret, 193, 195–196
Gibson, Mel, 151
Glorious Revolution, 55
Godthaab (Greenland), 15
Gray, Samuel, 133
Great Britain, 45, 66, 78, 131, 133, 138–140, 151, 154, 161–162
Greenland, 11, 13–20, 22–24; discovery of, 13–14
Greenlanders' Saga, The, 12, 17–23
Greenwood, John, 194, 204–205
Gunnbjorn Skerries, 14

Hale, Sarah Josepha, 85, 89–91
Hancock, John, 181, 183, 185–189
Harrison, Benjamin, 10
Havana, Cuba, 6

Hawthorne, Nathaniel, 83, 85, 94, 123
Heckewelder, John, 111
Helluland, 18
Henry IV, King, 120
Henry VIII, King, 58, 120
Holy Scripture, 60, 66
Hutchinson, Anne, 65
Hutchinson, Thomas, 71, 75–76, 121–122, 130, 143

Iceland, 11–14, 16–17, 19
Indian Removal Act, 32
Indians, 33–35, 39–41, 84, 86, 88, 100, 103, 110–112, 132, 135
Ingram, Dorothy, 196
Intolerable Acts, 133, 146
Irving, Washington, 153–154
Isabella, Queen, 3
Isles of Shoals, 57

James I, King, 29, 48, 59
Jefferson, Thomas, 167
Jersey Shore Volunteers, 167
Justice Act, 133

King Phillip's War, 53
King's Peace, 59

Lamson, William, 145
Lancey's Brigade, 164
L'Anse aux Meadows, 22
Leiden, 57
Leon, 1, 4
Lexington, 136, 163, 173, 177, 181–184, 186–188; battle of, 185, 189–190
Lincoln, Abraham, 85, 91
Little Red Riding Hood, 197
Longfellow, Henry Wadsworth, 174–175, 178–180, 182–184, 191
Lord Dunmore's Proclamation, 168, 170

INDEX

MacMurray, Fred, 125
Madison, James, President, 80–83
Malick, Terence, 36–37
Malleus Maleficarum, 119
Mandela effect, 196
Manhattan, 95, 98–101, 103–108, 113, 219; purchase of, 99–104, 106–109, 111, 113
Manifest Destiny, 7
Markland, 18–19
Massachusetts, xii, 51–52, 60, 64, 75, 118, 121, 129, 159, 175
Massachusetts Bay Company, 53–56, 58, 61, 65–66, 75
Massasoit, 71, 86
Mather, Rev. Cotton, 71, 121, 127
Mayflower, 66
Mayflower Compact, the, 66
McKean, Thomas, 163
Medical Museum in Washington, 197
Melyn, Cornelius, 108, 110
Meromocomoco, 30
Miller, Joaquin, 8
Minuit, Peter, 108, 110
Molasses Act, 138, 157
Mount Vernon, 194–196, 201–202, 204, 208

Native Americans, 2–3, 7, 11, 71–72, 86–87, 101–102, 105–113, 122, 130, 158–159
Native Americans and European newcomers, xiv, 111
Naumkeag, 53, 54
Navarre, 1
Netherlands, 105–107, 113
New Amsterdam, 98, 102
New Brunswick, 21, 153
New England, 47, 51, 54–56, 58–61, 63–64, 67, 89, 93, 117–118, 120–122, 157, 163–164, 166
New Englanders, 76, 89, 130
Newfoundland, 21–23, 159

New Netherlands, 67, 99–101, 110
New York State Senate, 96, 101
Nordic colonization, 22
Nova Scotia, 153, 159

O'Callaghan, Edmund Bailey, 99–105
Ogilby, John, 31
Olaf Tryggvason, King, 15–16
Old North Church, 130, 173–175, 177, 179–180, 186
Old South Meeting House, 143
Orkney Islands, 11
Outer Hebrides, 11
Owen, Robert Dale, 33

"Paul Revere's Ride," 174, 175, 179–184
Peace of Pocahontas, 28
Peggy Stewart, 137
Pequot War, 53
Phile, Philip, 7
Phips, William, 52
Pilgrims, xv, 51, 53–57, 60, 63, 65–68, 72–74, 76, 83–84, 124
Plymouth Colony, 52–54, 61, 66–67, 71, 73–75, 84, 86–89
Pocahontas (or Matoaka), xiv, 27–43, 45–49; animated film, 27, 33, 35–37; cinematic images, 35; conversion, 48; death, 30, 48; myth, 31, 33–34, 48; poem, 34–35
Potts, Richard, 44
Powhatan (or Wahunsenacawh), 27, 30–32, 36–37, 39–45, 47
Prayer, 29, 40, 52, 63, 73, 78–81, 84, 87–89, 93, 117, 127; daily family, 52
Prince Edward Island, 159
Proctor, John, 121
Provincetown, 140
Puritanism, 59–60, 68, 117–118, 123

INDEX

Puritans, xv, 51–56, 58–61, 63, 66–68, 75, 117–118, 123, 125
Puritans in Massachusetts Bay Colony, 60

Quakers, 64, 75, 125

Radical-Whigs, 163
Raleigh Register, 136
Ranney, William, 102
The Reporter, 194–196, 201
Revere, Paul, xiii, xv, 173–175, 178–179, 181–183, 185, 191, 194, 200, 203
Rip Van Winkle, 153–155
Robinson, Rev. John, 57
Rolfe, John, 32, 36–37
Rolfe, Rebecca (or Pocahontas or Matoaka), 37
Roman Catholic Church, 15, 51, 73, 119–120
Roosevelt, Franklin Delano, 11
Rotch, Francis, 140, 142–144
Rowe, John, 137, 141–143

Sabine, Lorenzo, 152
Salem, xiii, 51, 53–54, 60, 117–118, 121, 123, 125–127; Court, 120
Salem witch trials, xii–xiii, 117, 119, 121–127
Schagen, Peter, 98–103, 105–106, 113
Scots-Irish settlers, 164–165
Scrooby, 57
Seba, 34
Separatists, 51–60, 64–65, 67, 72, 75, 93
Separatists/Pilgrims of Plymouth, 54, 59
Seville Cathedral, 1, 3–5
Shetland Islands, 11
Skraelings, 19, 21, 23

Smith, John, Captain, 27–33, 35–38, 40, 42–44, 46–49
Sognnaes, Reider, 206
Sons of Liberty, 134–135, 138, 141–146, 166, 180, 184, 189
Stamp Act, 76, 138, 151, 159–161
Staten Island, 110; purchase of, 108, 110
Stoughton, William, 125–126
Strait of Belle Isle, 22
Sugar Act, 138, 157
Symonds, Rev. William, 31

Tammany Society, 10
Taxation, 129–132, 134, 138–140, 156, 159–162, 169
Taxation without representation, 168
Taxes, indirect, 139
Tea, 129–137, 139–147, 152, 185, 209, 215; British, 139, 152; consignees, 140–143, 145–146
Thackeray, William Makepeace, 34–35
Thanksgiving: Christian feast of, 72; Day of, 76, 88; Day of, holiday, 75, 79–80, 89–91; Day of, national, 90, 93; Elizabethan, 75; First, 71–73, 75, 84, 86; New England, 76–77, 89
Thanksgiving days, 74–75, 77–79, 82, 85, 88, 90, 92; national, 77–78
Thirty Years' War, 57
Thjodhild (wife of Erik the Red), 12
Thorvald (father of Erik the Red), 12
Thorvald Erikson (son of Erik the Red), 21
Townshend Acts, 76, 139
Trail of Tears, 32
True Relation of Virginia, 28–29, 39–40, 42
Tryggvason, King Olaf, 15
Tyrker, 19–20

Ulfsson, Gunnbjorn, 13
Underhill, John, 65
Uttamattamakin, 39, 47–48

Vespucci, Amerigo, 6
Vikings, 8, 12–14
Vinland, 12
Virginia Company, 27, 31, 40, 67, 73–74, 157

Walcott, Mary, 126
Waldseemuller, Walter, 6
Wallace, Brigitta, 23
Washington, George, xiii, 10, 77–79, 122, 149–150, 153, 155, 164, 193–210; "cannot tell a lie" myth, 193; correspondence, 206; dental problems, 193–202, 204–206; dentures, 193–197, 199, 201–207
Weems, Mason Locke (Parson), 193
Werawocomoco, 41–43
Werowance, 31, 43, 47–48
William, 145
William III, King and Queen Mary, 52, 55
Williams, Rev. Roger, 64–65
Wineland, 20
Winslow, Edward, 71, 83, 86
Winthrop, John, 53, 55, 58, 60–61, 63–65, 75
Witchcraft, 118–120, 122–127
Witches, xiii, 117–119, 121, 123–125

About the Authors

K. David Goss, MA, PhD cand., is a professor of history and museum studies at Gordon College, Wenham, Massachusetts. He is author of *The Salem Witch Trials: A Reference Guide*, *Daily Life during the Salem Witch Trials*, and *Documents of the Salem Witch Trials*. He is the 2014 recipient of the Dr. Marvin Wilson Award for Excellence in Teaching Humanities and a Society of Colonial Wars Scholar of Boston University.

A. A. Grishin, MA, is a professional multimedia developer, specializing in public history and education. Grishin created interactive experiences for dozens of museums around the country, including the William J. Clinton Presidential Library, the Smithsonian Museum, and the Mystic Seaport Maritime Museum. He has also made contributions to the study of Classical Latin poetry and original medieval sources.